TO PLEAD OUR OWN CAUSE

TO PLEAD OUR OWN CAUSE

Personal Stories by Today's Slaves

EDITED BY KEVIN BALES AND ZOE TRODD

Cornell University Press
Ithaca and London

Copyright © 2008 by Cornell University

All rights reserved. Except for brief quotations in a review, this
book, or parts thereof, must not be reproduced in any form
without permission in writing from the publisher. For information,
address Cornell University Press, Sage House, 512 East State Street,
Ithaca, New York 14850.

First published 2008 by Cornell University Press
First printing, Cornell Paperbacks, 2008

Printed in the United States of America

Library of Congress Cataloging-in-Publication Data

To plead our own cause : personal stories by today's slaves /
edited by Kevin Bales and Zoe Trodd.
    p. cm.
  Includes bibliographical references.
  ISBN 978-0-8014-4573-6 (cloth : alk. paper) — ISBN 978-0-8014-
7438-5 (pbk. : alk. paper)
  1. Slavery—Case studies.   2. Human trafficking—Case studies.
3. Forced labor—Case studies.   4. Prostitution—Case studies.
5. Slavery—History—21st century.   6. Slaves—Biography.
I. Bales, Kevin.   II. Trodd, Zoe.
  HT857.T67 2008
  306.3'62—dc22
                                              2007049029

Cornell University Press strives to use environmentally responsible
suppliers and materials to the fullest extent possible in the publishing of its books. Such materials include vegetable-based, low-VOC
inks and acid-free papers that are recycled, totally chlorine-free, or
partly composed of nonwood fibers. For further information, visit
our website at www.cornellpress.cornell.edu.

Cloth printing   10 9 8 7 6 5 4 3 2 1
Paperback printing   10 9 8 7 6 5 4 3 2 1

We wish to plead our own cause. Too long have others spoken for us. Too long has the public been deceived by misrepresentations, in things which concern us dearly.
Freedom's Journal, March 16, 1827

And this is the purpose, to tell my testimony…
so people will know that this thing is a real thing.
Ruth Kamara, a former sex slave, Liberia, 2006

CONTENTS

ACKNOWLEDGMENTS

This book would not have been possible without the work of Cornell University Press, especially Peter Wissoker, acquisitions editor, Ange Romeo-Hall, senior manuscript editor, Susan P. Specter, editorial assistant, and Katy Meigs, our copyeditor. We are grateful for research funding from the Northeast Modern Language Association, the Institute for Humane Studies, and the Charles Warren Center for Studies in American History at Harvard University. We acknowledge the assistance and great generosity of Peggy Callahan, director of communications at Free the Slaves, whose work gathering narratives and photographs was integral to this book. As well, we are grateful to Jean-Robert Cadet; Rajneesh Kumar Yadav; Benjamin Skinner; all those working with Anti-Slavery International, in particular Romana Cacchioli; the Coalition of Immokalee Workers; the Association of Albanian Girls and Women; Donna M. Hughes and the Coalition against Trafficking in Women; Yvonne Keairns and the Quaker UN; Kay Buck and the Coalition to Abolish Slavery and Trafficking; Jo Anne Lyon and Kristin Wiebe at World Hope International; and the Center against Violence and Human Trafficking. We also acknowledge the important antislavery work of Judy Hyde, Helen Armstrong, Lookie Amuzu, Supriya Awasthi, and—at Free the Slaves—Samira Tallandier, Marc Levin, and Nekose Wills. Our understanding of this issue has been developed in conversations with Doug Abrams, Holly Burkhalter, Rachel Cernansky, Austin Choi-Fitzpatrick, David Brion Davis, Claude d'Estree, Given Kachepa, Siddharth Kara, Heidi Metcalf, John Miller, Reggie Norton, Pam Omidyar, Julia Ormond, Jacob Patton, Ruth Pojman, Jessica Reitz, Kathy

Sreedar, Maurizia Tovo, and Gerri Williams. Warm thanks are also due to John Bowe, Ed Childs, Marcia Dambry, Clinton Fein, Henry Louis Gates Jr., Leon Gibbs-Avramidis, Lawrence Groo, Walter Johnson, Adrie Kusserow, Paul Lauter, Joe Lockard, Timothy Patrick McCarthy, Christine McFadden, Nathaniel Naddaff-Hafrey, Ann Mary Olson, Melissa Pritchard, Elliott Prasse-Freeman, Marliss Prasse, Werner Sollors, John Stauffer, Kate Takvorian, Tiffanye Threadcraft, Phyllis Thompson, and Alex Williamson. Zoe would like to thank her parents, Lyn and Geoff Trodd, and her siblings, Gabe and Bee Trodd. We want to celebrate the life and legacy of Winthrop Jordan, our friend and one of the great historians of slavery. Finally, it is difficult to express the profound gratitude we feel to those many slaves who have overcome bondage and then found the courage to speak out. Their voices are our truest guides.

KEVIN BALES AND ZOE TRODD

Washington, D.C. and Cambridge, Mass.

TO PLEAD OUR OWN CAUSE

INTRODUCTION

The Long Juneteenth

We could have told them a different
story...that would have touched their hearts.
   Harriet Jacobs, *Incidents in the Life of a Slave Girl,* 1861

I want you to listen...in the hope that
after you listen to me you can understand.
   Dina Chan, a former sex slave, Cambodia, 1999

In 1997, Roseline Odine was trafficked from Cameroon and enslaved in
Washington, D.C.[1] After escaping from her captors in 1999, she visited the
Lincoln Memorial. Standing in the Great Emancipator's shadow, she com-
mented on the irony of her presence there: "I mean, he fought to make

---

[1] Roseline Odine's narrative is in section 3 of this book. In some of the narratives we use
pseudonyms to protect the narrators' identities: Isra, Ada, Adelina, Elira, Flutura, Kimete, Miranda, Odeta, Sanije, Valdete, and Zamira in section 1; Kaew, Nuch, Pot, Seba, Alana, Bahar,
Maria, and Milena in section 2; Miguel and Faith in section 3; Aida, Dia, Manju, Chantha, and
Chariya in section 4. The narratives are also titled by the individual's first name only, as in many
cases we were not given their last names. The dates given after the narratives are their dates of
composition (rather than the dates when the narrators were enslaved or liberated), and the loca-
tions given are the places of enslavement (rather than the narrators' countries of origin or current
location). For the figure of 27 million (see next page) see Kevin Bales, *Understanding Global
Slavery* (Berkeley: University of California Press, 2005), 102–3. This number combines evidence
and data from Bales's original field research, the UN, the International Labour Office (ILO), the
U.S. State Department, and numerous studies by human rights organizations, anthropologists,
and economists. It is smaller than the estimates put forward by some antislavery groups, which
range as high as 200 million.

sure that slavery doesn't happen." As Roseline knows all too well, the Thirteenth Amendment is violated every day in the District of Columbia and around the world. Globally, there are 27 million slaves alive today; more than at any time in history, more than were seized from Africa in 350 years of the Atlantic slave trade. Making slavery illegal hasn't made it disappear, only disappear from view.

TO PLEAD A CAUSE

The ninety-five narratives that make up this book belie the notion that slavery is over. In narrating their stories, Roseline and others shift modern slavery out of Lincoln's shadow—the ongoing myth that slavery ended with the Emancipation Proclamation of 1863. Slavery continues, and so too does the slave narrative tradition. In giving witness to the fact of slavery, these new stories can be understood as continuing a tradition begun in the nineteenth century by Frederick Douglass, Harriet Jacobs, and the many former slaves who used narrative as a tool for abolition.

Recognizing this tradition, we have chosen to title our book *To Plead Our Own Cause*. The first issue of the abolitionist newspaper *Freedom's Journal*, on March 16, 1827, included a banner on its front page that read: "We wish to plead our own cause. Too long have others spoken for us. Too long has the public been deceived by misrepresentations, in things which concern us dearly." This phrase, "to plead our own cause," encapsulates the power at the heart of the slave testimony. And nineteenth-century antislavery organizations recognized that power by employing former slaves as lecturers and then publishing the lectures as narratives. With their calls for abolition alongside their firsthand descriptions of bondage and their assertions of humanity, the slave narratives were abolitionism's most popular and effective genre of writing. Now, modern narratives put the slave's voice back at the heart of the abolitionist movement.

Some narrators in this book told their stories to abolitionist groups in order to raise general awareness of slavery today.[2] Others were seeking specific changes: some told their stories at congressional sessions on the Trafficking Victims Protection Act (TVPA) and the End Demand for Sex Trafficking Act; Sam wrote his story to help end the ongoing enslavement of his wife; and Masha and Irina told their stories to protest the potential for increased trafficking during the 2006 World Cup in Germany. Dina

---

[2] See permissions and credits following the appendix for where and when the individual narratives were given.

Chan told her story as a member of the Sex Workers Union of Toul Kork (Cambodia), and followed it by recommending an end to police harassment and advocating legislation to protect sex workers. Beatrice told her story to the U.S. Congress and included calls for public awareness campaigns, the education of at-risk populations, greater monitoring of job agencies, and the removal of shame from slavery.

The narrators in this book are explicit in their desire to effect change with storytelling. "By talking out, people will be more aware and more able to help people become free," explains Mende. Ruth observes that her purpose after slavery is to "tell my testimony...so people will know that this thing is a real thing." Chantha hopes that "by sharing my story...I can help prevent others from the deep sadness of my life." And Rama wants to "tell the government that these kids exist," imagining the government surrounding "the loom on all sides" and rescuing children. With their protest literature, the narrators reach out to other slaves as well as those in power. "I write this story so that maybe someone who hears it will somehow be able to avoid the pain that was forced on me," explains Jill. Battis imagines being "an example for my friends" to "prevent them from getting into the trap of bondage." And Anita tells her story to "help other women who are forced into prostitution."

New slave narratives may also be considered within the explosion of storytelling in the human rights field over the last twenty years. Identifying this explosion in 2004, Kay Schaffer and Sidonie Smith noted that storytelling has become "one of the most potent vehicles for advancing human rights claims." *To Plead Our Own Cause* presents slave narratives performing the cultural work explained by Schaffer and Smith: "[intervening] in the public sphere, contesting social norms, exposing the fictions of official history, and prompting resistance."[3] Targeting oppression and silence, the modern slave narrative has emancipatory power as a linguistic weapon of the violated. Respecting, then, *how* the experience of slavery is narrated, as well as *what* the experience is, we are publishing the narratives—both written and oral—as they were told. We have made no additions or rearrangements to create happy endings or dramatic climaxes, no attempts to clean up oddities of phrasing.

Subtle, complex, and creative, these are voices telling "a free story," as William Andrews writes of nineteenth-century slave narrators. And, as Henry Louis Gates Jr. notes of earlier slave narratives, the texts are

---

[3] Kay Schaffer and Sidonie Smith, *Human Rights and Narrated Lives: The Ethics of Recognition* (New York: Palgrave Macmillan, 2004), 1, 4.

a "reversal of the master's attempt to transform a human being into a commodity," for they give "witness" to "the possession of a humanity shared in common" with nonslaves. Slavery makes a person "an object," in Dina's words. Nu has felt "like a piece of flesh, being inspected, bought, and sold," Beatrice and other women have been examined "as if we were vacuum cleaners," and Iliona has experienced the transformation of women into "senseless objects." But now the narrators make themselves *subjects* of a story instead of objects for sale and assert their humanity in the wake of being "less than human" (as Jill puts it) or "not a human being" (as William observes). Now, as then, former slaves are engaged in a process of "self-making" and achieve with their narratives what Andrews terms "literary emancipation."[4]

The book is divided into five sections. Section 1 offers what one narrator, Bin, refers to as the "strange scene" of slavery: narratives of prison camp slavery, war slavery, contract slavery in factories, bonded labor in stone quarries, sex slavery, fetish slavery in shrines, and carpet loom slavery. They are by men, women, and children, by individuals enslaved within their own countries (like the Sudanese and Indian narrators), and by individuals trafficked across international borders. Isra's narrative describes trafficking from developing countries into North America, while the Chinese prison camp narratives show slavery entering the global economy. The narratives are by individuals still held in bondage (Munni and Shanti), by slaves who were liberated by abolitionists (like most of the children from India), and by slaves who freed themselves (like Valdete).[5]

The narratives in section 2 focus on the particularities of the modern slave experience for women and girls—an experience that often includes sexual exploitation. Composed by women from Asia, Africa, the United States, and eastern Europe, who were trafficked internally and

---

[4] William L. Andrews, *To Tell a Free Story: The First Century of Afro-American Autobiography, 1760–1865* (Urbana: University of Illinois Press, 1986), 99; Henry Louis Gates Jr., *The Signifying Monkey: A Theory of African American Literary Criticism* (New York: Oxford University Press, 1988), 128; Saidiya Hartman, *Scenes of Subjection: Terror, Slavery, and Self-Making in Nineteenth-Century America* (New York: Oxford University Press, 1997); Andrews, *To Tell a Free Story*, 99.

[5] In the case of the Sudanese narrators, the narratives are also by slaves who were "redeemed" (bought out of slavery). In 1995, Christian Solidarity International (CSI), a Zurich-based international human rights organization, began a Sudanese slave redemption campaign. It paid $50 for every person liberated. In 1999 it went to North Bahr al Ghazal, in Sudan, and redeemed 1,050 slaves—including the individuals who provide narratives in section 1. Paying a slaveholder or a middleman to free a slave is regrettable, since freedom is a right and shouldn't need to be purchased. But sometimes redemption may be the only immediate answer and doesn't necessarily encourage the economic logic of supply and demand. In Sudan, for example, slave raiding can be an act of terror that happens to have an economic by-product.

across international borders, these narratives resist the idea that there can be any single voice or face of female slavery. As Kaew puts it in her narrative, "If you talk to different women, you will get very different stories." These women recount the varied origins of slavery, including poverty and sexual abuse at home or within marriages, kidnappings, and false offers of good jobs abroad. They describe a variety of slave experiences, from thefts of their passports and forced plastic surgeries to torture, mock executions, private and public rapes, starvation, forced marriages, abortions, drug addiction, and threats to kill their families. The narrators tell varied liberation stories and offer details of their lives after slavery: attempts to support their children, the decision to enter prostitution, time in prison, rejection by their families, or HIV infection.

Yet running throughout these stories is a sense of the shared impact of slavery on women. "No one in the world can get over sleeping with one man after another who does not love you," argues Nu. Seven months pregnant and living at a shelter in Bangkok, Nu offers a statement of despair for all girls born into her world: "I am waiting to give birth to my baby. I hope it is not a girl. She must not suffer like me." Christine, who refers to all sex slaves as her "sisters," describes the collective identity of trafficking survivors: "We are women in search of freedom." She imagines herself as a representative of the female slave experience: "I am not alone in my testimony, and I am not alone in spirit." Addressing other slaves directly, Christine shifts in her narrative from "we" to "you."[6] She forges a collective through the page itself, concluding, "You have my word that I will lend you my hand." Other women in section 2 use the same strategy: "I'll call myself Maria in this story....There are many Marias." And as a representative woman of twenty-first-century slavery, Maria, for one, believes her narrative might "stop 'Maria's Story' from happening again."

The narratives in section 3 take up the idea of a turning point from slave to free and offer different timetables, reasons, and processes for this turning point. For some narrators it was a sudden realization, and for others it was a gradual shift. Some craft the physical journey into and out of slavery as a psychological passage, and others explain the *psychological* passage in *physical* terms. Some focus on the moment of escape, and

---

[6] For a detailed discussion of pronouns in oral narratives, see Anne Salazar Orvig, *Les mouvements du discours: Style, référence et dialogue dans des entretiens cliniques* (Paris: L'Harmattan, 1999). Salazar Orvig discusses the dynamic shifting of personal pronouns (119–53), observing the displacement (*déplacement*) or gliding (*glissement*) of referential meanings as narrators "play" with multiple deixis in order to achieve specific discursive effects (144).

others explain that the real turning point occurred before they broke free from enslavement. And for some, the turning point comes a long time after their liberation, as though being free means more than just walking away from bondage. True liberation is often a process, not an event, and Roseline's narrative even has a double ending—as though her life after slavery is a long process of shifting from bondage to freedom. "It's good, after all, that everything happened. It actually made me strong, so I can face anything that comes to me," she observes, but adds that the "clock can't turn back," that the "damage...will stay with me for the rest of my life....I can never forget."[7]

The narrators in section 4 explore this problem of freedom. Formerly child soldiers, sex slaves, restavecs, and chattel slaves, they are in different stages of reaction and recovery. Their narratives reveal the self in flux, still shifting and reshifting across the turning point, and the self in stasis, trapped on the side of slavery even after liberation. Surviving the experience of enslavement, as Jill observes in her narrative, doesn't mean that individuals have "become safe from it." For the narrators, one problem of freedom is the vast gulf between their own experiences and those of free people. Jean-Robert extends this gulf of experience to encompass the ironic coexistence of slavery and abolition's bicentennial ("every Haitian will take to the streets to celebrate, except the children forced into domestic slavery"). He uses the second-person pronoun nine times in his first paragraph alone to extend this irony. Setting up a division between "you and us," "their and we," he hits home his message that restavecs are "observers instead of participants in their own society," forcing a recognition of the potential differences between the reader's experiences and those of the narrator, and demanding an effort of connection across difference.[8]

In spite of the struggle to find a clean psychological turning point from slavery to freedom, slaves look for a solution. For some of the narrators in section 5, a philosophy of freedom began in slavery and was the driving force behind their self-liberation. "Liberty was a thing that was necessary, that all the slaves must dream of....I always believed that I had to be free, and I think that helped me to escape," writes Salma. For others, like Ramphal and Tina, the solution is the antislavery movement and their

---

[7] In his famous narrative, published in 1845, Douglass describes "the turning-point" when he knew that "however long I might remain a slave in form, the day had passed forever when I could be a slave in fact." See Frederick Douglass, *Narrative of the Life of Frederick Douglass, an American Slave* (1845), in *Douglass Autobiographies* (New York: Library of America, 1996), 65.

[8] In her 1861 slave narrative, Harriet Jacobs expressed the same problem of freedom: "The dream of my life is not yet realized," she concludes. See Harriet Jacobs, *Incidents in the Life of a Slave Girl* (Cambridge, Mass.: Harvard University Press, 2000), 201.

own abolitionist work after liberation. And the narrators ask for the reader's involvement in that antislavery movement. "I want you to read this attentively," writes Salma, addressing the reader directly. Tina and William call for a shift from the reading experience to action. "You have to speak to people, to let them know," instructs William. "Now that you have the knowledge, what will you do with it?" asks Tina.[9]

The narrators in section 5 also insist on their own definitions of slavery and freedom. Choti defines slavery as "doing all the work…and not getting any assistance or any monetary benefit." For Ramphal, slavery means never being "free to…make our own choices," no longer being "individuals." Equally, Choti defines freedom as the opportunity to "study" and "learn." For Shyamkali it means "we work if we want to, and not if we don't want to," and for Sumara it means "we earn our own livelihood." And for Ramphal, freedom is "the fact that I can control my own mind, my own thoughts, my own movements" and have the chance to think ahead, "to not only live as I want to live but hope for a better future." That better future began in Ramphal's case with his new community. After liberation, Ramphal and other quarry slaves from the state of Uttar Pradesh, in India, founded the village of Azad Nagar, which means "the land that is free." In early 2006, an election was announced in rural Uttar Pradesh, and ninety-nine former slaves from the region surrounding Azad Nagar ran for office. Two weeks later, seventy-nine had been elected, including thirty-one women. "If you just stretch your eyes one day," notes Ramphal of Azad Nagar, "you might catch a glimpse of it."

SLAVERY NOW, SLAVERY THEN

The laws allowing slavery have been rescinded, but slavery occurs on every continent except Antarctica. Some selected hotspots include Albania, where teenage girls are trafficked into sex slavery by organized crime rings; Burma, where the military junta enslaves its own people to build infrastructure projects; Ghana, where families repent for sins by giving daughters as slaves to fetish priests; India, where children trapped in debt bondage roll beedi cigarettes for fourteen hours a day; Mauritania, where Arab Berbers or "white Moors" buy and sell black Africans as inheritable property; Sudan, where Arab militias from the north seize women and children from Southern Sudan in slave raids; Thailand, where women

---

[9] Douglass described this process of finding freedom as one by which a "man was made a slave" but a "slave was made a man." See Douglass, *Narrative*, 60.

and children become sex slaves for tourists; and the United Arab Emirates, where Bangladeshi boys are exploited as jockeys for camel racing. In the United States, a conservative estimate suggests that there may be 40,000 people in slavery at any one time, and the State Department estimates that 14,000–17,500 people are trafficked into the country each year. Slavery is prevalent in five sectors of the U.S. economy: prostitution and sex services (46%), domestic service (27%), agriculture (10%), factory work (5%), and restaurant and hotel work (4%). Forced labor operations tend to thrive in states with large immigrant communities, and victims come from numerous ethnic and racial groups.[10]

Between six hundred thousand and eight hundred thousand men, women, and children are believed to be trafficked across international borders each year, and trafficking is now the third largest source of income for organized crime, only exceeded by arms and drugs trafficking. The broad variations across regions and cultures mean that there can be no uniform answer to the question, What causes trafficking? But there *are* a number of commonalities. First, criminal groups choose to traffic in persons because it is high profit and often low risk. Unlike other "commodities," people can be used repeatedly, and trafficking in persons does not require a large capital investment. Second, many victims fall prey to trafficking because they are vulnerable to false promises of good jobs and higher wages. Third, political instability, militarism, civil unrest, internal armed conflict, and natural disasters may result in increased trafficking. The destabilization and displacement of populations increase their vulnerability to exploitation. Fourth, in some countries, social or cultural practices contribute to enslavement—whether through the devaluation of women and girls in society or the practice of entrusting poor children to more

[10] For the figure of 14,000–17,500, see U.S. Department of State, "Trafficking in Persons Report," June 2004 (Washington, D.C.: U.S. Department of State Publication, 2004), 23. Determining the exact number of victims in the United States has proven difficult given the hidden nature of forced labor and the government's practice of not counting the actual number of persons trafficked or caught in a situation of forced labor in a given year. Instead, it counts only survivors (defined by the Victims of Trafficking and Violence Protection Act of 2000 as victims of a "severe form of trafficking") who have been assisted in accessing immigration benefits. But multiplying the number flowing into the country by the average number of years spent in slavery provides a conservative estimate of around forty thousand people at any one time. For more on modern slavery see Kevin Bales, *Disposable People: New Slavery in the Global Economy* (Berkeley: University of California Press, 1999); Gilbert King, *Woman, Child for Sale: The New Slave Trade in the 21st Century* (New York: Chamberlain Brothers, 2004); Dale Tomich, *Through the Prism of Slavery: Labor, Capital, and World Economy* (Lanham, Md.: Rowman and Littlefield, 2004); Christien van den Anker, *The Political Economy of New Slavery* (New York: Palgrave Macmillan, 2004); and Kate Manzo, "Modern Slavery, Global Capitalism and Deproletarianisation in West Africa," *Review of African Political Economy* 32, no. 106 (2005): 521–34.

affluent friends and relatives. Some parents agree to take an "advance" on the wages their children will supposedly earn, not just for the money but also in hope that their children will escape a situation of poverty. Finally, the fear of HIV/AIDS is another factor—children are attractive to sex slavery traffickers due to the belief that they are free from the disease.[11]

A recent statistical study sought to determine the factors that most strongly predict trafficking in persons from and to countries. It concluded that the most significant predictors, in order of importance, are: the level of a country's governmental corruption; the country's infant mortality rate; the proportion of the population below the age of fourteen; the level of the country's food production; the country's population density; and the amount of conflict and social unrest the country suffers. This finding confirms much of the common knowledge held by experts working on trafficking in persons around the world—that traffic is most likely to flow from countries that are poor and suffering from instability and corruption. These are the powerful push factors. At the same time, the study found that pull factors were much weaker in predicting human trafficking. Those that did emerge as significant were: the proportion of the destination country's male population over age sixty; the level of governmental corruption; the level of food production; and low infant mortality. From a trafficker's point of view the perfect destination country would be a relatively rich country with just enough corruption to allow low-risk access across its borders.[12]

Beyond this traffic from poorer to richer countries (primarily the poorer global South to the richer global North), today's middle passage is made at several other levels: from poorer to richer districts within a country, and from poorer to richer countries within a region. One example is the complex passage of enslaved children in West Africa. Here, in what was the key origin region of the trans-Atlantic slave trade, the flow from the old Slave Coast is both internal and external. While the poorest children are moved into agricultural work, perhaps from Mali or Burkina Faso to Ghana, Ghanaian children may be sent as domestics to Nigeria or Cameroon, and Nigerian and Cameroonian children will be sent to Europe or North America as domestics or prostitutes. Children are moved

---

[11] For the figure of six hundred thousand to eight hundred thousand see U.S. Department of State, "Trafficking in Persons Report," June 2005 (Washington, D.C.: U.S. Department of State Publication, 2005), 6. For further statistics on human trafficking, see United Nations Office on Drugs and Crime, "Trafficking in Persons Global Patterns," April 2006.

[12] Kevin Bales, "Testing a Theory of Modern Slavery," presented at "From Chattel Slavery to State Servitude: Slavery in the 20th Century," the Gilder Lehrman Center for the Study of Slavery, Resistance, and Abolition, Yale University, October 22–23, 2004.

constantly from country to country into various forms of slavery and to other parts of the world.

The end point of the journey—whether around a region or from continent to continent—is slavery. Today, that slavery is most prevalent in three forms:

> 1. Chattel slavery, the form closest to old slavery, is described in the narratives by Tamada, Salma, Selek'ha, and Oumoulkhér. A person is captured, born, or sold into permanent servitude, and ownership is often asserted.
> 2. Debt bondage slavery, the most common form of modern slavery, is described by Ramphal, Choti, Shyamkali, Sumara, Shanti, and Munni. A person pledges himself or herself as collateral against a loan of money, but the length and nature of the service is not defined and their labor does not diminish the original debt.
> 3. Contract slavery, the most rapidly growing form of slavery, is described by Isra and Vi. Contracts guarantee employment, perhaps in a workshop or factory, but when the worker is taken to their place of work they find they are enslaved.

Then there are several other forms that account for a smaller proportion of today's slaves: 1) war slavery, described by William; 2) child soldier slavery, described by Aida, Dia, and Manju; 3) prison camp slavery, described by Shengqi, Sam, Ying, Jennifer, and Bin; 4) the *restavec* system, described by Jean-Robert; and 5) *trokosi* slavery, which is justified by religious tradition, described by Patience. Joy describes another use of religious ritual, whereby traffickers in Europe apply West African voodoo to discourage Nigerian women from attempting to escape.

Across all these forms, slavery's core attributes remain the same as they have always been: slavery is still a social and economic relationship in which a person is controlled through violence or its threat, paid nothing, and economically exploited. The essence of slavery is neither legal ownership nor the business of selling people but controlling people through violence and using them to make money. And slavery doesn't have to be permanent or lifelong. That has never been a requirement, even when slavery was legal. The ancient Babylonian law and the Louisiana Slave Code of 1824 both allowed for temporary enslavement.

Yet while contemporary slavery shares with the slavery of the past the essentials of violence and exploitation, it has—in addition to its illegality— three further characteristics that make it very different. First, while the slave traffic of the past provided a resource base and was an instrument for the achievement of colony and empire, today it does not play a key part in any country's economy and is instead the realm of small criminal businessmen. Second, slavery today is not dependent on race or ethnicity. In Pakistan, for example, many enslaved brick makers are Christians and the slaveholders are Muslim, but there are also Christians who are *not* slaves. In India, slave and slaveholder may be of different castes, but members of the same caste as the slave are also free. Enslaved prostitutes in Japan are more likely to be Thai or Philippine women, but they may also be Japanese. Though race, caste, tribe, and religion do initially look like markers of slavery, these differences simply make people vulnerable to slave traders: behind every assertion of ethnic difference is the reality of economic disparity. Only in a few countries, such as Mauritania, does the racism of old slavery persist: there, Arab slaveholders have black slaves and race is a key division.

Third, while chattel slaves were sizable investments, today's slaves are so cheap they are disposable. The fall in price has been so dramatic that the basic economic equation of slavery has been forever altered. The field slave who cost the equivalent of $40,000 in 1850s Alabama costs less than $100 in twenty-first-century Ivory Coast. When the price of any commodity drops so radically, the balance of supply and demand is radically changed along with concepts of value and usefulness. Today there is a glut of potential slaves on the market. That means they are worth very little but also that they are capable of generating high profits, since their ability to work has not fallen with their price. The amount of profit to be made on slaves in 1850s Alabama averaged around 5 percent. Now, profits from slavery start in double figures and range as high as 800 percent.

In spite of these differences between nineteenth-century chattel slavery and the new slavery of the global economy, history does inform the modern debate. Sam Lomax, a colonel in the security sector of Liberia, recently observed that trafficking in his country "brings us back again to those days when our fathers, uncles, were taken away, carried to plantations." Such memories, Lomax added, force awareness that "the issue of slavery still exists." Government officials see the power of historical memory as well. "We want to end [slavery] in the U.S. and take the lead to end it wherever we can in the world," commented John Miller, director of the Office to Monitor and Combat Trafficking in Persons at the U.S. State Department, in August 2006. "We've suffered the stain of slavery in this country and I think that makes us more sensitive to this issue," he said.

Likewise, in December 2006 UN secretary-general Kofi Annan acknowledged the past's unfinished work: "The 200th anniversary of the abolition of the slave trade in the British colonies…will be a powerful reminder of centuries of struggle and progress in combating slavery—but also of the fact that we still have not managed to eliminate it completely.…Let us pledge to draw on the lessons of history to free our fellow human beings from slavery." And in 2007, the U.S. State Department's 2007 "Trafficking in Persons Report" noted: "Two hundred years ago, the British Parliament outlawed the trans-Atlantic slave trade, culminating a decades-long struggle led by William Wilberforce.…Today we are again called by conscience to end the debasement of our fellow men and women. As in the 19th century, committed abolitionists around the world have come together in a global movement to confront this repulsive crime." And, as in the nineteenth century, former slaves work with these "committed abolitionists," pleading their own cause.[13]

A LAST JUNETEENTH

Many of the great obstacles faced by abolitionists of the past have either been torn down or blown away. The moral argument is already won: every country condemns slavery, and no major religious group attempts to morally justify it. In addition, the monetary value of slavery in the world economy is very small. The $13 to $30 billion in annual slave-based revenues is a drop in the world's economic ocean, and these funds flow to support not national economies or transnational industries, but small-scale criminal networks. The end of slavery threatens no country's livelihood, and the cost of ending slavery is just a fraction of the amount that freed slaves will be able to pump into the global economy. Another great advantage for contemporary abolitionists is that, for the most part, the laws needed to end slavery are already on the books. Bringing an end to slavery requires the political will to enforce law, not campaigns to make new laws. Political will (in most countries) is directly proportional to public awareness and concern. We might also take heart from the fact that while 27 million is the largest number of individuals ever enslaved at one time, it is the smallest ever proportion of the global population.

[13] Sam Lomax's comments were made to the Faith Alliance against Slavery and Trafficking (FAAST), January 2006, in Makeni, Sierra Leone; John Miller, quoted in Joan Delaney, "Canada Prone to Human Trafficking," the *Epoch Times,* August 10–17, 2006, A3; Kofi Annan, "Information Release 54/06: The International Day for the Abolition of Slavery" (United Nations Information Center, December 2, 2006); U.S. Department of State, "Trafficking in Persons Report," June 2007 (Washington, D.C.: U.S. Department of State Publication, 2007), 1.

Ramphal's "land that is free" *is* within reach for all slaves. The world is inaugurating another great antislavery movement. Though still in its infancy, it has made remarkable progress. In the United States, Ghana, India, Pakistan, Italy, Brazil, Japan, and a host of other countries, slaves are being liberated. Every time a slave comes to freedom we learn another lesson about how slavery can end. But there is no magic bullet that will stop slavery in every country or village; as Dina warns, we must not seek "easy solutions to difficult problems." Ending slavery in the United States will be different than ending slavery in India, Ghana, or Thailand. Like many crimes, slavery takes on the coloration and culture of its surroundings. Integrated into the local as well as the global economy, slavery has roots. Nearly every country will need to build a unique set of responses to slavery. Japan, for example, has the resources it needs to eradicate slavery very quickly inside the country, but it has an extreme shortage of political will. Poor countries may have the best intentions in the world but not enough money to take on the slaveholders.[14]

No revolution is needed to free slaves today, just adjustments. Some of these adjustments are as small, for example, as adding a line to the next Peace Corps appropriation bill in Congress announcing that in the next intake there will be a call for volunteers who want to work with slaves. Others are larger: the UN needs to appoint a "special representative of the secretary-general" on slavery; World Health Organization strategies need to be refocused through a slavery lens; foreign aid should be thought through with an antislavery focus, some of it targeting the underlying economic desperation that engenders slavery; and trade policies should reflect the idea that slave-made goods are taboo on the world market. Trade financing can be linked to demonstrable efforts to remove slavery from local as well as international markets. From local police to the UN, all can play a part in ending slavery.

Public awareness, education, honest law enforcement, government action, economic support, and rehabilitation are all key ingredients in the process. In many ways, it is public awareness and opinion that catalyzes the entire mix. Significant portions of the global population do not know or believe that slavery still exists, including large numbers of policymakers and law enforcement officials, who should be at the front line of response. In turn, this lack of awareness means that few resources are brought to bear. The U.S. government, for example, devotes around $200 million each year to combating slavery and human trafficking. Compare that to

---

[14] See the appendix to this book for a list of contemporary abolitionist groups.

the $40 billion spent on the "war on drugs," or the $102 billion that was spent on the occupation of Iraq in 2006. With so little spent to fight slavery it is not surprising that estimated detection and conviction rates rarely exceed 1 percent of existing slavery cases, even in the rich nations of the global North.

Sufficient public awareness would mean enough resources and enough pressure on politicians to make several things happen. One of the best guards against slavery is education. Many people are enslaved through deception. "Recruiters" hold out the chance of a good job to the economically desperate just long enough to take control of their lives. Women in the Ukraine, men in the slums of Brazil, girls in the villages of northern Thailand, and boys in Nepal all repeat this story. But against this deception a little education goes a long way. Young girls from Nepal are sold into prostitution in India. One organization that frees these young women also helps them visit villages to talk about their experiences. After hearing their stories, the parents who were ready to believe the lies of the recruiter, the girls who once yearned for jobs in the big city, and the local elders who were bribed by the con men are less likely to be tricked again. For the girls especially, meeting someone much like themselves who faces the death sentence of AIDS is an awakening. On a wider level, governments need to run advertising and education campaigns about slavery and trafficking in the same way they would in a public health crisis.

Alongside this effort of education, governments need to effectively rehabilitate freed slaves. In many countries, freed slaves are treated as illegal aliens or second-class citizens—kept poor and powerless within an informal apartheid system. In some languages, there is a special pejorative name for exslaves. As they decriminalize the victims of slavery and trafficking, governments need to provide support for them. When bonded laborers have been freed in India but given no rehabilitation, some slide back into slavery. But antislavery groups have seen that when children are equipped with skills and education, they return to their villages feeling empowered and committed to ending child slavery. These children often become village leaders. The adults come to rely on them because they may be the only people in the village who can read and write, and because they show no fear in confronting landlords or local police. The example and influence of a single rehabilitated slave can dramatically alter a whole village.

Consumers have a part in the process of ending slavery as well. Even the narratives of a country's internal slave system are often also narratives of the global economy. For example, Bin was enslaved within China, but he focuses on the final destinations of slave-made products. Insisting that slavery creeps into consumers' homes, he describes slaves packaging underwear with bloody fingernails and adds, "I was not sure if women would really look graceful in that underwear." He notes that slaves left their "diseased skin and sexually transmitted diseases" on light bulbs, and that when he saw beans imported from China in a U.S. supermarket he "wondered if our prison had made its contribution." For, although slaves like Bin were not trafficked to the rich nations of the West, slavery is often closer than we think. We can point to documented cases of slavery in cocoa, cotton, sugar, timber, beef, tomatoes, lettuce, apples and other fruits, shrimp and other fish products, coffee, steel, gold, tin, diamonds and other gemstones, jewelry and bangles, tantalum (a mineral used to make cell phones and laptops), shoes, sporting goods, clothing, fireworks, rope, rugs and carpets, rice, and bricks. We can use our consumer power to ask companies to examine their supply chains. If companies and consumers work with antislavery groups and everyone takes responsibility for the product chain, then slavery can be removed from the product at its source. For example, a method now exists for determining that a carpet was not made with slave labor. Known as the RugMark system, this is an inspection and labeling procedure certifying that a rug is slave free. Another example is the Harkin-Engel Protocol. Signed in 2001, this agreement states that there will be "credible, mutually-acceptable, voluntary, industry-wide standards of public certification, consistent with federal law" that cocoa is not being grown with child and slave labor. The protocol also established the International Cocoa Initiative, an organization that has channeled more than $15 million from the chocolate industry into effective antislavery projects in West Africa.

Another element needed to end slavery is training and resources in law enforcement. Laws exist but are not enforced. Pakistan, for example, enacted a strong law against debt-bondage slavery in 1988, but in spite of a large number of cases coming to light, not a single offender has been convicted. More than twenty-five years ago India enacted a law against bondage, setting a three-year prison sentence and a fine. But of the hundreds of cases prosecuted, no convicted slaveholder has ever served prison time. Today fines of just 100 rupees (less than $2) are common for those convicted, making a mockery of the law. And the chance of enforcing laws is most difficult in countries with corrupt law enforcement. In western Europe, Canada, and the United States, slavery happens *in spite of* the efforts of law enforcement; but in many countries slavery grows *because* of the work of the police. A simple payment to the local police allows the use of violence without fear of arrest—or sometimes the police themselves will provide violence for an extra fee.

Even in the United States, where the government spends more on law enforcement than any other country, a task force on human trafficking only appeared in 1998. The task force began to train police, but those who have been trained find that the government's response to slavery is haphazard and a low priority. A report by the CIA in 1999 found serious difficulties in information sharing and coordination and, worse, few resources to fight human trafficking. A small expansion of the "war on drugs" to include antislavery police could make a world of difference—the economic cost of enslaving others and the likelihood of punishment could be increased to the point that slaveholding would cease to be viable.

Finally, successful community-based solutions need to be scaled up as much as possible. Community-based freedom may be the best strategy of all. Rescuing individual slaves can leave the slave-based businesses intact, but when a whole community drives out the slave takers and slaveholders, freedom is locked in place. Small-scale programs for liberation and rehabilitation in a number of countries have demonstrated that slavery can be eradicated from communities and regions at a relatively low cost—slave families can come to freedom in rural India at a cost of about $130, and the cost of liberating and rehabilitating child slaves in Ghana is about $400 per child. Once a successful strategy is tested, it should be proactively offered to the world as an "open source" program, shared freely with all. Antislavery groups need to join together and cooperate, forming a wider movement with a shared identity. When slavery is linked to exports and products, the antislavery groups need to join with industries in working to stop slavery at its source on the farm or in the factory. When influence could help tip government policies, they need to work with international bodies such as the UN. As we begin the long process of turning around governments and building the international alliance against slavery, ending slavery means acting locally *and* globally.

Ramphal imagines emancipation "one day." Other narrators echo his phrase. Salma remembers telling her mother "that one day I would be free." Miguel remembers thinking that "one day we're going to have the opportunity." And Christina told herself that "one day everything is going to be OK" and prayed "for one day to come when I could be free." This "one day" in modern slave narratives is a reminder that those who remain enslaved now face what might be termed "a long Juneteenth." The Juneteenth holiday, still celebrated by some black communities, marks the day when news of the Emancipation Proclamation finally reached the people of Texas—on June 19, 1865. In the early 1960s, Atlanta civil rights campaigners wore "Juneteenth" buttons to insist that true emancipation was still delayed—by a century, rather than two and a half years. And now, in the twenty-first century, the delay in ending slavery within the United States and around the world has become even longer. As Ralph Ellison put it in his novel *Juneteenth,* which he wrote throughout the 1960s, the idea that slavery is over is "a gaudy illusion."[15]

The "one day" of a final Juneteenth has not yet arrived. But as we read these new slave narratives, we might remember the achievements of the nineteenth-century abolitionist movement. On the eve of the American Revolution, few Americans could envision a world without slavery. Yet, one hundred years later, slavery did become illegal in the United States. This achievement stemmed from the collective protest of countless slaves, ex-slaves, and abolitionists—from a crusade that created a new framework for equality and fostered a culture of dissent. The Juneteenth holiday reminds us that legal change is not enough. By seeking, achieving, and redefining freedom, the narrators in this book envision a new, global, and final Juneteenth.

[15] Ralph Ellison, *Juneteenth* (New York: Vintage, 1999), 115.

SIGHTS AND SCENES

Modern Slave Experiences

I was born amid such sights and scenes.
  Frederick Douglass, "What to the Slave Is the Fourth of July?" 1852

It was such a strange scene.
  Wang Bin, a former prison camp slave, China, 2005

PRISON CAMP SLAVERY

Hundreds of thousands of people are trafficked across international borders each year, but millions more are enslaved within their own countries. Between four million and six million people are slave laborers in China's "laogai" (reform-through-labor) camps, according to the Laogai Research Foundation. Most likely, China has about one thousand of these forced-labor camps. Created by the Chinese Communist Party under Mao Zedong, the laogai system is intended to "reeducate criminals" and uses prisoners as a source of cheap labor. The camps produce major consumer goods and pay no salaries. Prisoners work for up to sixteen hours a day and experience solitary confinement, torture, gang rape, sleep deprivation, malnutrition, drugging, and brainwashing.

Some of the laogai prisoners are practitioners of Falun Gong, a spiritual movement that was banned in China in 1999. Human rights organizations claim that Falun Gong practitioners are often targeted for arrest, along

with ethnic minorities, Catholics, Protestants, and Tibetans. By some estimates around one hundred thousand Falun Gong practitioners have been
sent to the laogai. Sam Lu, Chen Ying, Jennifer Zeng, and Wang Bin were
four of those individuals. Sam, who now lives in the United States, was
imprisoned in 2000. Ying, a student in France, was imprisoned in 2000
while visiting her family in China. Jennifer was held in Beijing's Xin'an
Female Labor Camp and forced to make toys. Bin, a reporter for a newspaper that reported on Falun Gong, spent two years in the laogai. Labor
and prodemocracy activists are also targeted for laogai imprisonment.
Fu Shengqi was held repeatedly between 1981 and 1995 on charges of
counterrevolutionary propaganda and was granted political asylum in the
United States in 1996.

Shengqi (CHINA, 1997)

From January 1983, I was a prisoner at the Shanghai Municipal Prison
because of my political statements. The government had devised a system of work points to control the prisoners. Prisoners were forced to
labor. Work points were deducted for failure to fulfill quotas. Once or
twice a week, a prisoner could watch TV. Once a month they could watch
a movie, buy foodstuffs, or meet with their family. These benefits were
deprived for failure to fulfill quotas or for bad performance in reform.
Hence, many prisoners were forced to labor overtime to maintain the
work points. Those who were slower could have only three or four hours
of sleep a day. I witnessed how the prison established a radio assembly
shop. As I learned from the other prisoners and policemen, the prison
also ran a regular print shop and other shops.

From July 1993 to April 1994, I was incarcerated at the 2nd Company,
3rd Battalion, Shanghai Reeducation-through-Labor (Laojiao) Farm located in Dafeng County, Jiangsu Province. Again, my political activities
were my crime. In cooperation with Shanghai No. 18 Knitting Mill, the
battalion made interlock jerseys. Laojiao inmates were forced to labor
and reform their thinking. In the busiest time, they had to labor nearly
twenty hours a day. Inmates, while working at sewing machines, often fell
asleep. In slack season, several hours a day inmates sat on benches studying, writing a report of what they learned from the studies. The 1st Company, 3rd Battalion, established a shop for making the teaching slides.

In April 1994, I was transferred to the 5th Battalion. In 1994 and in
1995, I witnessed how from June to October the battalion's 2nd Company
assembled multicolored Christmas lights for export for Haiman Lamps

Factory and a lamp factory in Jiangsu Province. Each box consisted of thirty-six, fifty, one hundred, or two hundred lights on a string. The lights I have at hand are similar to those processed at the 2nd Company. The task was hard. Every inmate had to labor overtime, many laboring until one or two at night. Those who failed to fulfill quotas were punished. Inmates at the woolen sweater mill also often labored overtime. Inmates in farming had to labor overtime even more. For instance, inmates who transplanted rice seedlings often labored from seven in the morning until eight at night.

On laojiao farms, inmates were often beaten and cursed. The government cadres cuffed and kicked them at will. Those laojiao inmates trusted to supervise other inmates beat and cursed them even more. I was also beaten by them. In China, laogai and laojiao facilities are not common prisons but are the Communist Party's tool for consolidating its one-party rule. Not only do the facilities force prisoners to labor for profit, they also force inmates to accept brainwashing. The thought-reform made them surrender to the Communist Party.

Sam (CHINA, 2003)

I used to be a graduate student at Georgia State University in 1996. I'd like to share my personal experience to let people know why some products from China are so cheap. Before I returned to the United States in February 2001, I worked as a tax auditor in China for nine years. On June 7, 2000, I was arrested in China only because I handed in a letter at the State Appeal Bureau in Beijing to express my opinion about Falun Gong, which is a traditional exercise based on "Truthfulness, Compassion, and Forbearance" and which is being persecuted in China. I was put in a jail in Guangdong Province for almost two months. Here I will not mention how the Chinese government persecuted family church members, Tibetan monks, and Falun Gong practitioners. I only want to let you know how some products from China are made and why they are so cheap.

In prison I was forced to work on export products such as toys and shopping bags without pay....The cell was only about three hundred square feet in size, with twenty prisoners and one toilet inside. They slept and worked in the cell. Sometimes we were forced to work until two A.M. to keep up with the schedule. They only provided two meals a day (only once a week you have meat in your food). In other words, being hungry, you still need to work more than fifteen hours per day. The police used a wire whip to beat you if you did not do a good job or you could not keep up with the schedule.

Sam Lu (photograph
by Sam Lu, 2004)

During this desperate time in prison, I was always wondering who gave them the business and who helped them to abuse us. Now the same kind of tragedy is happening to my wife. She was sentenced to forced-labor camp for three years without any trial and without a lawyer only because she handed out flyers in the street to clarify the truth about Falun Gong. She has already been detained for more than thirty-four months. In my wife's letter to my parents, she mentioned that she was forced to do embroidery work for export. The hard work, malnutrition, and torture made my wife almost lose her eyesight.

In that female labor camp alone, where my wife is detained now, about three thousand female Falun Gong practitioners have been detained there and forced to work for export business. According to human rights organizations, there are more than one hundred thousand Falun Gong practitioners detained in China's forced-labor camps. How many people other than Falun Gong practitioners are detained in forced-labor camps and prisons and are forced to work without pay for China's export business? Who knows?

Ying (CHINA, 2004)

I was imprisoned between November 2000 and November 2001 for refusing to give up Falun Gong practice. During that period of time I was held in servitude at the Tuanhe Prisoner Dispatch Center and the Xin'an

Female Labor Camp in Beijing. While there, I was forced to do slave labor. I was forced to make various types of slave-labor products.

Products Made at Tuanhe Prisoner Dispatch Center
1. Packaged large quantities of disposable chopsticks. Most of them are being used in restaurants and hotels while some are being exported.
2. Made Florance Gift Package [a cosmetic product].

Products Made at Xin'an Female Labor Camp
1. Packaged large quantities of disposable chopsticks. Most of them are being used in restaurants and hotels while some of them are being exported.
2. Knitted sweaters.
3. Knitted woolen gloves (60 yuan per pair, exported to Europe).
4. Crocheted cushions for tea sets.
5. Crocheted hats for a company at Qinghe Township, Beijing. Knitted seat cushions.
6. Reprocessed sweaters; removed sundries from yarn.
7. Made large quantities of slippers. The job was mainly gluing the sole and the instep together, and the labor camp demanded a high-quality product. When I was there, it was the hottest time of the summer. Many practitioners and I were working in our prison cells. Working in a humid prison cell full of irritating glue odors was suffocating. We worked until midnight or one o'clock in the morning every time there was a shipment.
8. Made stuffed animals such as rabbits, bears, dolphins, and penguins, etc. Major steps included putting the stuffing material inside, stitching the doll together, sewing the eyes, and stitching the mouth, etc.

Sanitation and Living Conditions at Tuanhe Prisoner Dispatch Center
I was locked up with over a dozen Falun Gong practitioners in a cell that was about twelve square meters (130 square feet) in size. There were only eight bunk beds in the room; thus, some of us had to sleep on the floor. While we were sleeping, we had to keep our heads visible to the guards. We did everything in this cell including working, eating, drinking, and using the toilet; therefore, there were many flies and mosquitoes. At the dispatch center, we were only allowed to eat at certain times. Water was rationed; drinking water was limited. The prison guards never allowed us

to wash our hands before meals. After a meal, we had to get back to work immediately. Twice a day we were given five minutes for personal hygiene. When the time was up, we were forced to stop and drain the water. We were not allowed to take any water back to our cell. If we could not finish the work assigned to us, we were not allowed to clean ourselves. When there was a rush to get products out, we had to work late and go to sleep without washing.

There were fixed times for the whole group of practitioners to go and use the toilet. Even then, we still had to ask for permission from the guards. We were allowed two minutes to use the toilet each time; thus, many people did not even have enough time to have a bowel movement. Those who had constipation could only have bowel movements several times a month. We could go to bed only at the specified time; otherwise, we would be scolded and not allowed to sleep. At night the guards locked up all the cells; a small bucket in each cell was used for a toilet. We were watched even during sleep. Several times, I was woken up because I propped up my legs while I was sleeping. They thought I was doing Falun Gong exercises, so I had to keep my legs flat.

We were allowed very little sleep each day; we were forced to start working the moment we opened our eyes. My hands had blisters and thick calluses from working long hours to finish the assigned quota of packaging disposable chopsticks. I often worked until midnight. We were not allowed to sleep unless we finished the quota. We were forced to work over sixteen hours every day, and everything was done in our cells where we eat, drink, sleep and use the toilet. The sanitation condition was extremely poor. Even though we were packaging disposable chopsticks and the label said the chopsticks were disinfected at a high temperature, the entire process was unhygienic. We could not wash our hands, and we had to package those chopsticks that had fallen on the floor. In order to seek a huge profit, Tuanhe Prisoner Dispatch Center and Female Labor Camp disregarded the health of the general public and knowingly committed such wrong doings. Many restaurants in Beijing are currently using these chopsticks. I heard they are even being exported.

Many female practitioners were usually forced outside; all of their clothes were taken away and they stood outside, naked, for a long period of time. In the winter, some practitioners were forced to freeze outside until they lost consciousness. During these long-term tribulations, I finally reached the limit of my endurance. I signed a guarantee that I would not practice the exercises. The pain of giving up one's own belief and being transformed cannot be described in words. The next day I cried all day long.

Female practitioners are forced to perform excessive physical labor. We were forced to unload trucks full of bagged materials that weigh over one hundred pounds each. We had to carry the bags on our shoulders from the truck to our cells. Other physical labors included digging pits, planting trees, and transporting fertilizers. The police exploited our labor to create illegal income for themselves. The dispatch center did not compensate us for any of our work. In fact, we were forced to do long and hard labor without any compensation.

Sanitation and Living Conditions at Xin'an Female Labor Camp
Both our bodies and minds were imprisoned and severely persecuted under the excessive workload. The police [guards] often kept us from sleeping at regular hours. When there were work orders, we had to work day and night to produce the best product with the shortest amount of time. The police even said, "You are trying to be good people, you should do the best under every circumstance." The torture and inhuman treatment of Falun Gong practitioners by policemen is widespread and serious. While in prison, the first thing they have to do is take off all of their clothes in public and have iced water poured all over them. Everyone has to go through this severe routine, including menstruating women. This may cause them to later have problems when giving birth, but the policemen didn't care.

All the work in the labor camp is labor intensive. Falun Gong practitioners are forced to work until midnight under dim lights, and everyone has a quota to meet. If a practitioner cannot finish the quota, he/she is not allowed to sleep. One time we were making gift items...knitted products and crocheted cushions. In order to meet the shipping deadline, we were forced to work in the hallway or lavatories until one or two o'clock in the morning; we sometimes worked through the whole night. The police used this method to control our thoughts. They would not let us have a single moment of idle time to think calmly, and we were not allowed to talk to each other. They had drug addicts and ex-practitioners monitoring us. They only wanted us to work.

In order to evade people's attention, [we had to] to [go to] sleep on time every night. We got up very early in the morning to work. During summertime, our cells were so hot that people sometimes collapsed from heat exhaustion. Many practitioners developed symptoms of hypertension and heart disease from overwork. Their entire bodies twitched.

We had to say "Report, yes" loudly whenever going in and out of the jail cells. If the sound wasn't loud enough, we would be punished by being forced to shout one hundred times at the wall. Then we had to lift our legs up at a 90 degree angle while walking and then stamp down with all our strength. Before eating, we had to kneel down on the ground, hold the bowl over our head and shout loudly, "Reporting to the leader, prisoner XXX asks to have her meal."

Once they handcuffed me to the window and forcibly injected medicine into my left arm. When the medicine got into my bloodstream, I felt severe pain in my heart, and then my heartbeat sped up and beat severely. Every heartbeat felt like it would cause my heart to explode. After that, I clearly felt that I was having difficulty thinking. My reactions and memory became dull. My left side also twitched frequently and it became more and more fierce. What we were fed in jails and labor camps may have had medicines mixed in. The food smelled strange. After eating it we would feel like throwing up, and we would become very drowsy. In addition, there was brutal beating and torture. Once they beat me so badly that the prisoners who watched the beating cried and asked the policemen to stop beating me.

With some kind-hearted people's help, I was eventually able to leave China. I only want to follow the standard of "Truthfulness, Compassion, and Forbearance" to be a good person, but they forced me to change from a respectable person to an accomplice who persecuted my fellow practitioners. It is Falun Gong that will save me once again.

Jennifer (CHINA, 2005)

In the labor camp, we were forced to do all kinds of heavy labor work, including planting grass and trees, clearing garbage, digging cellars for storing vegetables in winter, knitting sweaters, knitting cushions, making toys, producing disposable syringes, wrapping sanitized chopsticks, and so on. Most of the products were for export. In particular, the sweaters we knitted were large sizes only suitable for foreigners who are big in build. In February 2001 we received an order for one hundred thousand toy rabbits....The rabbits were about thirty centimeters long, brown in color, with a long neck, wearing a large bright red collar made from fleecy material, with two black whiskers on each side of the face, about five to six centimeters long. Some of the rabbits wore cowboy vests, some wore dustcoats, and some had one eye patched up like a pirate. There were English letters on their chests, with their fists clenched, thumbs up. There were three toes on their feet, canary yellow in color. Their tails were white in color and very short.

Usually the toy rabbits for processing were delivered to the labor camp by a middle-aged woman riding a tricycle. The steps we did included: flip over the rabbit that had already been stitched from inside; stuff the man-made cotton wool into the back, neck, ears and the five-petal small flower on the head and in the collar; thread a soft steel wire into the ears; stitch together the back and collar; sew on the whiskers; use thread to stitch the mouth so as to make the gaping mouth close a little bit; sew the eyes to make them more firm; glue on the eyebrows; use thread to shape the fingers and toes on the hands and feet. (The hands and feet of the half-made product are in one piece; we used thread to pull back parts of the hand and foot tightly, so the dent looks like a finger groove.) We stitch on the tail, stick alphabets on the chests, and so forth. The tool used to stick the eyebrows and the alphabets on the chests look like a hot-air gun. Except for sticking on the eyebrows and the alphabets and stitching on the tails, I did all the other steps. The ears, five-petal small flower, and collar were separate from the body when they came to us. We stuffed man-made cotton wool into them. After filling the ears, we flipped them over and threaded a soft steel wire (or aluminum wire) into them.

The rabbit's collar is a circular loop—the diameter is about four to five centimeters. After stuffing in man-made cotton wool, it is directly sewn onto the rabbit from the outside with red thread. This is the first time I learned this method of sewing in the labor camp. The thread is pulled after sewing and the two sides will appear very even. You cannot see any traces of the stitching. This method is also used to sew the rabbit's body from the back (if you can get hold of a rabbit and carefully pull it open, you can also see if a certain section of its collar and the section slightly above its back is sewn together using this method). Before sewing it up, it is first stuffed with man-made cotton wool. There is a wire in the body of the rabbit (slightly thicker than that in its ears, the wire seems to be two-ply, all the way through to the back of its head).

The whiskers are made using black nylon string one millimeter thick. This kind of nylon string is about fifty centimeters long before being cut up for making the whiskers. It is threaded through a needle that is stuck into one side of the rabbit's cheeks through underneath its nose and out from the other cheek, leaving a five- to six-centimeter-long nylon string at the beginning spot where the needle was pricked into, thus forming the rabbit's whiskers. Then the nylon string is knotted so that it does not move and it is threaded back to the other cheek and cut off. The string is cut off so that it is around one centimeter shorter than the one above. After making the whiskers on one side, the two whiskers on the other cheek are completed using the same method. When the nylon string in the needle is used up, another is threaded in and the process is continued.

It would take over thirty processing steps to make a rabbit like this, and it would take over ten hours to make one. But the processing fee for each rabbit was only thirty cents. The processing fees were paid to the labor camp. We didn't get anything. Usually we began work after getting up at five o'clock in the morning, and we worked until two or three o'clock in the morning the next day. Sometimes we had to work overtime, otherwise we could not finish the job. At the busiest time, I did not dare to wash my hands after going to the toilet, in order to save a few minutes. At night sometimes I was so exhausted that I could not even count clearly from one to nine. Yet I still had to force my eyes open to knit sweaters. The pattern of the sweater was quite complicated; sometimes we finally finished the knitting after much effort only to discover the next morning it had been knitted completely wrongly. So, we had to unpick the stitches and redo it. Long hours of highly intensive workload and severe lack of sleep made me feel, for a very long period of time, that the only thing I needed in my life was sleep.

Bin (CHINA, 2005)

I was kept in a gloomy prison cell, about thirty square meters, with over thirty people locked inside. When I was first imprisoned in this cell, I could smell all kinds of foul odors from feces, urine, mold, rotten flesh, and materials. After a few months, I could no longer smell anything. The smells permeated everything in the cell all day and I had gotten accustomed to them. Occasionally, it would be so quiet in the cell that one could hear a pin drop. Everyone took advantage of this brief silence to ponder over his past. Day after day, quite a few people were getting closer and closer to execution day.

During the years of 2000 and 2001, following orders given by Jiang Zemin and Luo Gan, the National Security Division of the Beijing Police Department had arrested a large group of high-ranking intellectuals who practiced Falun Gong, including professors, people with PhDs and master's degrees. They were detained in the Beijing Police Department until they accepted the education of the "Party and people." This was proclaimed to the outside world as being done gently as "a breeze and rainfall in spring." I was one of them.

The prison cell had two doors, the front and the back. The front door was a thick iron door and an iron fence. The iron door was about one inch thick and the fence was made of iron poles, as wide as an adult's thumb. The back door was also an iron door, as big as the front door. The front door was an entrance-exit where prisoners were escorted in and out, or dragged out for execution. Ten armed policemen guarded the door against potential runaways. Every time the front door was opened, it could mean someone was going to die soon. Once, a "criminal" secretly sharpened the handle of a toothbrush. He poked a policeman's neck with the sharp toothbrush in an attempt to use him as a hostage to gain his release. However, hostages mean nothing to the Communist Party, and without giving it a second thought, another policeman immediately shot the prisoner to death.

The policeman who was held as hostage was terrified to death. Since this incident, the prisoners detained at the No. 1 Detention Center of the Beijing Police Department are given only the brush end of the toothbrush; the handle end is cut off.

The "wind cage" is connected to the back door of the cell. It was square-shaped and about ten square meters (about 108 square feet) in size. All four sides of the wind cage were thick concrete walls. The top was flat and made of big iron pipes on which policemen could stand in a line. The police standing on the top of the cage could open the back door to let prisoners out for fresh air and sunshine. The wind cage wasn't even opened once a week.

"Open the wind cage!" the loud shout came from a policeman standing on the top. It broke into my thinking and the temporary quiet of the cell. The pale, unkempt prisoners started to show a hint of happiness on their faces. One by one, prisoners walked outside of the back door. They nodded and bowed to show their gratitude to the policeman on the top of the wind cage. Then they quickly occupied a place with more sunlight.

The first time I was let out, I was shocked by what I saw. After they secured a place, the first thing the prisoners did was get naked. The scabies, sores, and psoriasis on their bodies were fully exposed. I was not too surprised by this. What truly shocked me was that many people quickly flipped their genital organs up into the sunlight. Then, they kept flipping them back and forth. It was such a strange scene.

If they were not sentenced to death, the criminals surviving the detention center would be sent to prisons to complete their sentence and do slave labor. At the same time, they brought sexually transmitted diseases with them to the prisons. There, they are an absolutely cheap work force. An amazing number of products made in China are produced in prisons and forced-labor camps.

In May 2002 I was sent to the Beijing Repatriation Division of Provincial Criminals with several others and Shao Ping. Shao Ping earned his master's degree from the Chinese Academy of Science. In the repatriation division, we were waiting to be repatriated to other formal prisons to serve a sentence. From this experience we gained a real understanding of forced labor in prisons.

The strict management system, frequent insults, and degrading treatment were meant to cause fear and mental trauma in the prisoners. The prisoners were expected to labor tirelessly. To labor for fifteen or sixteen hours a day was routine. If a prisoner had trouble finishing the assigned work, he was punished by having to "sing until the dawn" (that is, he had to work around the clock without sleep). Since the cells were more than full, the prisoners had no time to take care of personal hygiene. They counted the days, with their diseases worsening day by day.

I was arrested for my belief. I had committed no crimes. Nor was I a criminal. I simply considered myself a "correspondent" sent there to seriously observe what was happening around me. I hoped that one day my observations would enable the world to have a better understanding of what is going on in Chinese prisons.

Various jobs of manual labor involved packing women's underwear, making copies of audio and video materials, attaching trademarks to various products, processing books, binding books, and making for export fishing floats, colored Christmas bulbs, and accessories. I participated in all of the manual labor and had a good understanding of each working procedure. During one hot summer, the prison authorities ordered us to make packages for Gracewell underwear. It was really hot and the prisoners hadn't showered for a very long time. They scratched all over their bodies while being engaged in manual labor. Some of the prisoners scratched their private parts every now and again. When they took out their hands, I saw blood on their fingernails. I was not sure if women would really look graceful in that underwear.

Another time, the prisoners processed a kind of packaged food called "Orchid Beans" for self-employed people. This snack was made from broad beans. Self-employed people kept trucking broad beans in to the prison. In the prison there were barrels in which the broad beans were soaked in water until they were swollen. To spare themselves some trouble when changing water in the barrels, sometimes the prisoners would dump a whole barrel of beans into a dirty urinal and then pour water into the barrel putting the beans inside. When the beans became swollen in water, the prisoners would start to peel the beans. In front of everyone there was a set of parallel knives. One picked up a bean, rolling it over the knife and removing the bean skin on either side leaving a "golden belt" in the middle. In this way beans look good, though dirty and muddy. Then, the last step was to throw beans back into the basket. At least ten thousand beans had to be peeled in one day to meet the government's quota. The prisoners bustled around peeling the beans, with their snot and sputum mixed with beans. Then the processed beans were put into a big bag to be taken to the stores of the self-employed people where they would be fried. The fried broad beans looked golden and shiny. The self-employed people packed them in beautiful packages and sold them to customers. The broad beans are in demand in the market and thus of high profit to sellers. Consumers enjoy the beans. In a U.S. supermarket, I saw fried broad beans imported from China. I wondered if our prison had made its contribution to those beans.

Annually, a large number of Christmas items and clothing for Western countries are made in Chinese prisons. Once the prison in which I had been detained was assigned to make light bulbs. Every day prisoners were supposed to tie copper wires tightly around a plastic tank in a fixed shape and then connect all the light bulbs together. The prisoners' hands were usually bleeding. Needless to say, their diseased skin and sexually transmitted diseases were left on the light bulbs.

Once the prison I was in made strings of beads as accessories. The prisoners used needles and thread to string colored beads and then connected the two ends to make a string of beads. The strings of beads looked beautiful. But I hope that children will not put them in their mouths and women won't put them around their necks.

WAR SLAVERY

Along with the three main types of modern slavery (chattel slavery, debt bondage slavery, and contract slavery), war slavery is another form of contemporary bondage. For example, in Burma there is widespread capture and enslavement of civilians by the government and the army. War slavery is also a feature of the ongoing civil war in Sudan: thousands of women and children have been taken into slavery during the decades of Sudan's civil war, mainly from North Bahr al Ghazal (where these nine individuals were liberated) and the Nuba Mountains.

Slave taking was revived in 1985 in Sudan by the ruling National Islamic Front; it was used primarily as a weapon against counterinsurgents in the south, and secondarily as a way to reimburse its mercenary soldiers for neutralizing this threat. In 1989 the government created the Popular Defense Forces (PDF), militia trained to raid villages and take people as slaves. PDF recruits were allowed to keep whoever they captured, along with booty of grain and cattle. One study documents twelve thousand abductions by name, while NGOs offer estimates ranging from fifteen thousand to two hundred thousand. The female slaves were often moved to large towns in the north on weeklong journeys, during which time they were repeatedly raped. Then they were sold to new masters who used them without pay for farming and sexual services.

The ongoing peace process has brought these PDF abductions to an end, but intertribal abductions continue in Southern Sudan. In addition, Sudanese children are used by rebel groups in the ongoing Darfur conflict; Sudanese boys from the country's eastern Rashaida tribe continue to be trafficked to the Middle East for use as camel jockeys; the rebel organization Lord's Resistance Army continues to forcibly conscript small numbers of children in Southern Sudan for use as combatants in its war against Uganda; and the institution of chattel slavery continues on a large scale in South Darfur and South Kordofan. The number of chattel slaves in Sudan is estimated to be in the tens of thousands.

Abuk A. (SUDAN, 1999)

My master was called Mohammed. I never heard the rest of his name. He lives in Aliet. He had eight other slaves. One of them was Adut Tong, a woman from Warawar. He and his wife Howeya called me Miriam and made me do everything like a Muslim. Howeya was an unkind woman. I had to do all kinds of work in their home. During the rainy season, I also had to do a lot of cultivation. Mohammed often beat me. He also raped me many times. I had to sleep outside with the cows and the goats. He would come outside at night and have intercourse with me. Whenever I resisted, I got a bad beating.

Mohammed and Howeya wanted me to be a Muslim woman, so they forced me to have my genitals cut. A man did it. I don't know who he was. He tied my hands and legs down very tightly. You can still see the marks. It was so painful. I cried and cried. That was the worst thing they did to me.

I am so happy to be here now. I will go back to Warawar and Bac, and I will go back to church again. I can remember going to church in Warawar. The catechist there was Akuei Deng.

Yei (SUDAN, 1999)

I was caught together with my mother, Abuk Acueri Yei. It was three years ago at the beginning of the rainy season. I tried to run away when the attackers came. I damaged my eye while I was running away through the bush. My master was Abdullah. He lived in a village called Acharob. Abdullah gave me the hat that I still wear. He would become very angry with me if I ever took it off. He wanted me to become a Muslim. I was called Naim, and he sent me to a khalwa [Koranic school], together with other slaves.

I rejected my new name and didn't like to visit the khalwa. Because of this, my master beat me severely and sent me to a cattle camp where I had to stay. Some of my master's other slaves who had been captured before me had to wear hats too. Some of them were recruited into the *murahaleen* army [progovernment tribal militiamen] after spending some time at the khalwa. A man who had come to visit my master pierced my ears. He accused me of not listening properly to him. My mother was also released today. She stayed with a different master and I only saw her again on my way back. One of the subchiefs told me that my father is around.

Abuk G. (SUDAN, 1999)

I was captured in my home village Kur Awet near Warawar. It was early in 1997. We were suddenly surrounded by countless horsemen. A lot of my people were shot dead. The attackers who caught me were dressed in military uniforms. They raped me and many other girls. Our village was burned down completely. I lost my parents as well as my four brothers and two sisters in the attack. I don't know whether they are still alive. The attackers killed my uncle Alou Alou Deng right in front of me. We walked for about ten days; I had to carry a heavy load of sorghum grain. They had looted it from our stores.

My master was Mahmoud Mahdi. I was mistreated terribly by him. I, together with fifteen others, had to stay in an open pen near his house. He lived in Sidam. My master repeatedly raped me. Various other men who came at night also did this to me. I was given the name of Fatima. I was forced to pray the Islamic way, and now I can speak some Arabic. Slaves who tried to escape were immediately killed by my master. I saw the execution of some of them.

Achai (SUDAN, 1999)

I was at home when the soldiers came. I heard guns and started to run. Everyone else was running too. Some went in this direction, and others went that way. I ran to the forest, but I was caught by two soldiers. I had to walk to the river Kiir and then on to Daein. They made me carry a sack of durra [sorghum] on my head. The journey was about ten days long. I was together with a lot of other girls. The soldiers would take them away for sexual intercourse. The leader of the soldiers, Musa, did this to me. On the way, Musa did not beat me, but he gave me hardly any food. Musa kept me for himself. He called me "Sudan." He took me to a camp for soldiers near Daein. Musa had a home in Daein town, but he never took me there. I had to stay at his home at the army camp. It was a place where soldiers marched and learned how to prepare their guns and to shoot. There were both Arabs and Dinkas there. I had to do housework for Musa.

I could not leave the camp. Many times each day, he would say that he would shoot me or cut my throat if I tried to escape. I was very sad and couldn't help crying. He would beat me when he caught me crying. Musa used me as a concubine. I am now about five months pregnant. Musa let me go away with the trader. I think he did this because I was so sad and tearful that he didn't want me any more. I am a Christian and used to go to church at Nyamlell. One of the catechists named Mario is my friend.

Ajok (SUDAN, 1999)

I was visiting my younger sister's home near Warawar when I was captured. It happened two years ago during the dry season. The soldiers came early in the morning. Everyone was asleep. My sister and I woke up with the sound of gunfire. We ran out of her *tukul* [circular adobe house] as fast as we could. But we did not get very far. We were surrounded. There were a lot of Arab soldiers all around us. Some wore uniforms, others wore jalabeyas. They had come at night on camels and horses. Six soldiers grabbed me. I struggled with them and tried to get away. But they beat me with a big stick. I had to submit. You can see the scar on my back. I got that wound during the beating.

They tied my hands together with a rope and led me away to the bush. They raped me in the bush, one after the other, all six of them. After that, I had to walk beyond the river Kiir with the other slaves. My hands were tied to a long rope. My sister was tied to it too. Along the way we were beaten and raped. We walked for four days. Then we reached a place where the soldiers divided us and the cows and goats among themselves.

I was given to Musa. My sister was given to a man named Ibrahim. Musa was a good friend of the leader of the raiders, Mahmoud Issa from Zeri. Musa had a bodyguard and was responsible for distributing slaves and cattle among the Popular Defense Force. This meant that he was away from home a lot. Musa took me to his home in Gos. I had to do housework for his wife. She is an Arab woman named Howah. She is a very bad woman. She always loved to hit me with a big stick, even when I was ill. She made me sleep outside in the courtyard. There was no shelter over my head. Only when it rained did she let me sleep in the covered cattle pen. Sometimes Musa would come to me at night and take me to the cattle pen for sex. Whenever Howah discovered that her husband was missing at night, she would give me a good beating on the next day because her husband had come to me and not to her.

I had Musa's baby. He is now seven months old. Musa called him Ahmed, but I call him Thiop. Musa called me Howah, so he had two Howahs. The worst part about being with Musa and Howah were their threats to kill me. Whenever they told me to get water from a far place or do some other hard labor, they would say that they would cut my throat if I didn't obey. Musa would threaten me like this when he wanted to have sex with me. My sister's throat was cut by her master. Howah's children told me they saw her body when they were going to the well. They said she had tried to escape but was caught.

My sister had a very strong will. I remember that she always showed displeasure when the soldiers called her Fatima during the walk to the north. I was so afraid, I thought I have to get away from there. I knew that Musa loved Thiop and would never let him go, so I wanted to escape with him. One day, I was told by a woman who was cultivating in the fields that a trader was looking for slaves to return to their homes. I decided to escape and ran with Thiop to the forest. There I came across a Dinka man who took care of me and helped me find the trader. He brought me back here. I like being back and hearing my own name again. I also like it because no one calls me "slave" or "nigger" anymore.... Now I will go to Warawar to try to find my children and my father.

Anyang (SUDAN, 1999)

I was captured in April 1998. Several hundred Arab *murahaleen* attacked our village in the afternoon. They came on horses and many wore army uniforms.

My husband Garang Acuil Atany was at Warawar at the time of the attack. I don't know whether he is still alive. The attackers took me, my children Acien Garang and Garang Acuil, and a son of my sister who happened to be with us at the time of the attack. I was pregnant at that time.

The raiders ordered me to milk the stolen cattle on the way. I also had to lead the cattle with a stick and carried loot on my head at the same time. Some of the stolen children had to lead the goats. We were forced to march fast because the raiders feared that they would be attacked by our people from behind. We walked for five days until we reached Adeela. I thought that I would die on the way because I was totally exhausted. In Adeela we were divided. The two children stayed with me. I was given to an Arab by the name of Hamid. He ordered me to milk his cows.... It will be good to die in my own land. I am very happy now.

Abuk K. (SUDAN, 1999)

I was captured together with Anyang Anei during the last dry season. All the girls were kept separate from the boys on our long walk. I had to lead the goats and was beaten on the way. The boys were beaten even more. Their legs were tied at night. We were given leftovers from slaughtered goats.

I was taken to a man by the name of Hadi in a village called Adeela. Hadi treated me well and said he would give me in marriage to one of his sons one day. Hadi had many other slaves. I was not allowed to play with other children. I slept in the kitchen on a plastic sheet. My master didn't call me by my Dinka name but, instead, called me Howah—I have no idea why. I refused to attend the mosque and was beaten for that. But they didn't send me there again.

Hadi is a rich cattle owner and has a big house surrounded by a fence. His family ate three times per day. My job was to wash the plates and do other domestic work. I was given only leftovers to eat.

Mary (SUDAN, 1999)

I used to live in Aweil town. I was married to Michael Nyong Akol. He was a student there. I am a Christian. My husband and father were Christians too. I used to go to church in Aweil. The priest there was Father Matong. I was very happy when I was at church.

We fled Aweil some years ago when there was insecurity in the town. We went to Marin village and survived by farming. In Marin I had three children. Their names are Nyibol, Akon, and Abol. I was five months pregnant when the soldiers came and caught me. It happened when the train came to Wedweil last summer. I tried to run away, but they threatened to shoot me dead. I obeyed and stopped running.

Five soldiers grabbed me. I did not struggle with them. They then tried to tie me to a rope. I refused to cooperate, so they threw me down on the ground and beat me. I almost had a miscarriage. I knew because I started to bleed from the womb. After the beating, I could not walk and was put on a horse. They took me to their camp near Wedweil and put me in a big pen with a lot of other people. I spent two days in the pen.

Then everyone had to start walking to the north, together with the cattle. I was still not able to walk, so they again put me on one of the horses. It took us many days to get to Matarik. We were all divided up there. I was given to Mahmoud Abdullah. He called me Zeneib and took me to his home. It was nearby in Matarik. He is a trader there. In his shop he sells sugar, grain, soap, and things like that.

I had to clean his house, wash clothes, cook, and fetch water with the donkey. Mahmoud had four boy slaves to look after his cattle. Their names are Yel Ngor Akol, Aciek Kuol Tong, Dut Angok Angok, and Macol Chan Atak. Mahmoud has two Arab wives. They are Asha and Kadija. They were kind to me. They gave me clothes to wear. But Mahmoud was very unkind. Whenever he was unhappy with me, he would beat me. Once he wanted me to go to the Koranic school and cook for the boys there, but I refused to do it because I am a Christian. He did not force me to go there.

One day the trader Ibrahim came and took me and my baby to the forest and then brought us back here. I am very happy to be back here. I thank everyone who helped me come back. I am sure I will be even happier when I find my husband and children. I will now return to my village and look for them.

Marco (SUDAN, 1999)

I was captured three years ago at the beginning of the dry season. I was caught in Marim. I had gone there to visit my aunt. When the Arabs came, I tried to run away. But I was surrounded. About eight men grabbed me. They all wore uniforms. They tied my hands to a long rope. Other people were tied to it too.

Then they took us to the train station at the bridge over the river Lol. This station is between Ariath and Wedweil. The soldiers put us in the cars of a train. There were about twenty-eight people in my car. We had to stay inside the car for four days. They only let us out at night for a short time when they gave us food. After we were finished with our food, they put us back inside. It was very hot and dirty in there. The train was then on its way to the north from Wau. When it was ready to leave the station, we were taken out and had to walk to the north. I was tied up, like before, for the walk.

On the way, I had to carry a sack of durra, and I was beaten by the soldiers. It took us eight days before we reached Daein. We were divided up there. The one who organized it was Mohammed Abdullah. He was the leader of the Popular Defense Forces. He gave me to Jima Mahmoud. He was one of the soldiers who caught me. Jima Mahmoud took me to his home. He lives in Daein town.

Life was very hard with Jima and his wife Howah. They made me grind grain and look after their goats. Every night they tied my hands and legs together and put me in a small outhouse without windows. Jima had another slave. He called him Jima, but his real name is Garang Ngor Bol. He was also tied up and put in the outhouse. We were able to speak Dinka secretly to each other in the outhouse. One day, Garang disappeared. Howah told me was sent to Khartoum. In the evenings, they made me go to the Koranic school. I had to memorize the Koran. Teacher Bakhiet would beat me with a whip if I could not memorize well.

The khalwa was only for slaves. There were fifteen of us, twelve boys and three girls. All of us were teenagers. We were not allowed to speak to each other in Dinka. The teacher said we are now mujahadeen and would be given guns and money, and would be sent to the south to fight against the Dinka who have no religion. He said the Dinka are not good people and that he did not want them in the south anymore. I did not like the khalwa. I am a Christian. I used to go to church in Yargot. Sometimes Father Jervis would come and visit us. I was baptized and confirmed by him. I will go to church again when I get back home.

INTERNATIONAL SEX TRAFFICKING

Between six hundred thousand and eight hundred thousand people are trafficked across international borders each year, according to the U.S. State Department. Some NGOs claim the figure is four million, and the UN puts the average estimate of international organizations at two million. Perhaps the most well-publicized form of this international trade is sex trafficking. By some estimates, as many as two million women worldwide are currently trapped in forced prostitution. And for those who are trafficked across international borders (many of them from eastern Europe, South Asia, and South America), they are doubly bound, not only by the brothel owner but by the restrictions of a foreign country where they cannot speak the language, have no knowledge of their legal rights, and often fear the police.

In the global market for people, the vulnerable are trafficked from poorer countries to richer countries, and many thousands of these trafficked women arrive in western Europe, the United Kingdom, Canada, and the United States. Isra, a Thai national, was a sex slave in Canada. She is one of around 600 to 800 trafficked people who arrive in Canada each year. A further 1,500 to 2,200 people are trafficked through Canada to the United States. Canadian officials note that both these estimates are conservative, for very few victims of trafficking report the crime. Most trafficking victims who arrive in Canada come from South Korea, Thailand, Cambodia, China, Malaysia, and Vietnam, and most are women trafficked for commercial sexual exploitation.

In 1996 Canadian law enforcement officials learned that a Toronto-based sex trade ring was procuring young women from Thailand and Malaysia aged sixteen to thirty. Agents sold the women's services to brothel owners for Cdn $16,000 to $25,000 each. Before they could keep a percentage of their earnings, the women had to work off the cost of their transportation and a "debt bond" that ranged from $30,000 to $40,000—which meant servicing five hundred customers. Their travel documents were confiscated and their movements were restricted. On December 2, 1998, police officers arrested sixty-eight people at ten brothels in Toronto, including Isra. One of the charges laid against the brothel owners was forcible confinement.

Isra (CANADA, 1999)

When I first arrived, I worked and stayed at a place on Kennedy Road. I stayed with the owner who had bought me. Later on, there were quite a number of women who worked there—about four other girls. I used to serve four to five customers per day. Some days, I had eleven customers. I wanted to finish my contract quickly. Once there were more girls, I did not have to work as much, and the owner decided to move me to another place, which was where I was arrested.

At this place, I had to put up with all kinds of customers. They were all drunk and stupid. I had to do everything they wanted. At first I could not stand it. I went back to the first place because one of the girls who had come here a month before me had finished her contract. At the time, the owner of the parlor was going to the United States. At first she told me that she would take me back to the second place to work, and I just had to let her do that. She let me go back, however, when one of my regular customers was going to spend the night. When I came back the next day, she told me that she would like me to finish my contract fast and she would take me to her friend's parlor in the Sheppard area. I had no objection. She could do anything to me because I wanted to finish the contract as soon as possible. However, instead of taking me to her friend's, she sold me to a Thai girl who had a Vietnamese boyfriend, in Mississauga. I could not stand staying there because I did not have enough customers. After two or three days, I could not stand it anymore.

At the time I owed $12,000 more. It took seven or eight days before my former boss bought me back. The boss bought me for $10,000 and wanted $2,000 from me. Every day, I had to work. I had no time to rest even when I had my period. Sometimes when I got really tired, she asked her boyfriend to take me to her place for some sleep. I could not sleep at the massage parlor because the owner had fights with her boyfriend. I had to put up with my circumstances because I owed them money. If I finished paying her back I could leave. I had to work every day because they forced me to. I had to have my period in one day; I had to take three or four birth control pills per day. Actually, I did not want to work at all. When I told her that I hurt, and where, she still made me work without stopping. I had to be patient and I never had a fight with her. The owner was a workaholic. If we did not have enough customers on any day, she would start to complain and use abusive language saying that I did not do a good job. I just had to be patient and listen to her. When we had lots of customers, she was happy and went out with her boyfriend, but when they came back, they started fighting again.

One day I woke up early in the morning to launder my clothes at a place near my work. On that day, the owner of my massage parlor went out to advertise our phone number—that hadn't been done for one to two months. At that house, one of my friends was making a dish called *kanom jeen man nguew*. That day the house was strangely quiet. I felt like going out; I did not want to stay at this parlor. One of the reasons was that all day we had had only two customers. I worked for one and my friend worked for the other. The owner of the parlor, my friend, and I played a card game. We finished the game. I was lying down on the sofa. There was a Vietnamese man who came to see the owner. This person was looking for a girl to work at his place. After the conversation was over with the owner, the Vietnamese man walked out the door. After about five minutes, there was somebody knocking on the door. The owner of the parlor opened the door and thought that it was a customer. She did not look through the cat door. That was the moment we were about to be arrested. It was about eight or nine at night. There was a middle-aged Vietnamese-Chinese man who knocked on the door. She opened the door. As soon as she opened the door, the police, about ten of them, raided the place. They ordered us to be still and not move.

The owner of the place turned very pale, like a boiled egg. Some of the policemen searched for evidence. They broke the glass windows in two rooms—the workroom and the room that the owner and I stayed in. The officers who restrained us shouted very loud saying that we should not do anything. My friend and I and the owner of the place sat on the sofa with our hearts sunk and lost. I told myself that I was arrested and would accept the situation later on. The owner of the place could not control herself and cried.

CONTRACT SLAVERY

Contract slavery is the most rapidly growing form of slavery, and probably the second largest form today after debt bondage. Contracts guarantee employment, perhaps in a workshop or factory, but the workers arrive to find themselves enslaved. In 1999 Vi was one of about 250 workers brought from Vietnam on a labor contract. A South Korean businessman named Kil Soo Lee had bought a garment factory called Daewoosa near Pago Pago, in American Samoa, and required sewing machine operators. Vi was recruited by a Vietnamese government-owned enterprise called Tourism Company 12 and was told she was heading for the United States. Like the other recruits, she paid $5,000 to cover the cost of airfare and work permits and signed a three-year contract in exchange for monthly paychecks of around $400, plus free meals and housing and return airfare. But on arrival in American Samoa, the recruits were forced to work to pay off smuggling fees. Lee confiscated their passports to prevent them from escaping, and he quickly stopped paying them altogether, though he kept charging them for room and board. He withheld food, ordered beatings, and forced them to work fourteen to eighteen hours per day. Female employees were sexually assaulted, and those who became pregnant were forced to have abortions or return to Vietnam.

Vi's story of slavery is also one of prosecution. In 2000 two workers at Lee's factory sought legal help from attorneys. On behalf of more than 250 factory workers, the attorneys filed a pro bono class-action lawsuit against Daewoosa and the Vietnamese government. The case was publicized by human rights groups. The two workers who asked for legal help disappeared. Their bodies were never found. Then, in November 2000, a group of workers refused to return to their sewing machines and a fight ensued between workers and factory guards. During the incident, one woman lost an eye and two other workers were hospitalized. This gained the attention of local law enforcement, and the FBI field office in Honolulu began investigating Daewoosa in February 2001. Enforcing the Trafficking Victims Protection Act of 2000 federal agents closed down the factory and arrested Lee on charges of involuntary servitude and forced labor. He was sent to Hawaii for trial in March 2001.

Though the recruiting companies and the Vietnamese government refused to pay for the workers' flights home, they left American Samoa. Some returned to Vietnam, and more than two hundred, including Vi, were flown to the United States and admitted as potential witnesses for the prosecution at Lee's trial. In April 2002, the High Court of American Samoa ordered the factory and two Vietnamese government-owned labor agencies to pay $3.5 million to the workers. Lee claimed bankruptcy. In February 2003 he was found guilty of involuntary servitude, extortion, money laundering, and bribery and was sentenced to life imprisonment. The court also ordered him to pay $1.8 million in restitution to the workers. Vi and the other Vietnamese workers who came to the United States applied for T visas, issued to victims of trafficking after passage of the TVPA. Lee remains one of the few employers prosecuted for human trafficking.

Vi (AMERICAN SAMOA, 2001)

My name is Vi and I am twenty-eight years old. I arrived in American Samoa on July 22, 1999. Two other groups of Vietnamese workers had been brought to this island before us. When I signed the contract with Tour Company 12, they told me that I would go to the United States, and its deputy director promised that I would get paid $408 a month. I had to borrow $4,000 to pay to Company 12 and another $2,000 to pay the company official in charge of recruitment.

We were taken to American Samoa and not the United States. As soon as we landed our passports were confiscated. At a Daewoosa shop, I had to work from 7 A.M. to 2 A.M. and sometimes to 7 A.M. the next day, and also on Saturdays and Sundays, without pay. We had no money to buy food, amenities, or soap. We had to pay $200 per month for room and board, which they should have provided according to the contract.

Meals at Daewoosa consisted of a few cabbage leaves and potatoes cooked with a lot of water. Those who were at the head of the line could get some cabbage and potato; latecomers got only water. Hungry, we planted some vegetables to supplement our meals, but Mr. Lee, president of Daewoosa, destroyed our garden. Undernourished, I lost thirty-five pounds within one year and weighed only seventy-eight pounds.

Working and living conditions at Daewoosa were very suffocating. There was no air ventilation. Workers slept right next to each other. The temperature in the rooms sometime went up to over 100 degrees. We were not allowed to step out for fresh air. The supervisor even kept count of how many times we went to the toilet.

We lived thirty-six people in one room. Another worker and I shared one tiny bed. We could only sleep on our sides. If we lay on our backs, we would pile on top of each other.

Most of us were women. At night Mr. Lee often came into our room and lay next to whoever he liked. Once he forced me to give him a massage right in our bedroom.

He called pretty ones into his office and forced them to have sex with him. Three women have publicly denounced him for that. Once, several of his customers arrived in American Samoa. Mr. Lee pressed several female workers to sleep with them. They resisted. At the workplace, he regularly groped and kissed female workers in front of everyone.

There were three pregnant women among us. Mr. Lee demanded that they have abortions. He fired them when they refused. Evicted from Daewoosa, they had to seek refuge at a local church.

Movement at Daewoosa was very restricted. Everyone leaving the compound was searched by American Samoan guards. Female workers were groped all over their bodies. Those who protested were strip-searched. Those coming back from the compound after 9 p.m. were beaten up. I was once slapped.

Mr. Lee used big American Samoan guards to terrorize us. Once, several workers staged a strike because they were not paid. He threatened that he would send these guards to short-circuit electric cables and cause a fire to kill us all. Everyone was fearful because two female workers, Nga and Dung, involved in the lawsuits against Mr. Lee had just disappeared.

On November 28 of last year, there was a dispute between the supervisor and a female worker. Mr. Lee ordered the supervisor: "If you beat her to death, I will take the blame." The supervisor dragged the female worker out by the chest. Other workers came to her rescue. The American Samoan guards, already holding sticks and scissors, jumped in. Everyone was so frightened. We ran for our lives. Mr. Lee ran after to beat the fleeing workers. We were terrorized for days after that.

The guards paid special attention to the five or six workers known to have supported the lawsuit against Mr. Lee. They beat them the hardest. Ms. Quyen, the key witness in this lawsuit, was held by her arms on two sides by two guards. A third guard thrust a pointed stick into her eyes. As a result, she lost sight in that eye. A guard beat a male worker with a stick, breaking his front teeth and bleeding his mouth.

Another male worker was pinned down to the floor and repeatedly beaten at his temple. His blood was spilling all over the floor. The next day, an FBI agent took pictures of the bloodstains. During the assault, Daewoosa's lawyer and the police were there but did nothing. Only when the lawyer representing the workers showed up did the guards stop the beating.

From 1999 to the above incident, Tour Company 12 and the International Manpower Supply, another Vietnamese company hiring workers for Daewoosa, forced us to continue working without pay and threatened to send us back to Vietnam if we disobeyed. Everyone was deeply in debt. If we got sent back, how could we pay our debt?

Since my arrival in the United States, I have sent every dollar earned back to Vietnam to pay my debt. However, this has barely made a dent because the interest rate is so high, 50 percent. My parents in Vietnam are very worried. Their hair has turned all gray. They told me that it is fortunate that I have come to the United States; otherwise, we would be in a hopeless situation.

If sent back, it would be hard for me to find employment. My previous workplace will not take me back. Because of my involvement in the prosecution of Mr. Lee, I am afraid of running into trouble with the government if repatriated to Vietnam.

I am getting used to life in the United States. Here I am free to choose where I want to work. If dissatisfied with one workplace, I can always go to another one. I have been thoroughly helped in my first step toward a normal life, and I find everyone to be very kind. I now live with a Vietnamese family without having to pay rent. That family offers me employment. They take care of my food, transportation, and other things. They also give me a phone card to call my family in Vietnam once a week. Staying with me are six female workers from American Samoa. Two of them are here today.

I have received a certification letter from the Department of Health and Human Services for public benefits. I have a temporary visa that will expire on October 30, 2002, and a work permit. I work at a nail salon in the District of Columbia to pay my debts. If allowed to remain in the United States, I would like to go back to school, because in Vietnam I had to stop schooling at seventh grade. I also wish to be reunited with my child left behind in Vietnam. I am thankful to everyone who has helped me get out of American Samoa and everyone who has assisted me in this new life in the United States.

DEBT-BONDAGE SLAVERY

Debt bondage is the most common form of modern slavery. Found predominantly in South Asia and South America, it typically occurs when a person pledges their labor or that of a child as collateral against a loan of money. There are around 10 million bonded laborers in India and another 2.5 million in Nepal. Debts arise from two main sources: an urgent crisis such as illness, injury, or famine; and the need to pay for death rites or marriage celebrations. Technically, bonded laborers can end their servitude once the debt is repaid, but this rarely occurs. Since all labor belongs to the lender as collateral against the loan, it is impossible to repay the initial debt, and the debt usually increases because the employer includes charges for equipment and living expenses or fines for faulty work. According to India's laws, families can simply walk away from debt and bondage, but this is usually impossible. If families try to leave, the slaveholder's thugs retaliate with beatings, rape, and forced eviction. If a family survives the beatings, they are free to starve. Without access to jobs, health care, community support, or credit, independence is impossible to sustain, and they reenter debt bondage.

Though the Bonded Labour System (Abolition) Act of 1976 criminalizes the use of the system, which is at least 1,500 years old in India, those in debt bondage face involuntary servitude at brick kilns, rice mills, carpet looms, and embroidery factories. Bonded labor is also widespread in the quarrying of granite and other stones. Workers are required to purchase their own materials and are forced to borrow money from the contractors or quarry owners. Children aged four to fourteen are required to work along with their parents for up to fourteen hours a day, carrying loads of rocks, in order to maximize production. Bonded children are sometimes sold to other contractors, and female workers are frequently raped. Accidents caused by explosions or drilling are common, and workers suffer from respiratory illnesses due to inhaling stone dust.

Munni Devi and Shanti narrated their stories while enslaved as bonded laborers in the rock quarries of Uttar Pradesh, India. Both find the idea of escape impossible. But the day before Munni told her story in November 2004, Ramphal—an abolitionist and former quarry slave in Uttar Pradesh, whose narrative is in section 5—explained of slaves like Munni and Shanti: "We keep...showing them...the life we lead now, and they're keen to get out of bondage, so it'll happen. It's just a question of time."

Shanti (INDIA, 2001)

My name is Shanti. I do not know my age. I have five children. My contractor has said, "If you die I will take your dead body out of the mud and make you work to return my debt." My husband died in September or October this year, and the contractor gave me no money for his burial. The head contractor came the day before yesterday. I have a nine-year-old daughter, and the contractor caught her hands and said that he would force her to work to repay my loans. He says I owe 8,000 rupees [$180]. My husband took the loan, and now that he has died the contractor is forcing me and my daughter to pay it back. I tried my best to work somewhere else, but if he does not let me go, what am I to do? He forces me to work for him. I break stones. The problem is that those big stones need to be brought out of the mountains. Some stronger person needs to do that job. My husband was doing it, but now there is no one to bring those stones. So whatever small pieces are lying there, I break those. I break enough to earn 400 rupees [$9] and it takes me ten or twelve days to achieve that. I don't even have a place to stay. I stay on someone else's land. And when they tell me I have to move my little hut, I have to move it.

Munni (INDIA, 2004)

My name is Munni Devi. I'm thirty-five to forty years old. I have four children—two boys and two girls. I've been working in the quarry for a long, long time, many years. Maybe twenty years, maybe more. I'm not sure. My husband died while working there, and now I have to work there myself. Life is tough. I've taken a loan because of which I'm a slave to the person from whom I took it. And now the situation is getting even worse. I'm in debt. I can't work that much, and he threatens to throw me out of my house. My poor son is just running from pillar to post to organize things. I don't know what's going to happen.

Munni Devi (photograph by Peggy Callahan, Free the Slaves, 2004)

I've been working under the same contractor, and I've taken one loan and now it seems to have doubled to become two loans. I'm not really earning too much and my debt is increasing. My original loan was for 9,000 rupees [$200], and I've been trying to repay it for a long, long time. It just seems to be increasing. I took it for the marriage of my daughter. I'm not paid any money or salary except once in a while; when the lorry comes to be loaded, I'm paid about 400 or 500 rupees [$9–11] depending on his mood. The lorry only comes when all of us are able to break down the hard rocks into tiny pieces. As and when the tiny pieces are ready, the lorry turns up. I would say the process of breaking hard rocks into tiny pebbles takes about fifteen days.

I am forced to work. If I have something important to do at home, I am forced to work. Even if I'm sick, I'm made to work. They don't look after my expenses, my food. There's no nourishment coming from that side whatsoever. When I'm not working, my loan amount is escalating monthly. I have been threatened, verbally that is. The threat has been that he's going to throw me out of my house. He keeps coming over once in a while and saying he'll throw me out, put a lock on my door so I can't use my own house. We're trying to do something about it. Once when he did come, earlier, we all got together, abused him and made sure he went out of the village. But I'm not sure how long that tactic will work. I am scared. I am scared because at least in the daytime I have my children around me and it's possible they will protect me. But then that's the daytime. In the night when my children are not around me, I'm more vulnerable and somebody could just come and do anything. Beat me up, thrash me.

I think I must have paid about half the loan by now and half might still be due. But then again that's not taking into account the fact that he may be cheating me. If that's the case, I'm not sure how much of my loan has been repaid. What he's doing is not right. I don't know what the law says, but I don't think it's right. I have no choices. Where will I go? What will I do? This is my house. This is my home. This is the only way I can survive, because I have no money and that is all I can do. I can't run away. How will I run? Where will I run? What will I run towards? I'm here. I spend my whole day here.

EUROPEAN SEX TRAFFICKING

Human trafficking is Europe's fastest-growing criminal activity. Many women are brought to the richer western countries from the poorer eastern European countries, including Albania, which is now one of the top ten countries of origin for sex trafficking. The fall of communism in 1991 led to a rise in organized crime in Albania; in 2001 it was estimated that one hundred thousand Albanian women and girls had been trafficked to western European and other Balkan countries in the preceding ten years. More than 65 percent of Albanian sex trafficking victims are minors at the time they are trafficked, and at least 50 percent of victims leave home under the false impression that they will be married or engaged to an Albanian or foreigner and live abroad. Another 10 percent are kidnapped or forced into prostitution. The women and girls receive little or no pay for their work, and they are commonly tortured if they do not comply.

The eleven narratives in this chapter are all by Albanian women in their teens and early twenties. Adelina and Sanije were trafficked within Albania. Valdete was trafficked to Greece, where victims are also trafficked in from Nigeria, and then into Italy. Ada, Elira, Flutura, Kimete, and Odeta were trafficked to Italy, where trafficking victims also arrive from Nigeria, Romania, Bulgaria, China, and South America. One NGO estimates that 48 percent of the prostitutes in Italy are from eastern Europe, that 35–40 percent are minors, and that 26 percent have been kidnapped and taken from their countries of origin by force. An Italian social research institute estimates that there were 2,500 new trafficking victims in 2005.

Miranda and Zamira were trafficked to Belgium, where Albanian girls aged fourteen and fifteen make up nearly half of the foreign women forced into prostitution. Maria was trafficked to Italy, France, and the Netherlands. In France, there are an estimated ten to twelve thousand trafficking victims, primarily from Romania and Bulgaria, but also from Albania, Nigeria, Sierra Leone, and Cameroon. In the Netherlands, victims are trafficked from eastern Europe, Nigeria, and Brazil. Local NGOs estimate that up to 70 percent of the twenty-five thousand individuals engaged in prostitution in Amsterdam are trafficking victims.

Several narrators explain the process of making a new life. For Zamira this means putting slavery "in my past" and closing "that door behind me." For Maria, however, closing the door on slavery seems almost impossible: "The shame for our parents and us is too large.... What man will marry me?... It is difficult to smile." Instead, she reopens the door to her slave past and tries to help other trafficking victims—telling *them* that "they must make a new life" and inviting them to share their stories.

Maria (ITALY, FRANCE, AND NETHERLANDS, 2002)

I'll call myself Maria in this story. This is a real story about my life, and I am not the only one who could be named that name. There are many Marias like I am, and that is the reason to bring this story to daylight—to stop "Maria's Story" from happening again. I come from a little village in Albania where my parents and my sisters still live. They probably think I am dead, and I hope so. It is easier than the truth—I have done things they never can imagine. I shall never see them again.

It was only four years ago when a young man from Skopje came into my father's shop. He was very polite and well dressed and he asked about life in our town. When I said there was little to do, my father asked if he was there to talk or to buy something. My father is very old-fashioned and he was always protecting me from boys, which I did not like. I was almost seventeen years old and did not need my father's protection. The smile the young man gave me said he understood. But he talked to my father politely, paid for some items, and I saw him going away in a Mercedes-Benz car. I was very angry with my father and many times thought of the young man in his expensive car.

Perhaps two weeks after, the young man arrived again. This time my father was away in a café and we talked (later, I wonder if he watched the shop to see my father going out). His name was Damir and he spoke of the famous cities he often visited. Rome, Paris, Madrid, and many other ones I could only dream about. I said how much I wanted to see them, and Damir said that he worked for a modeling agency that looks for pretty girls like I was (my face became red, but I liked him to say such things). To live and work in Paris!!! If I wanted to do it, he would arrange for a colleague to speak with my parents. I was very excited and said yes. Some days passed and a woman entered the shop. She was Damir's colleague. Her jewels and expensive clothes made me embarrassed of my own. She spoke to my parents and showed them a contract. I will earn a certain amount of money, so much to me for living and the rest to my parents. When my father asked about safety, Vanja said that young models live together and always with chaperones. I begged them to allow me, and finally my father signed. I remember he was very sad about me going away. Vanja took me to a photo shop for passport photos and said Damir hoped to see me soon. I was in Heaven! The next week Vanja returned. In her car were two other girls, one gypsy girl, younger than me, and another Albanian, a little older. I kissed my parents good-bye. It was the last time I saw them.

We drove some hours to Durres on the coast of the Adriatic Sea. Damir was waiting for us. The other girls knew him also and I was already jealous, but too excited to be angry. He had our new passports but told us he must keep them. It was the first time I saw the sea and my first time in a ship. It seemed very big and beautiful. We followed Damir, who had our tickets and travel documents. He spoke with an official and gave him something before we went into the ship and down many stairs. I thought we were near the engine—the smell of oil was very strong, also rotten food and the smell of clothes not washed in a long time. He said for our safety he must lock the door but will return in the morning. Two of us had to share a bed, but only for one night, and the next day we shall come to Italy! The sound of the engine was very loud and soon the ship was moving very fast. We wished to talk about the handsome men we are going to meet and how the girls at home will be jealous, but the bad smells and moving ship made me and the gypsy girl very sick.

The next morning we arrived in Bari. Damir took us to a house where the streets are dirty and we saw beggars and even rats during the day. We were nervous because we were expecting something very different than that. When we entered the house it smelled as bad as the ship. There were many girls' magazines, wine bottles, and cigarettes on the floor. Some men were sitting inside, they laughed and looked at us in a bad way and spoke to Damir in Italian, which we did not understand. I asked him who they are, but the polite young man from my father's shop grabbed my arm and said something very bad in Albanian. He hit me on the face. I fell on the ground and he pulled me by my hair into a room and hit me more than once until my face started bleeding. I did not understand what had happened. I heard other girls screaming. And then he raped me. Then the other men came in and did the same. After that event, each day the same men came again, and then others, who paid money to be with us. If we said no, Damir would hit and kick us and give us no food. He said THIS was modeling that we must do for anyone.

He paid for our passports and documents. They belong to him and to be without them in a foreign country means going to prison if the police find us. If we try to escape, he and his friends will kill us and no one will ever know. If we succeed and go to police, bad things will happen to our families and everyone will hear we are prostitutes. He laughed and said we were stupid girls from farms. He asked what our parents and friends would say if they knew with how many men we have had already!? It was very cruel to make us feel ashamed for what he makes us do.

One night Damir took me and the gypsy girl to the truck and said another man owns us now and if we thought he is a bad man, this man is worse, so we better do always what he says. He gave our passports to this man and we traveled all night and next day to Marseille in France, where we stayed in a house with the other girls. There I learned that if I am quiet and do what he says I won't be punished. Some were given drugs to make them addicts. If they were bad, they did not get the drugs they wanted.

I was in Marseille for almost one year and was sold to a man and a woman who took me to Amsterdam. I slept in a small room with no heat and little food, sometimes only what is left over from their meals. Sometimes I did not eat for one or two days. They were drug addicts and would forget about me—except to bring men. When there were no customers, the man would hit me and burn me with cigarettes and force me to do things, sometimes with the woman there also. He said this was to make me remember that he is the master.

I made no trouble, and after some time the woman took me to carry her shopping. I liked these shopping trips with her and did everything she wanted me to do—it was wonderful to be away from my small, cold room. After some time she began to give me some small money for treats. One day I saw a poster about a charity for women. I begin to pray that I will find them and they will help me. But I was frightened because I had no papers. My owners always said to me how without a passport I will go to prison and then be sent to Albania if the police find me. Even after more than two years I cry with shame of my life and shame for my parents if they ever know about me.

One day the woman was looking at clothes. She gave me a small amount of money to buy a treat. But I found a telephone and with the money called the number of the charity. It was difficult to understand me, but a Bulgarian came to the telephone and asked where I am. SHE SAID SHE WAS COMING FOR ME!!!!!

I worked for this charity for more than one year and helped girls like me. I talked to them every day, and I tell them they must make a new life. They wept very much. I also, but waited until night so they do not see. We all wanted to go home but we cannot. The shame for our parents and us is too large. I dreamed to be a model. Now I dream about a nice man, but what man will marry me? Even if he accepts what happened to me, I can never have children because of it. It is difficult to smile.

My new friends in the charity all say that girls like us must be warned. I came to Bulgaria with the person who saved my life. It is not the Albania I remember and love more than any other place, and where I can never return, but it is in many ways closer to my home than Italy or France or Holland. My friend and I talked about my experiences and those of the girls we helped in Amsterdam and wondered how we could help others before they made the same mistakes. My Bulgarian friend said perhaps the way is the Internet. And we decided to make a website. My English is not good, but she helps me.

We pray that young men and women who are tempted by people who are the lowest animals to smuggle them to the west will find it and listen to what we suffered. If it saves only one person it will be worth it. We hope many people will find it. Send me your stories of how you traveled from your beloved homeland. What you saw and what happened to you. We should also shame those who tricked, hurt, and stole your life from you and your family. These people who think they are above the law—send their names and their crimes.

Adelina (ALBANIA, 2005)

I am fifteen years old, and I became a sex worker when I was thirteen. I am writing my story for you. When I was a little girl, I had a good family, but later on everything in my life changed because my mother fell in love with a terrible man. After having a relationship with this man for some time, my mother decided to leave my father for him. When we were leaving, my mother fell from the mountain where we were passing because we were in such a hurry. Fortunately, my mother survived the fall and we were able to send her immediately to a hospital. One day the doctor said that she couldn't be treated adequately there and she must go to Tirana for medical care. My mother told me that I should not tell my father that she was being sent to Tirana. We went to Tirana in an ambulance, and one day my grandmother came to the hospital. My mother told me to go and live at her house until she was better. When my mother was released from the hospital, we had to leave my grandmother's house because my grandmother didn't accept my mother's boyfriend as her husband. We didn't have any house, so sometimes we lived in the houses of others, and sometimes we lived on the street. My mother and I were begging because we didn't have any income. We did this for several years.

Once we went to the house of a friend of my mother's, but she was poor, too, and we couldn't stay there permanently. One of the neighbors was economically better off and asked my mother to let me live with them and later on marry their son. My mother didn't think anything bad would happen and thought I would be safer there, so she let me live there. I was only nine years old. At the beginning, they treated me very well, but later on they began to mistreat me and not give me enough food to eat, and so on. I was really in a very bad condition. They told me to tell my mother that her boyfriend raped me. I did as I was told, even though it wasn't the truth, because I was afraid of them, so I hurt my mother. She had trusted her boyfriend, and she started crying and left me. I felt so bad to lie to my mother, but I felt I was forced to lie.

I stayed almost one year at that house, and the marriage promised from them was not realized because my mother saw their son one day kissing another girl. My mother then understood that I shouldn't stay anymore in that house, and she came and got me and took me to her house. Thanks to God she helped me leave from that hell.

My mother was living in a very bad house with her boyfriend. All the rain always came inside, but I felt very happy because I was with my mother. My mother was begging. One person whom my mother knew promised my mother a better house. He seemed like a good person, but he lied to my mother about better work, and he exploited her. My mother had to work in the streets as a sex worker for his interests.

But something else even worse happened during that time. My mother's boyfriend raped me during the time when my mother wasn't in the house. He told me not to tell my mother what happened, and I didn't dare to tell my mother because I was so ashamed. I just couldn't find the ability to tell her.

Later on we left from that place, and went to stay at the house of another friend of my mother's. We stayed there for some days and then left together with my mother's friend to come to his house. His nephew fell in love with me. He was twenty-one years old and I was twelve. I told my mother's friend all the problems I had passed in my life and that my mother's boyfriend raped me. He then told my mother that her boyfriend raped me. During this time, my mother's boyfriend was in Tirana, and when he came back, my mother's friend quarreled with him because my mother and I didn't want to stay with him anymore. He hit my mother's boyfriend with a car and he died. After this unfortunate situation, we went to my grandmother's house to live. My grandmother was living in an apartment that had been a hotel, but many families were living there. We got a room there. I met a friend, but she and her mother were working as sex workers there. I found out I was two months pregnant. I aborted my baby because of these terrible conditions. I was twelve years old.

Later on, I worked as a sex worker with my friend and her mother because my mother was ill, and I didn't want to see her always suffering. When my mother heard about what I was doing, she told me not to do that work, but I said to her that I was doing this thing for her. I didn't know anything about my future, but God helped me, and I survived that time. I went to Italy with a guy I met, and he sent me to a convent. The Mother Theresa sisters there helped me very much, but I wanted to come back to Albania to my mother. They referred me to the shelter here, and I was able to see my mother again. She was in a bad condition and told me that my father was dead, so I was so sad. Her leg was cut badly, and it was hard for me to see her. She is now living in the same house and begging again as before. I have stayed two years in the shelter now, and I learned how to read and write here. I know how to use the computer now and can speak English and Italian. I have also successfully completed two vocational training courses, one on cosmetology and one on cooking. I feel good about myself, but I am sorry for my mother. I want to help my mother in the future, when I will be able to work. This is my story.

Sanije (ALBANIA, 2005)

I am seventeen years old. I was born in a city in the south of Albania. Four sisters, two brothers, my mother, and my father compose my family. My parents do not work; they used to live by begging in the streets or by the money that one of my sisters as well as one of my brothers sends to them. They are working as illegal immigrants in Greece, I think. We used to change our residence frequently; we never had a real house. We used to live in just one room with the toilet outside.

When I was fourteen years old, my family (my father, I mean, because he was the one who decided for the family) arranged for me to marry someone who was living in Greece. I married him even though I had just seen him a few times when he came to Albania. We got married, and we went to live in Greece illegally. Even my marriage was not a formal one; it was an agreement between my father and him.

I stayed with him for one year. During this time he was emotionally abusive of me and physically violent toward me. He used to spend money by going to discos, and it seemed to me that he didn't do any work at all. I did not know where he used to find the money. He had regular documents; I didn't.

I worked for one month in a bar as a cleaner. My husband used to go to this bar, and he used to steal things there, so after one month my employer fired me. My husband threatened me by saying that he was going to put me to work on the streets as a prostitute. At this point I decided to denounce him to the police. I denounced him for his abusive treatment of me, the physical violence even while I was pregnant, and for all the rest. The Greek police deported me to Albania through the crossing point of Kapshtica. I was left on the border of Albania near a village. I didn't know anybody there, and I did not know any place to go. I was pregnant and scared. A family there hosted me for one night. The next day I went to the city of my birth, by minibus. I couldn't find my parents because they had changed their home again. I contacted my sister who lives with her family in a village. My sister paid the driver of the minibus.

When I arrived in Albania, I was five months pregnant. I stayed with my family until the birth of my child. Even my parents were against it. They wanted me to have an abortion because they said they didn't have money to raise my baby. I gave birth to a baby girl. I called her Sara. Meanwhile my family arranged for me another marriage with an old Italian man. He was sixty years old. He wouldn't allow me to leave the house and he abused me sexually. I was distressed. I decided to leave him when I met a guy from the same village, someone I had known since I was ten years old. This guy was a friend of my father and used to serve as a translator between me and my Italian husband at the beginning. He offered to help me go to Italy where I could meet my other sisters. Though he was married, he told me he would abandon his wife and children to stay with me and my daughter. He took me to live in hotels for five months. He told me he loved me, and I believed him. He promised to find me a good job in Italy, and I believed him.

Later on, I found out that he wanted me to be a prostitute when I met some other girls who were staying at the last hotel where I stayed in Vlora. They were both Albanian and foreign girls. He began to beat me and told me that I must abandon my daughter. I did not want to do that, but he threatened to kill my daughter and me. I was all alone and scared. Then he promised me that if I left her somewhere, it would be better because she could never survive the trip through the sea by speedboat to Italy. He promised we could take the baby back after some months. I did what he told me. I could not do any other way. He cheated me and forced me to abandon my daughter. One night we woke up at three in the morning and went by speedboat. Fortunately, the police caught us, and they referred me to a safe place here in Albania.

Valdete (GREECE, 2005)

My story started because of the deep poverty in my house. We were living on my mother's pension payment, since my father was unemployed. When I was sixteen I had to go to Athens and work there for my living. There I was introduced to a guy from Fier [in southwest Albania], who first promised to marry me, but very soon cheated me and made me a prostitute.

I was unlucky, living with a cruel person who treated me as a slave. I stayed with him for more than two years. During that time I was working ten to twelve hours a day, and he got all my profits. The first thing I experienced in the morning was beating and torture by him. He would hit me with his belt and tie me up with rope for twenty-four hours at a time without anything to eat. I hate him and sometimes think that his bad life made him criminal.

I wanted to escape but had no other place to go. Once I did escape and spent the night at the train station on a bench. As I was tired and exhausted I fell asleep, but I got up immediately because it was so cold. Where could I go? The roads of Athens are the property of my trafficker or his friends. How can a person escape from them? When my trafficker found me, he thought that I had been working and asked me for the money. I told him I didn't work that night because I was sick, and he didn't wait until I even finished my sentence; he caught my hair and hit me on the sidewalk. He beat me so much that night that I couldn't move from the bed for fifteen days. So it is hard to get away from traffickers.

Finally, after two years, I escaped and came back to my city in Albania to get a job, but it didn't work well. I left Albania again, this time by a speedboat to go to Italy. There I met a guy from Vlora, who even though he exploited me as a prostitute, treated me better by giving to me half my profits.

If I had a good job I would never begin the profession of a prostitute. I would even be a street cleaner, but there were no other jobs, especially for a young Albanian girl like me. You may ask, how is this thing possible in Italy and Greece? I couldn't get any other jobs. What do you think, that once you get to Italy or Greece, they present you a long list of jobs and then ask you which one you like the best? I am telling you: there is only one job there for young girls, the most difficult one, the most humiliating thing for a girl. I have always faced two paths—to sell my youth or to turn back to Albania. But I thought, where can I go in Albania and what will I do there? My family was so poor that we were never full and satisfied.

You might think it is embarrassing to be a prostitute, but to me it is embarrassing to live on somebody's shoulders, and that somebody is my paralyzed mother, who gets only 3,000 lek [$31] a month. My situation and the situation of many other Albanian girls like me should make the Albanian government think and create jobs in order to employ Albanian young people in Albania. Why did they make us sell our honor abroad? And they say that Albania is going to Europe…but I saw Europe. We Albanians are going to the gap of poverty. If there was an agreement between the Albanian government and other foreign governments on immigration issues, we Albanian girls wouldn't have become prostitutes. We sell our honor to make money, because we cannot live on 2,000–3,000 lek [$20–30] a month. I am feeling that this profession is making me sick.

Every Albanian girl has her own mind. I don't want to make statements, but I want to tell you that this profession of the prostitute is the dirtiest of every other profession, and every girl understands what I mean. I would never wish my fortune on anybody else.

Ada (ITALY, 2005)

I am twenty-one years old. I have my parents, four sisters, and three brothers. My father is sixty years old and my mother is fifty-five. When I was thirteen years old, my father raped me. It was at two at night. All the members of my family were in the house. I was terrified about what happened to me. From that moment I was afraid to stay at home, to look my father in the eyes. I was afraid to stay alone with him. I did not tell anyone what happened to me, even my mother.

After that, my attitude toward my family changed, and so did my behavior. After I finished middle school, I went to my sister's home to stay there to help her because she had a lot of work to do. There I knew a boy and fell in love with him. I told my sister about that.

When I came back to my family, I told my father about that boy, but he did not listen to me at all. He treated me very badly. So one day, I decided to leave the house. I went to the city where I knew another boy. Together we went to Italy. He was stopped by the police and brought back to Albania, while I was accommodated at a center where nuns stayed. I was very satisfied there. I wrote a letter to my family and gave them the telephone number to call me. While I stayed at the center, I started learning Italian, and I also took a tailoring course. One day my family called me, but I was not in the center; I was at school. When I came back from school, I was told that my family had called me. I was so sad; I started to cry. After some days I decided to come back to Albania.

When my family found out that I was back in Albania, my brother came to the city to pick me up. I went with my brother to the village. Everybody from my family was so cold to me. They tried to find somebody for me to marry, but I did not agree. I still loved that boy I met at my sister's village. My father told me that if I ever met him again I should kill him. It was the first day of May when this boy came to meet my parents and the family. My father was so angry that he killed him in the yard.

Both my father and I were put in prison. I was kept there only two weeks. When I got out of prison I did not go home. I met another guy and asked him for help. We created a plan together. We went to Vlora where he sold me to another person. I stayed some days in a hotel in Vlora; then we went to Italy by speedboat.

First we were placed in Genova [Genoa]. Very soon I started to work on the street. One night when I went to work, another girl was in my place. I approached her and asked her who she was working for. She worked for the same person. I said nothing to her, but when I met him I picked a quarrel with him. From that time I moved to another place in Novare. I denounced him. I had no money, so I went on working in the street— not in Novare, but in another place not far from it. There I was stopped by the police and deported to Albania.

Elira (ITALY, 2005)

I am from Elbasan. When I was fifteen, my parents married me, against my will, to a man aged thirty-five, whom I did not love. So started my miseries. Not too long afterwards, I abandoned him and returned to my family. But my parents did not accept me back because I had dishonored them by leaving my husband. I had no support and nowhere to go. I got acquainted with a boy who was twenty who said he loved me and promised to marry me. He convinced me to go to Italy for "a better life."

I thought my sufferings now were at an end, but I did not know the real hell that was expecting me. I was compelled to work on the street. I did so for nearly three years. My exploiter savagely battered me frequently, mainly when I did not bring home the required sum or when he faced drug trafficking problems. During that time I gave birth to a son.

Once he beat me so hard that I cannot remember, and I fell on the floor. A friend of mine, passing by to meet, me found me on the floor, covered in blood. She saved my life by taking me to the hospital. I gave evidence in Italy and returned to Albania with my son. Again, my family did not accept me. They took in my son only, and I could not take care of him.

Being destitute on the street again, I was forced to prostitute in Tirana, in the hotels and motels. I slept wherever I could—on the street, in the park. I decided my condition would be better in Italy. When I returned there, I worked on the street again and was caught by the police and taken back to Albania a second time. I find calmness and support in the shelter, and I now contemplate my future. I do not want anything else except to go home, to see and take care of my son, to be the mother he missed for so long.

Flutura (ITALY, 2005)

I am twenty years old. I was born in a northern city of Albania. I have three sisters and two brothers as well as my father and my mother. We have always been living under a patriarchal mentality where the man of the family has the right to judge and decide for everything and everybody. We had good living conditions, though, so I managed to finish high school with an average of marks 8.7. My desire was to proceed to the university, and I was interested in pursuing law. During the summer after I finished high school I started to work in a fast food restaurant in order to help my family, as we moved to the capital city for a better life. In the meantime I met a boy who I used to like a lot, but my father did not allow me to see him, so I respected his wishes and I broke with the guy.

After one month or so a neighbor next to my house told my father that a cousin of hers was interested in marrying me. She told my parents he was rich and had serious intentions towards me. I could not stand this woman; indeed, she seemed to me a very cheating person. So I told my father I was not going to say yes to her and her cousin. I had other plans for my life than getting married. We quarreled for some days; then it seemed everything was settled down. One day as I was coming back home as usual, a car stopped at my feet and two men kidnapped me by force. They used violence; it was late afternoon and for my bad luck nobody was walking by. They kept my eyes closed and I found myself in a city near the seaside.

We stayed there for one week. When I opened my eyes I could easily tell who the persons were. One of them was the guy that was supposed to marry me. I could not believe my eyes at first, and then I understood their real intentions. In the meantime they abused me physically, sexually, and psychologically as well. Then we moved to the city of Vlora. Once there we stayed one night only, and we left for Italy by speedboat. As soon as we arrived there we met some other girls that were there for the same reasons.

We all had to work as prostitutes in the streets. For sure I refused to work, but you would never believe what kind of persons they are and what methods they use to keep you feeling as a prisoner, as a victim. One time when I could hardly withstand the torture, they threatened to kill my family and to kidnap my little sisters who were only children at that time, so I accepted the work.

They took all the money I used to earn. I used to work every night in the streets and used to earn enough money for them, or this is what I believed. But they were never satisfied, and no deal to make with them was ever possible. So I started looking for ways to escape by myself. Once I tried to get hidden in the house of a priest, as he offered to help me. There were some other girls there as well. He called the police in order to help us. We stayed at the police station one night and they deported us to Albania. But very soon the pimp found out were I was and for a second time we went illegally to Italy, where I worked for about nine months.

During this time I met with a guy who used to be my regular client. He used to behave well to me; he respected me and showed compassion for my story and experience. So by passing the time we became good friends, and then we fell in love with each other. He proposed that I leave with him, and I reflected quite well and escaped with him. I did not denounce anybody because I was still very afraid and unsafe. I lived with him for one year and a half. I met his parents and his sister.

We did not tell them anything about my story. I was afraid they would prejudge me even if it was never my fault. I tried to contact my family in order to say to them I was living a normal life, but only my mother and one of my sisters would accept to talk to me. I had not spoken to my father and brothers for two years.

We decided with the guy about the possibility of getting married one day, sooner or later, but I was still an illegal immigrant, without regular papers. So I decided to come back to my country. I went to the police and told them about my situation. They deported me to Albania. I went to live with the nuns for some time and then in a safe place in Albania. There they helped me to contact my family, to set up the relationships with them. This was a hard process at the beginning, but after time, things settled down.

Now, after some months, I get along well with them, although it's still not so easy. In the meantime I contacted the guy to tell him I was fine. He promised to come and marry me here in my country in order to have the possibility of preparing the documents to go back with him to Italy. Now I am trying to start a new life with him as well as with my family.

Kimete (ITALY, 2005)

I was born in 1985 in a village in southwest Albania. My biological parents had divorced several months before I was born. Being unable to raise me, my father took my sister who was four, and my mother took me to an orphanage where I stayed until I was four years old. After that, my mother married another man who had four other children and gave birth to another child, my second sister. This second marriage lasted only two years. Again my mother took the only child she had with her and went to live with another man who had no children of his own. This time she decided to take me out of the orphanage. We were four people living in a shack.

This husband of my mother did not have any affection for us; he was always quarreling with my mother, saying he could not stand me being around, and he suspected my mother of continuing to have contacts with my real father. He hit us children, and my mother did not work or provide anything for the family. I had three other siblings from this marriage—two brothers and one sister. My parents did not have money to buy books, so I was not able to attend school regularly. Besides, I was told to pasture the cow, so I was not left time to learn or do my homework. After the third grade, my stepfather started to build a house, and I helped him although I was a small child. The relatives of my mother did not help her because they disliked her for her divorces; we were out of money most of the time.

Once, with the help of my aunt, I met my real father, and at that time my stepfather got so angry that he treated me as if I had committed a crime. It was 7:30 in the evening and I did not know where to go. I came to Tirana to tell my aunt, and she brought me back home.

When I turned sixteen my mother and my father arranged for me to marry a man who was thirty-three years old and mentally ill. He took drugs every day. After some months he was hospitalized, and I turned back home feeling ashamed, crying all the time for my fate and thinking that my parents did not love me. Some months later a salesperson came to buy the products of our garden. He came in to have coffee with my parents and asked for me when he saw me looking depressed. He said that he had a nephew who was living in another city and whose wife had died during childbirth. He said that he could arrange for me to marry him. That same day he brought this so-called nephew for us to see him.

The next day, my parents went to that city to see if the nephew's family lived there, but they did not find anybody at that address. When the salesperson came back again, my parents expressed that they felt he was lying, but he got a taxi and took my parents to that city and showed them a half-finished house, saying that this was his nephew's house but that his mother was not there because she went to a hospital in Tirana to see her sister. There my parents met only one person, who said that he was the salesperson's father. My parents were convinced, and that afternoon when the nephew called me he said that his father did not like me but that it was OK because he had fallen in love with me and he would disobey his father.

The next day he took me to a family, introduced them as his relatives, and left me there. These people used to hide me when they had guests in their house. He was telling me that since his father did not agree with our marriage, that we would live better in Italy. He made me a passport and arranged that another person take me to Italy by speedboat. He took a plane because he said he had documents.

There in Italy he paid 450 euros [$591] for a house and told me that I had to work to pay for the rent and also to help my parents. He told me he would find a job for me and soon brought home a girl to teach me. When I realized what kind of job he was talking about, I refused, saying to him that when someone loves his wife, it would not be acceptable for him to allow her to do this kind of work. He promised me we would buy a house in Tirana and we would live together in Tirana. I accepted and started working with that girl, giving all the profits to him. After a week or so I found a picture of him and his wife and started quarreling with him.

He got a telephone call from his father telling him that my mother had made a denunciation and that many persons were arrested, so he had to bring me back. He gave me the ticket and told his brother to bring me back to Durres. A person was waiting for us who took me to his relatives and introduced me. A good man who was their relative felt compassion for me and took me to the police station of my city.

Odeta (ITALY, 2005)

I was born in a city in the south of Albania in a very problematic family environment. I am sixteen years old. My father used to drink a lot, and he only worked sporadically. He still faces alcohol problems. He used to be violent when he was drunk and would physically abuse me, my mother, and my brother and sisters. Meanwhile, my mother worked as a garbage collector, but all her salary was appropriated by my father in order to drink and gamble.

About six years ago, my mother decided to leave my father, and she went to Italy illegally. We stayed with our aunt and grandmother. They raised us. Three years after my mother left Albania, she married an Italian man and was able to obtain all the necessary documents. She sent money for us to my aunt in order to help a little bit in our living. During this period of time my grandmother died. After that, I went to live with my father again. He kept beating me regularly. I was expected to take care of my little brother and sisters; the youngest one was only four months old when my mother left. I have never been to school, although I wanted to.

One night a man came to our home asking to take me away. He was armed and threatened my father, who did not accept what he was asking for. Then my father called the police, and then the man left because he was afraid of the police. In the meantime, I met a guy and fell in love with him. I felt he was in love with me, but my family never accepted this fact, so they found me another man to marry. I had never met him before. My mother and my aunt decided on this. This marriage was not legal at all, because I was only fourteen; that's what I learned later on. My father went illegally to Greece, and I went to live with my so-called husband and his brothers. This lasted only three weeks because he began to beat me regularly.

After this, a neighbor of mine promised to go and find a job in Italy for me. He also proposed to me and asked me to marry him. I accepted and ran away secretly from home, hiding with him in the same city where I was born. There was a Russian girl hiding in this house as well. I was not comfortable with this new situation, but I had no other way, so I just stayed and waited for things to happen. An Albanian boy brought us to Vlora and then illegally from Vlora to Italy by speedboat. We slept one night in a house that belonged to a friend of the boy, and the very next day they took us to a city in Italy. We stayed there in another house where there was a woman who used to teach us how to work in the streets. At the beginning I refused to do this type of work, but I was beaten all day and night. They threatened to kill me as well. So I was obliged to work as a prostitute.

I worked in the streets for about three weeks. I was forced to give all the money I earned to the Albanian boy. After three weeks the police caught me, and I denounced him. The police guys took me to a center for minors. I stayed there for about a year and a half. During this time, I tried to contact my mother because I wanted to live with her and my other brothers and sisters. I found out that my mother took them from Albania to Italy. I went to see where and how she was living. I found out in the meantime that she was living with a man, a guy younger than she is, and working as a prostitute herself.

I then told all my doubts and fears to the social workers in the center where I was sheltered and decided not to live with her. I miss her and love her so much, but I cannot accept the way she earns the money. Then I contacted my aunt in Albania and told her that I might want to come back to my country of origin and live with her. I returned from Italy and am trying to start a new life here.

Miranda (BELGIUM, 2005)

I was born in Korce in Albania in 1984. I lived with my family in the outskirts of Korce. Last summer when I was walking to a friend's house a car drew by and two men offered to drive me to my friend's house. One of the men was a cousin of my brother's friend. Instead of driving me to my friend's place, they took me to a house in Vlora, where a few other girls were staying. They told me that my brother wanted me to go to Italy, where I could work for an Albanian family and earn money to support my family. They also threatened me that bad things could happen to my family if I would resist them or try to run away. I lived for two weeks in this house. I stayed with two other girls in a small room and we were not allowed to go out. One girl came from Moldova and the other girl came from Berat [in south-central Albania].

One evening we were taken from the house and brought to the seashore. There we waited for two hours before embarking on a boat. We were accompanied by one of the men who took me to Vlora. There was also another man whom I had never seen before. There were about forty people on this small boat. We were not allowed to speak to the other passengers, but I heard that we were heading for Italy. I was scared, as it was night and the boat traveled at a very high speed.

We arrived the same night in Italy and had to jump out into the water about thirty meters from the coastline. There were cars waiting to pick up some of the passengers. We were taken to a house where we stayed overnight. The next day two other men took us to the train station and we left for Milan. There was a car waiting for us and we were taken to a house where we stayed for two days. We then took the train to Paris. The men who had transferred us to Italy didn't go with us. Only me and the girl from Moldova took off to Paris. The other girl from Albania remained in Milan. Two Albanians who accompanied us told us that if we would be safe on the train we had to pretend to be their sisters. There was no safety on that train. In Paris we took a train to Brussels where we were picked up by another man. He spoke Albanian, but I don't think he was from my country. They drove us to a house in Antwerp.

The same night one of the men told us that we had to work in prostitution. I told him that I didn't want to work in prostitution, but he threatened me severely. That very night I was forced by another man to have sexual intercourse. He told me that this would be a preparation for my new job. I cried and said that my brother would never agree to this. They told me that my brother was in Albania and wouldn't be much of a help.

I worked for one month in a window. I had several clients a day and was forced to hand over all the money they paid me. I was heavily guarded by those people and beaten up on several occasions. They often threatened to kill me or harm my family if I wouldn't comply. I was afraid of them, as I knew they carried guns and were on drugs.

One night police came in the window and took me to the police station. I stayed for several hours at the police station and told my story. They referred me to the Payoke shelter where I have been staying for three weeks now. They helped me to contact my family. My father told me that my brother had been receiving threats by this gang in Korce. I want to return as quickly as possible to my family in Albania. My father is planning to move to another place as it might be dangerous for us in Korce. The social workers from Payoke are assisting me and are currently arranging my return to Albania. They also contacted an organization in Albania to assist me upon my return home.

Zamira (BELGIUM, 2005)

When I was a senior in high school here in Tirana, I met a boy who did not go to my school. He was kind, attractive, and treated me well. After a time, we fell in love with each other—or so I thought at the time. He was my "first love," and I hadn't had much experience with boys romantically prior to that.

After dating for a time, he convinced me to go to Belgium with him. He said that he could get a good job there and told me about what a wonderful place it was—how clean, how beautiful, and how many opportunities there would be there for us. He proposed to me, and our plan was to leave Albania illegally (since we would not qualify for visas) and get married once he found work there. I was in love, and I believed him. Once we got to Belgium, however, he totally changed. He became abusive of me and violated me many times. He threatened my life and the lives of my family members. I did not speak the language there and was totally dependent on him; I had nowhere else to go and was afraid. He trafficked me for six months. I don't want to talk anymore about that time. It was the worst period in my life. It is now in my past, and I have closed that door behind me.

I was able to find a shelter there with people to help me return to Albania. I wanted to return to my family here, but my father would not accept me and was abusive to me and my mother. My mother decided to leave my father to help me, even though this is something unheard of in Albania for a woman to leave her husband. Women here can't really find work to support themselves and have to rely on their fathers or husbands for their livelihood. My mother gave up everything for me, and for this I am grateful. After living in the shelter for as long as we were allowed, my mother and I are now living together and trying to support ourselves.

TROKOSI SLAVERY

Religious and cultural practices are sometimes used as a justification for modern slavery. In Sudan, for example, women and children enslaved during the 1980s were given Arabic names, and some of the women were circumcised. While the purpose of enslavement was not Islamization or Arabization, the authorities abused Islamic conceptions to continue slave-raiding activities in the name of the holy war of jihad. But sometimes religious and cultural practices go beyond justification and are at the heart of modern slavery, as with the system of *trokosi* ("wife of the gods").

The trokosi practice has existed in the Volta region of rural Ghana for centuries. Fetish priests (traditionally Ewe priests to the war-gods) who run shrines insist that only by handing over a virgin daughter—typically aged between eight and fifteen—can families atone for alleged offences committed by their relatives or ancestors. These offences range from murder to petty theft. Once the girls are handed over, priests turn them into slaves and impregnate them repeatedly. They are beaten when they try to escape and are denied education, food, and basic health services. Most remain in slavery for between three and ten years, some for their whole lives. If they die, the family must offer another virgin daughter, and if they are ever released, former trokosis are considered unmarriageable. Any children born to trokosi become slaves of the priests, and trokosi are passed on to the next priest upon one priest's death. During the late 1990s, the number of trokosi reached about six thousand, most native to Ghana. The practice also exists in Togo, Benin, and southwestern Nigeria.

Until July 2002, Patience was a trokosi. Brought from Togo to a shrine in Ghana at the age of ten, she worked without pay, performing labor and sexual services. Patience was released by the Christian organization International Needs—Ghana (IN), which has liberated several thousand trokosi from shrines across southeastern Ghana since 1996. The trokosi practice was banned in Ghana in 1998, but enforcement of the ban has been ineffective; officials are hesitant to restrict the practice because they view it as an integral part of their religious beliefs, and fetish priests claim the right to preserve their forefathers' culture. Togo and Benin have done little to stop the practice, and practitioners in Ghana bring girls from these countries. Several former trokosis now campaign against the practice.

Patience (GHANA, 2004)

I want to now be called Patience. This will be my new name because I want to forget about all my past and start a new identity in life. I was about ten years old when I was brought across the border to become a trokosi. I was abandoned in the shine by my relatives for the rest of my life. When I was being brought I was given no reason; I only remember that I had a lot of beads on my waist. I brought a bundle that was stuffed with a stool, cloth, broom, plates, and some other items and placed on my head to carry for the journey. We crossed the border into Ghana, and when we got there I was taken through some rituals and was finally left in the shrine. My relatives came from Togo to visit me a few times, but I never saw my mother. They only told me she lives at Togo.

At the shrine there were some other trokosis, but I was the youngest. They sent me on errands and gave me food to eat. Later I started joining them on the farm. My education ended when I came to the shrine. When I grew up, I asked the priest why I was brought to the shrine in Ghana, because my relatives came from Togo to visit and I got to know that

I belonged to a different country. He said I came to atone for the death of my relatives who were involved in a land litigation case with another party. My relatives were cursed at the shrine for trying to possess a piece of land that did not belong to them. Many people had died, including my father. I was therefore brought here so that people would stop dying rapidly under strange circumstances. I was not given any definite time to serve at the shrine after which I should return to my country.

Life at the shrine was not easy. As a child, I had to fend for myself, apart from going to farm for the priest. My basic needs were provided by myself. I went to the bush to cut trees and burnt charcoal for sale. I also sold firewood. As a trokosi you had no rights over the fruits of your labor. We were threatened that if you earned money for yourself you would die. Thus, whatever we sold, we gave it to the priest. He collected all the money, and if it pleased him, he would determine how much to give you. I saved and bought soap, food, panties, and so on, from this. The only times that I worked extra hard to make some money from farming was when some fruits were in season. I picked baba fruit from the bush, which I pounded for sale. I picked mangos for sale when it was the season.

When I became an adolescent and had my second menstruation, the priest instructed me to be sending food to his younger brother in his hut. One day when I sent the food again, he seized me and raped me. I cried and complained but was told to shut up. This continued until I got pregnant. I later realized that it was an arrangement between the priest and his brother. I had a baby girl later. I continued to cohabit with him and now I have three children. My husband does not take care of us. He beats me up mercilessly and there is nobody to complain to. I enrolled my children in the primary school in town and they are schooling.

When life became tough for me, I decided to run away from the shrine for a while. The priest heard this and he cautioned that the curse I came to redeem from my family would follow me. Misfortune would follow me and I would fall sick and die. I was frightened but later on gathered courage to leave my children and go, because we were hungry. I followed a woman from our community to Accra. She gave me some money, which I paid back later. I slept on the floor in a long room with many other strange people. The next day I paid for the floor, a bucket of water for my bath, and rented a bowl. I joined other porters. We carried loads for people and they paid us what we bargained with them. I saved some money from this and sent some provisions and clothing to my children. While I carried foodstuff for one of my customers one day, she engaged me in conversation. She sympathized with me. She requested that I leave that job and work with her to sell eggs. I felt very sick and returned to the shrine. The priest said it was the curse, and he told me it would follow me. I went through some rituals.

When I recovered I left for Accra again, because I was committed to paying the debt to the egg seller. I explained my problem to the operator, and we entered into an agreement that she would pay the debt while I would work for her for one year without pay. She would however provide me with free meals. I had joined the woman for four months, when I heard my daughter was very ill. She gave me some money to buy provisions and send my daughter to the hospital. When my daughter recovered a little I returned to Accra but paid her visits with money from my employer. I had worked for the woman for about eight months when I had information to return to the shrine to be liberated from the trokosi system. I was liberated on the 9th of July, 2002.

CHILD SLAVERY

The International Labor Organization estimates that around 120 million children worldwide are involved in the "worst forms of child labor"— including prostitution and mining. More than three hundred thousand children are estimated to be trapped in India's carpet industry in India, and there are also an estimated five hundred thousand children in the same industry in Pakistan. Most of India's carpets are woven in Uttar Pradesh, where the majority of workers are low-caste Hindu boys. Some are lured into bondage by agents' promises to their parents that they will receive good wages, and others are kidnapped. The boys are forced to work for no pay, for ten to eighteen hours a day, seven days a week. They are beaten, tortured, branded, kept half-fed and half-clad, and are usually made to sleep in the loom shed. Cuts and wounds are frequent.

These narratives are by children trafficked into carpet looms in Uttar Pradesh, except one, by Arvind Kumar, which tells the story of a failed attempt at trafficking. While Rama escaped on his own after three years in slavery, the others were liberated in 2004 and 2005 by activists from Bal Vikas Ashram (BVA), a relief organization that liberates and rehabilitates child slaves. The boys were found weaving carpets, wearing only underwear, and had been forced to weave rugs for twelve to fifteen hours a day, beginning at 6 A.M. After their liberation, the boys—including Arvind and Rama—were taken to BVA, in Uttar Pradesh, where they received medical care, counseling, literacy training, and basic rights education. They returned to their villages after six months. BVA continues to liberate children; since 1999 it has rescued and sheltered around four hundred. It carried out ten liberation raids in 2002, releasing 78 children from carpet looms, and in 2005 it carried out nineteen raids and released 111 children.

Arvind (INDIA, 2004)

My name is Arvind. I am ten years old. The middleman came and took me from home to the station. He gave my parents 500 rupees [$11]. He told us that they're going take us and let us study, and we were very happy. But after some time they showed us a knife. When they showed us the knife, we were eating our food and we all starting crying. We were on the train and that's when Ratnaji came and he took us off the train and took us to the police station. They saved our lives. We were very happy.

I like it very much over here. We get to study, we do a few light chores around the place, and we get to play. I want to study further, but when I get holidays I'll go back home. I told father that I'll be good and I won't fight with anybody, I'll stay happily over here and study some more. I want to study Hindi and math and I want to become a collector [district magistrate] after studying so I can help people who are sick. I'll sing a few

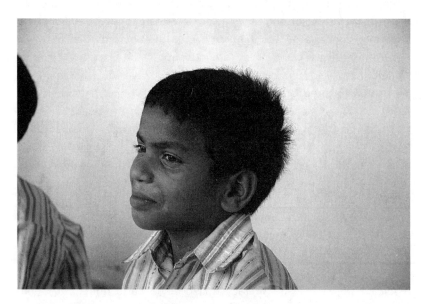

Arvind Kumar (photograph by Peggy Callahan, Free the Slaves, 2004)

lines of a song. Yama, yama, ya...a, a, a. I feel bad about kids who are sold. It happens only to the people who are poor and need the money.

Rambho (INDIA, 2004)

My name is Rambho Kumar and I am eleven years old. I used to work at home, and I also used to play and roam around with the kids living nearby. A man named Shankar and the owner of the loom came one day to my house and gave 700 rupees [$15] for me. They told my parents that they were going to educate me and make me do some work. I didn't want to go to the looms. I wanted to stay at home. But there was no money at home for us to eat, so my mother told me to go. I was crying and saying that I didn't want to go there. They said that they're going to give me money. He'll send money home and then after some time I can come back. But after a very long time, he told me that I'm not going to be able to go back home ever.

Rambho Kumar (photograph by Peggy Callahan, Free the Slaves, 2004)

After two days I reached the loom and they made me sit. They told me to learn how to use the loom. My hand got cut, and the owner and his brother shut my eyes and put my finger in boiling oil and said: "Now it's all right, now you get back to work." If I made any mistake, the loom owner used to take a stick and beat me with that. I kept asking the loom owner when I would go to school, and he kept telling me, "There is no school for you. You will spend time weaving carpets."

I used to work from four in the morning till eleven in the night. I wasn't allowed to play or roam around or anything. At about ten in the morning we used to get our first meal, which was not good, and then I would go back to weaving the carpets till about ten at night. And that was all we did during the day: weaving carpets, eating food, and going to sleep. I was there for one year. I wanted to go back home. I always used to want to get away. The owner used to tell us, "If the police ever come, run away before they can catch you." So I knew that when the police came I'd be taken away from there. When I saw them coming I was very happy. As soon as they came, the owner and his father and his brother and all the other people ran away. About ten of us were surrounded by the police. Six of us ran away but four of us were brought to the ashram. When I came here I liked it because you get time to eat, you get time to play, to study. I like studying the most.

I haven't seen my mother for the last thirteen months, and I miss my family a lot. My father has passed away. We put 6,000 rupees [$130] into expenses for his treatment, but still he passed away. Now we don't even have a place to stay over there in the village. I want to help my mother find a house. I want to go to my village and be a guard there, and I think I'll be able to study and earn money. And I won't let anybody go to the looms even by mistake. I'll tell them: "They hit you and they beat you." I would not let them go there, ever. If the children make any mistakes they beat them up. I won't let them go there.

Rama (INDIA, 2004)

I will absolutely not let my parents send any of my brothers to the loom. When it comes to the loom owners, I was badly beaten. They did not provide any of the facilities they talked about in the village. In fact, they made us work day and night on the loom. I will make sure that none of my brothers get caught in the same trap again.

Before I was taken I did not go to school. I would take the cattle of my neighbors for grazing. I would have fun. We would go in a large group of

Rama (photograph by Peggy Callahan, Free the Slaves, 2004)

boys. We would just let the cattle graze while we had fun and went and did our thing. In the village I had five brothers, my mother, and my sister. I was in the village when a man came and offered food, clothing, shelter, money. My parents sent me even though I didn't want to come. I didn't know what was happening to me—where I would land up. I was very scared. The journey took a long time. I didn't know how to weave, but I was taught by being beaten up repeatedly—they beat me up each time I made a mistake. I was beaten with the wooden portion of the knife. I wasn't allowed to go out to play outside and had no friends. The food was really bad, stale and two-days old. I didn't like it at all.

I always had hope that I would be rescued, but nobody came while I was there. Once I got a call from father. He asked if I was alright. I lied and said I was OK. I didn't want my father to worry about me. I would think about running away every night. One morning something snapped. I took my blanket and ran for my life. I jumped on a tractor and it took me to a place I didn't know. A woman sheltered me for the night and sent me to her father's house. The owners of the loom chased me. I was lucky and lived with my parents for the next two years. The loom owner actually came to the house but didn't see me. My brother tried to escape before me—he was caught and beaten.

What I have learned at the Bal Vikas Ashram, I will take back home: how to behave, not only with myself but also with others. That is what I want to take home, interaction with other people. I can read now a little bit. When I do go back, I intend to enroll in school and learn a whole lot more. The happiness and joy that I have found at the ashram may never come again. I don't think I can find the joy back home. I will go, but I know I will have to come back here one day. Now there are no thoughts about running away in my mind. I am just so happy here on my daily basis. I just think about my work and what tomorrow will bring. The work I do here I want to continue when I go home. I want to work as an electrician.

I want to tell the government that these kids exist. It's time for you to take these children out of the loom. And it's not so difficult. All you need to do is surround the factory on all sides, come in and take the children. That's all you have to do.

Ravi (INDIA, 2004)

My name is Ravi Shanker Kumar. I think I am between twelve and thirteen years old. My maternal uncle's son was working in the loom and it was he, in fact, who told my uncle to go back to the village and talk to my parents so they could send me here. Eventually the loom owner landed up in my village and met my parents. He went to my father and told him that he should send me to the loom. I was very happy in my village, playing, having a good time until the loom owner showed up.

My parents came up to me and asked me if I wanted to go. I refused. They agreed. The loom owner refused to take no for an answer, however. He argued that he didn't agree with my parents. They succumbed to his demands. He paid them a sum of 500 rupees [$10] and then they asked me to leave. Once he had paid the 500, the loom owner and I took off from the village. We boarded a train, and throughout the entire train journey he refused to feed me. He just didn't give me any food. It was only when I got up to Allahabad that he gave me four samosas to eat.

After the train journey we went from the station to the loom owner's house. We went inside and sat down and ate some dinner and went to sleep. The next morning I woke up without any food or any full nourishment; we both went to the place where the looms and the machinery were kept. That was the first time I saw the loom.

I was made to sit at a loom, and the very first day that I sat there he made a little mark on the loom itself. He gave me clear instructions that up to that mark I had to weave a carpet. If I was unable to do so, I had to

Ravi Shanker Kumar (photograph by Peggy Callahan, Free the Slaves, 2004)

work under candlelight to reach that particular mark. Because I was made to work late-night hours, I would never be able to sleep adequately in the night. As a result I was always sleepy when I was on the loom and my work would get spoiled. The whole morning I would be weaving and I would only get some basic food at about 12.30 P.M. The food wasn't good. I didn't like it at all. Every day I had to force myself to eat it. Once in a while the loom owner would ask me, "Ravi, have you eaten your food?" And I would say, "Yuh, I have." Basically, he would give us half-cooked rice, and the dal would be not well cooked and full of water—not at all what dal was supposed to taste like.

In fact, things were so bad that once in a while, while [I was] working on the loom, my fingers would get cut and they would get nipped. Each time I got cut on my finger, I would go up to my boss' wife and say, "Look, I've got a wound on my finger. Can you give me some medicine, some ointment you can give to me?" The boss' wife would not put any ointment for my wound. In fact, she would take a little bit of kerosene and put it in my wound and strike a match to it. That would hurt terribly. The wound would not heal, and we were made to go back and resume weaving again. Very often, because the wound was in raw condition, the blood would start oozing out of my finger. But then we could not stop. With the blood running down my finger I was made to weave. Only when it became so bad that I could not possibly weave anymore, would I stop. And the moment I did stop, I was beaten up. There were two ways he would beat me up. With the stick of the loom, he would lift that up and beat me up with that. Or, there was an instrument called a *punja* with which we would put the threads down and snap it with the loom. It's a sharp instrument, and he would use the wooden portion of that and beat me with that.

I didn't get any money, but I did get a bed. We were confined in one room and made to work for a period of twelve hours. Once in a day we could go and maybe use the bathroom, but those bathroom stops were limited in number. In the evening, once I would finish working on the loom, I would go up to him and ask for a little bit of money so I could go to the market and have a good time. He would always refuse. No matter when we went to him, he would just refuse to give us any money. At the maximum he would give us a rupee. Or he would say, "Don't worry, we will go tomorrow." He was always lying to us. My father came to visit me once. He asked the loom owner to release me, but he refused: "Until such time as the carpet is completed, I can't let him leave because he's the only one who knows the pattern." My father went away. So that was it. That was the only time I spoke to my father.

I would think, there has to be something better. I would think of running away. But the thought of running away would always be followed with the thought of what if I get caught? If I did get caught I would be beaten up mercilessly. Therefore I never ran away. I was rescued in a raid operation conducted by Dajna Kurooji, a person who works in the Bal Vikas Ashram. He came in a raid and picked me up from there and got me to the ashram. I was very scared during the raid. I thought I was going to get beaten up again and they're going to throw me away. I was terrified. The loom owner would tell us, "If and when the police come, run away, run away because they are going to be mean to you." The police official was smart enough to park the vehicle about three kilometers away from the loom and made his way slowly. We were surprised because they crept up on us slowly. The kids were working on the loom. We didn't have any option to run away.

The first day I came to the ashram, the other kids showed me around the place, where the bathing area was, where the bathroom was. They showed me where the cocks and rabbits lived. I was fed a good meal and I went to sleep. It was just beautiful the first time I knew that I was not going to be beaten or tortured. What I like best here are the studies, the playing, the food, the interactions. I love it. I don't think I'll like my home anymore. I think when I do go home, I'll miss this place. Before I sleep, I always make a comparison between this and home. I've fallen in love with this place. I don't want to leave. But then also I do. I want to go back home. I have no clue—this or that? I'm also trying to learn how to be an electrician. I like the electricity idea. I like the fact that the teacher gives us notes and lessons that we have to memorize. He asks me questions in class, and when I'm able to answer, it feels good. When I go back home, I'm sure I'll join a school and continue my education. I dream to teach my brothers, to teach my sisters. I dream to teach my fellow village people. I dream to learn and teach, and do them both together.

I would like to tell the children who are working right now on the loom to stop, to do what they want, to stop. If I got a chance to talk to the world, I would relate my life story. I would tell them that I was working on the loom. I would tell them about my rescue. I would talk to them about how I came to this wonderful place and how I was given the opportunity to study, to learn. I would tell them about my life experiences. And I want to simply tell Father Louis, "Six months, six months of my life I've spent with you. But you've turned it around. You've given me a whole new life, a fresh lease." This ashram is such a great place. Not only is there the education, but physical training, prayers, growth in all aspects. Now I know for a fact that every child in entitled to study. I know for a fact that no child should be subjected to any torture from anyone. I know for a fact that you should not be made to work for anybody else for food.

Shahnawaz (INDIA, 2005)

I will give a great punch on the face of the trafficker if he enters my village again. I will be a great trouble for him. He has tortured me very much; he did not allow me to play with my friends. I was a very small child in the loom, eight years old. I was there for one month. This one month was very scary for me. My family is at the breadline, hence my parents fell easily into the trick of the trafficker. He told my father that I will be getting 200 rupees [$4] a month and I will be working in good conditions at a good place. But that man has cheated me and my family. I was forced to work for more than sixteen hours a day, with insufficient food to eat and in a room where there was too much suffocation because of the smell of the woolen threads used for weaving carpet. Every day we were made to complete at least 200 rupees worth of part of a carpet. Once a week or so, I was paid 10 or 20 rupees [$.20–.45] by the broker who brought me. He was getting all my money, about 110 rupees [$2] from the owner. Same was done with the other children too.

Being a small child I was getting beatings from the broker and sometimes from the owner. Most of the time that broker was there to supervise our work. I never dreamt of such a poor condition at this age when other children play and enjoy. I was working continuously on the loom for more than sixteen hours daily. I feel that this is an injustice to we poor children.

Ashok (INDIA, 2005)

I was fortunate to work for a little period at the loom compared to the other children. I came to the loom with one of the owner's family members eight months before the date of rescue. As usual, my father was tricked by a trafficker, through his false promises of a better future for me—food, education, and income. I was sent with the man for just 2,000 rupees [$45]. Due to the poor condition of the family and a huge debt after my brother's marriage, I decided to go with the man to rescue my family from debt.

It was a very fearful experience for me when I entered the loom, which was very dark. I was not able to see things clearly. I was amazed to see children working in such a miserable condition, but now I was also part of it. I was forced to work in miserable conditions at the loom with no proper food to eat. I was provided with poor quality as well as poor quantity of food. Sometimes there was no salt and sometimes a full packet of salt. The food was watery with no nutritious value and of such a bad quality that even animals would also not wish to eat it.

I was made to work continuously from seven in the morning to seven in the evening. I got only one hour of break either to take rest or lunch. My master tortured me both physically and mentally. When I was not able to finish my work, I received beatings with a slipper and bamboo sticks from the owner of the factory.

One day his torture crossed its limit, both my hands were tied to the trunk of the tree and I was beaten very badly. I was not able to come out of that situation for more than one and a half months. I felt that I had been so happy at my house. At the time of any illness and sickness such as fever, pain in my legs, hand, backbone, I was treated badly and also not given any proper care to recover from the sickness.

I tried to escape from the loom but was caught by the owner's father who used to do guard duty during the night. This made me very disappointed, and very often I thought of my past days when I was free to play, free to go anywhere I wanted and enjoy my life in the field when I used to graze my cattle along with my friends. I was not allowed to go anywhere. Even when there was a problem in my family, I never got any leave. Whenever I asked for leave, the owner clearly said, "First return my money and only then you will be allowed to go home." I was getting mentally depressed and used to get angry very quickly whenever I talked with other boys working along with me. But I was not able to understand what was happening to me.

The world is too cruel for those who don't have money and education, hence I ask you to please support us and stop child labor. I hope I will become an army officer to fight for the children and my country. Please pray to God for my success.

Battis (INDIA, 2005)

I was beaten at my school by the teacher and decided not go school again. I was so happy when I left the school, but today I am facing a problem. If I had not left the school I would not be in child labor and separated from my family.

I was brought two years back by the broker, whose name is not known to me. Before coming to the loom I was working as a daily wage labor. I was getting 10–20 rupees [$.20–.45] per day in the field. The poor condition of the family compelled me to work from early childhood. The broker gave 1,000 rupees [$20] to my father and took me with him as a product in his carry bag. He assured my father that I would be getting proper education and small work to earn my daily bread. Being unfamiliar about the coming situation, my father sent me along with him, and seeing the miserable economic condition of my family, I also did not refuse to go. When we were on the way the broker did not give me any thing to eat; rats were jumping inside my stomach, but what can be done to prevent them from jumping?

From the moment I stepped inside the loom I was made to knit the carpet. I was supposed to knit three square feet of carpet daily with my small fingers, and if I failed to do so, I was beaten with sticks and an iron rod. I had to work ten to fourteen hours daily, with a break of one hour in the morning, and was not allowed to go outside. I was not even allowed to talk with my parents on a phone line. One day my father made a phone call and my owner told him, "Battis has gone somewhere." It was very irritating to me. My friends told me that the owner does this with every child.

I never got sufficient food to eat. I always felt hungry. The quality of food was also not good: dal full of water and rice; sometimes we used to get puffed rice to eat. While doing work, whenever I felt hunger I used to think of my home where I was free to eat anything anytime. I tried to escape from the trap of the owner and I succeeded, but unfortunately I was caught at a place nearly twenty-five kilometers from the loom. I felt bad about my condition before the rescue operation but am now feeling happy. I will open a tailoring shop and stitch clothes for my villagers. They will give me money and I will definitely not come into bondage again. I will set up an example for my friends and children of the village and prevent them from getting into the trap of bondage.

Sandeep (INDIA, 2005)

I was twelve years old when brought to the loom. My father was working in brick kilns as a daily wage laborer without sufficient money to fill the stomachs of his five sons and one daughter. The miserable condition of the family was very disappointing for me. I always felt bad about the situation but not able to help out.

Day came when one of the agents of the loom owner arrived to meet my father. At that time I was very curious to know why this man has come and started dreaming about my better future without knowing the consequences of it. The agent told my father that I would be in a better place than the present situation. Tricked by the man, my father decided to send me with him. I also agreed to go since many other children were going along with him without knowing the upshot of it.

When I came to the loom, I came to know that the agent was the owner's younger brother. From the time I entered the loom I was told very harshly to learn to weave carpets of the required length. It was a very bad experience for me. Anyhow, I tried to adjust to it. But the things were not going in the right direction, I felt. I was made to work on looms from early morning, 4 A.M., to late at night, 10.30 P.M., with only two hours of break for daily activities and lunch as well as dinner. The owner's father made me wake up early in the morning along with the other boys to work, and by chance if I was not able to wake up and do the work at that time I was given hard thrashes on both my cheeks. One day I was beaten so badly by the owner's father, I got a fracture in my hand and no treatment was given for my recovery.

I always demanded education as per promises made by the agent, but I received beatings on my knees and elbows rather than a pen and books.

This went against my self-respect. Hence I tried to escape but was unfortunately caught. I tied the rope from the terrace of the house in which we were working and came down through it at midnight. I ran from that place and came nearly twenty-five kilometers away from that place. Since I was walking across the road and did not have a single penny to go by bus, I was caught by the man who was a watch dog for us. I failed to escape and was again in the trap of bondage. During the night, after work, I always used to think of my family and cry, but there was no hope for me. I wish that in the future I will become a policeman and break the knees and elbows of these slaveholders, and not allow any children to go along with them even if he gives scores of money.

AIN'T I A WOMAN?

Female Slaves and the Dynamics of Gender

I have borne thirteen children, and seen most all sold off...ain't I a woman?
   Sojourner Truth, "Ain't I a Woman," 1851

We are a sister to someone, a daughter, a granddaughter...we are women.
   Dina Chan, a former sex slave, Cambodia, 1999

THAI SEX TRAFFICKING

Of the estimated six hundred thousand to eight hundred thousand individuals trafficked across international borders each year, some 80 percent are women and girls. Nuch, Pot, Kaew, and Nu, were several of the thousands of women trafficked annually out of Thailand for sexual exploitation. The major destinations include Japan, Malaysia, Bahrain, Australia, Singapore, and the United States. Internal trafficking occurs within the country as well, usually from northern Thailand (where hill tribe women and girls are denied Thai citizenship) to the large cities. In Japan, where Nuch, Pot, Kaew, and Nu were enslaved, women are trafficked from Thailand, the Philippines, Russia, and eastern Europe—and on a smaller scale from Colombia, Brazil, Mexico, Burma, and Indonesia. Of the 150,000 foreign women who are part of the Japanese sex industry (around 30,000 of whom are Thai), most likely 25,000 are enslaved.

Kaew entered Japan on a tourist visa in May 1992 at the age of thirty-one, after meeting an agent in Bangkok. She was kept in a "snack bar," or brothel, in Nagano Prefecture, west of Tokyo. Nu, who was repeatedly raped by a relative and escaped to Bangkok at the age of fifteen to work as a prostitute, was tricked into leaving for Japan with the promise of waitress work. She spent ten months enslaved in a "karaoke bar" in Shinjuku, a major Tokyo commercial district, and another four years working as a prostitute after her escape. Nuch left for Japan in March 1992 at the age of twenty-seven and was held in Tokyo. She explains that—like Kaew, Nu, and Pot—she apparently owed money for the trip and had to work off her debt with clients. After three months in slavery, she was taken to a police station, detained for several months in solitary confinement, and transferred to an immigration detention center, where she was held until the Thai embassy issued travel documents. She flew back to Thailand in March 1993. Pot was introduced to an agent in Bangkok in 1990 at the age of twenty-seven and was flown to Tokyo via South Korea. There were up to twenty women working in her brothel at any given time, and she was held there for eighteen months.

Pot's pimp was female. Whether through initial deceptions by female recruiters, or experiences like Pot's of a female pimp, these narratives describe the involvement of women in the process of enslavement. Nuch's experience was at the hands of a long series of women: a Thai woman who got "extra points" by betraying her, a female agent, a woman who was the "boss," and the Taiwanese "mama" (brothel manager). Equally, Nu describes "peer bonding" and help from a Japanese nun, but also the involvement of women in trafficking—a hairdresser friend and the "mama-san" (brothel manager). The percentage of female traffickers is rising. Some have been trafficked themselves and then reappear on the scene as recruiters or pimps. Others are blackmailed by criminals. Female traffickers are often the most convincing at deceiving women and girls into accepting fake job offers and so beginning the journey into slavery.

Nuch (JAPAN, 1995)

The agent told me she could find a job for me in a Thai restaurant in Japan and that I could make several tens of thousands a month. She agreed to pay for all of my expenses, saying that I could pay her back once in Japan. I didn't know anything about exchange rates or different currencies so I didn't know how much 380 bai [$30,000] was, but it didn't sound like a lot. I asked how long it would take me to pay it back, and the agent said five months.

I didn't carry my own passport to go through Thai immigration. The agent gave both of our passports to immigration and talked to them. I arrived in Japan at night. At Narita airport immigration the agent told me to go to a specific line, and she went in another one. She went through first and then came to help me. She spoke Japanese and got me through. Then we took a taxi to a hotel in Tokyo. She told me I would work at a Thai restaurant that belonged to a Thai woman named Ice. Ice told me I was to stay there and that I shouldn't speak Thai outside the apartment. She told me I couldn't escape and not to even try.

Another woman took the three of us. We traveled all day by train. Once off the train, I was separated from the others and brought straight to a snack bar. I was very cold because I had no winter clothes. The snack bar was very small and had only four other Thai women there. They worked and slept at the snack shop. The mama was a Taiwanese woman. They told me there was no way out and I would just have to accept my fate. The snack bar had many customers who I saw drinking alcohol and singing. I was told I had to go to sit with them. I knew then what had happened to me. That first night I had to take several men, and after that I had to have at least one client every night.

When I first got to the apartment a Thai man slapped my face and said, "They told you not to meet other Thai." Then Ice took me into another room. There Ice beat me, mostly by kicking me everywhere, while I sat in a chair. Ice beat me for over an hour saying, "I told you not to speak to any Thai." I couldn't fight back because there were many men outside the room. When Ice finished she took a visa photo of me and forced me to write a contract. I said I couldn't write, but Ice forced me to write the contract by telling me each letter in Thai. I was forced to write that "if I try to escape again, I agree to be killed," and then Ice forced me to sign it. Then Ice photocopied it and said she would give a copy to the next mama I was sent to work for. Ice then asked me, "Do you want to go into a brothel where you'll never come out or pay back a debt of 700 bai [$55,000]?" I didn't know what a brothel was, but it didn't sound good so I agreed to having my original debt doubled.

I had to take all the clients that were introduced to me and was never given a day off. I was given birth control and charged 1,000 yen [$8] per month. The only money I ever had was the tip money I saved. With the tip money, I had to buy my own food, except for rice, with the other women. Once I slipped and said I was from Thailand. The client asked the mama if it was true that I was from Thailand. It was a big problem. The mama's daughter slapped me, and the Japanese husband of the mama told me, "If you tell another person you are Thai again you will have a name, but no body." This meant he would kill me and only my name would be left. The mama's daughter slapped me again another time, when I was told to serve a very rude, drunk, and dirty client whom I had been forced to have sex with several times before and couldn't stand it. She slapped me because I wasn't eager enough to take this particular client.

We were watched at all times. When we had to go out with clients, the mama hired taxis to wait for us at the hotel and bring the women back. There was never any chance to escape. We worked at the snack bar from 6 P.M. to 3 A.M., and at 9 A.M. we were woken up to clean the house and the snack bar before lunch. After lunch we worked in the field out behind the snack bar until dinner. We were given birth control pills and told not to take the white pills. So we never had our periods while working there. We worked and took clients every day.

I asked another Thai woman to help me write a letter to send to my mother. It had been a long time since I had written to my mother. I had never told my mother what I was forced to deal with or the details of my life. I just wanted to tell my mother that I was well and everything was OK. But, while I was telling the other Thai woman what to write, I slipped and said, "Sorry I haven't written to you for a long time. I have moved to another restaurant." The Thai woman who was transcribing the letter asked me for more details. I told her then that I got sick and my blood was positive [for HIV]. Then this Thai woman went and told the mama—to get some extra points by telling on me. In all my time in Japan only about ten clients ever used condoms, and even then they broke a couple of times. I did not know about AIDS then or what "blood positive" meant.

One morning, the police came to arrest us. They asked me and the others in Thai if we wanted to go home, and if so to get our clothes. Only myself and one other woman got our clothes. Everyone was arrested, the mama, her husband, the two Taiwanese friends, and the seven Thai women. One Thai woman had just finished off her debt after two years and was about to be paid for the first time for twenty clients. She was especially upset.

Pot (JAPAN, 1995)

A friend I knew from the market in Nakhon Sawan told me about the opportunity to work in factories in Japan. I had divorced my Thai husband when I was four months pregnant, and now my son was three years old and I had to raise him by myself and was finding it difficult to make enough money. My parents asked me not to go, but I thought if I went for just one year I could make money for my family and son. I didn't realize what kind of work I was going to do until I was on my way to Japan, and I didn't realize I was in debt for 380 bai [$30,000] until I arrived at the snack bar. I was told by the recruiters in Thailand that I would work in a factory and would get 50 percent of my salary until my debt was paid off. I was angry and freaked out about my situation. I was surprised to be locked up because I was not allowed any chance to say good-bye to my family, even over the phone. I heard the agents talking about the price for each woman being between 150 and 160 bai [$10,000–11,000], but I couldn't really understand what they were talking about and did not realize that we were being sold into prostitution. I was feeling suspicious but still wasn't clear about what was going on. In hindsight I believe that the immigration officer at Don Muang airport in Bangkok knew what I was going to do in Japan better than I did at the time, as the officer was buddy-buddy with my escort and just kept smiling at me and the other Thai women as he stamped our passports.

Most of the women were under twenty years old and from the north of Thailand. All fifty women were guarded, controlled, and watched by the men at all times. I knew that there was something wrong and began talking to the other Thai women there. This is where I learned that all of the women were going to work in prostitution, because some of the women had worked in prostitution before and knew that they were going to do so in Japan. I didn't know what to do. I just thought that once I got to Japan I would change my job immediately.

Chan was trying to sell me and the others like cattle. Then, on the fifth day, a Thai woman bought me and took me to another woman named Chan in Ibaraki Prefecture who paid 380 bai for me. I had known since Korea that I was being sold as a prostitute, but I didn't realize until I got to the snack bar that this 380 bai that I was bought for was to be my debt.

In all, I worked for eight months to pay back my debt, and I had calculated that I must have paid it back long ago, but the mama kept lying to me and said she didn't have the same records as I did. During these eight months, I had to take every client that wanted me and had to work every day, even during my menstruation. The mama also made me and the other women work for her during the day and wouldn't allow us to eat much, saying we would get too fat. I was like a skeleton during that time. While I was under contract, the mama paid for everything except for my health care and birth control pills. This was all added to my debt. I tried to keep track of my own records quietly, but I didn't know all the additional expenses that the mama was adding to my debt. And I did not want the mama to know I was keeping track for fear that she would get angry. I did not have any money to send home unless a client gave me a good tip. I just wanted to pay off my debt and get enough money to go home. But the mama was always swearing at me for saving money. The mama threatened me, saying that if I made any trouble she'd sell me again and double my debt. During the first three months I was never allowed out of the apartment except with the mama or a client. Even after three months I was allowed out only along with others and was warned not to make any friends.

Once a Yakuza member took me out for the night. He brought me to a hotel room and first injected himself with heroin and then tried to force me to inject. I refused and struggled. He beat me until I was almost dead. Then he took a rubber band out and strapped it around my arm and was just about to inject me when he passed out. I tried to move and after some time was able to get out of the hotel and fled back to my apartment. I didn't dare tell anybody what happened or seek medical help for my injuries.

When the Japanese police came around I knew that I had overstayed my visa and that the mama had my passport. I never dared to run away or even considered running to the police without my documents. Without my documents I was sure I would be arrested and jailed. I tried to be cooperative with the mama and not make any troubles for myself.

Kaew (JAPAN, 1997)

I had three kids, my husband drank, and we had no money, so I had to do something. I went back and forth several times trying to make money, leaving my children with my mother. The agent in Bangkok decided I was beautiful enough to go to Japan, though I had to get a nose job first and they kept messing it up; they had to do it four times to get it right. The agent wanted me to get my eyes done too, but I refused. Other women got plastic surgery for their breasts, eyes, or other body parts. Women who were not beautiful enough were given a bus ticket home to their villages. They used me because I was older, so it was easier for me. I got five passports for other women—each time getting married to change my surname. If I think about it now, the agents were very, very clever. They could even make birth certificates; they could do everything. They were so clever, and in Japan the brokers are even more clever.

After seven months, I threatened to go home because I wasn't making any money, so they sent me to Japan. My escort was a Western man named Gary. He took the women to Japan one by one. He had many passports and worked with the airline. He had a visa that allowed him to go back and forth between Japan and Thailand through his banana business. He was handsome and dressed up and spoke Thai. I told the immigration officials that I was going to visit a banana factory in Japan to see how it worked and I had a letter from the company in Thailand. Gary had 150 bai [$12,000] with him. Gary and I were separated by the immigration officers at the airport and asked questions about the company, but we had prepared before. I had practiced for two or three nights before I left and learned to write my new name in English.

At Narita airport, someone was waiting for me and took the clothes and jewelry that they had given me to wear. The person took me to the mama's house in Tokyo. There were lots of women there, and people came to choose women and buy them. I was bought on the third day and told that my price was 380 bai [$30,000]. After three or four days of working at the snack bar, I realized how much 380 bai was. The other girls said to me, "That's a lot of debt and you're old; you'll never pay it off." Then I prayed that it would only take six or seven months to pay it off, and I went with all of the clients I could. The mama said to me, "Don't let your period come, or you'll never finish paying your debt." The boss would tell me to go with a man, and I couldn't refuse. Girls were beaten if they didn't agree, and the owner was close to the Yakuza so he knew how to fight. Women were also fined for coming back late, fighting with each other, or not agreeing to sit with a client, so I did what I was told. Other women were beaten so badly they had to take days off; I wasn't beaten or given fines because I obeyed.

Some clients were good, and some were abusive. I had up to three clients a night because I needed to pay off my debt, and after six months the mama said I had paid off 250 bai [$20,000]. I kept track in a notebook and this sounded about right—I was paying back about 40 or 50 baht [$3,000–4,000] per month, and I could have paid off the rest of the debt soon. But while I was working, I met a man who was a friend of the owner. He came to the snack bar often, but he never took women out, he just talked to them. I had to talk to him, and at first I was upset because I knew he wasn't going to pay to take me out, but then he gave me tips just to sit and talk. He told the owner that he liked me and asked to buy out my contract, and the owner agreed since it was his friend. Usually, they didn't allow men to buy women out.

So he paid the 130 bai [$10,000] that I owed and set me up in an apartment. He gave me money, and I also continued to work at the same snack bar, but I wasn't in debt so I earned money. Women working without debt still had to go with a customer if he picked her out, but I didn't have to try flirting and all anymore because I wasn't so worried about money. On Tuesdays, I spent the day with my boyfriend, and the other days I worked. I continued to work there for almost two years after my debt was paid, and then I was arrested.

All of the local police came to the snack bar, just like in Thailand, and they were very nice—there were no problems. But then police came from Tokyo. They were cleaning up in preparation for the Olympics in Nagano, and an undercover police officer from Tokyo came to the snack bar. She said she was a tour operator from Tokyo—there were a lot of tours from Tokyo—and that she wanted to see the women. When the women lined up, the officer took out her ID and arrested us all. I always kept 10 bai [$980] in my pocket to pay for my ticket to Thailand in case I was arrested and deported, so I had that with me. I also had my passport—the mama had kept it while I was in debt, but after my contract was paid I carried it at all times. I gave my money and passport to the officer, and she let me get my stuff, and then I was taken to jail. Five days later I returned to Thailand. I didn't have to stay long because I had my passport and enough money for the trip home. When I left, I just got on to the plane like other passengers. There were twenty-four of us arrested together at the snack bar, and we were sent back to Thailand in groups of three or four.

Whenever I think too much, I get sad. But then I remember when I could only feed my children rice and soup. My husband didn't help, so my kids had to stay with my mother while I went to earn money. That guy was physically abusive too. He would come home drunk and beat me. I tried to work it out with him. But things never changed. The oldest son knows everything I did. He remembers before, knows the choices I've made. I worry that my children will be embarrassed by me, by the fact that I was a prostitute. But I tell my kids, "I had many men on my chest and I cried, but I closed my eyes and thought of my kids." I don't know if they really listen or if it's in one ear and out the other.

It's all good luck or not. It was good luck that I had a good snack bar, and bad luck that I got arrested, and good luck that I found a good boyfriend. If you talk to different women, you will get very different stories. Some women start to gamble, spend their money, and drink. It gets difficult to remember why you're there, for the young especially. Some are less obedient than me, so they have problems. The snack bar next door to me was run by the Yakuza so it was worse. Some women are killed or followed if they escape, or even if they are arrested. Some are followed to Thailand, so many don't go back to their families right away, but wait. Now I want to go back to Japan to visit, but only legally. When I was in Japan, I had no rights because the job was illegal. I'd like to go back to see, independently. I'm trying to go legally, with a passport, so that I'm allowed to be there.

Nu (JAPAN, 2000)

I am waiting to give birth to my baby. I hope it is not a girl. She must not suffer like me. I was abandoned by my parents and left to be brought up by distant relatives. I studied up to the primary level and did all the housework. When I reached puberty the son of the family I lived with began making advances towards me. He raped me several times and began sending me out occasionally with clients for short periods, warning me never to tell his parents. I was already "spoilt" and decided to run away and entertain clients on my own instead of living under his control. I came to Bangkok at the age of fifteen, rented a room, and began seeing clients independently. But getting enough and good clients was difficult, and operating independently without any protection was risky.

A hairdresser friend suggested that I find a well-paying job outside the country that also took care of my food and accommodation. She said that there were plenty of Thai women who worked in Japan and returned rich. She said that if I didn't know how to go about things, she would introduce me to an agent who would help me secure work in Japan. I was willing and an appointment was fixed.

The agent interviewed me on my background. I told him that I had no relatives, that operating independently in Bangkok hardly got me good clients and money, and that I was worried that I wasn't smart and good-looking enough to go to Japan. He assured me that this was no problem at all but that he would have to physically examine me before a final decision was made. He asked me to undress behind a makeshift screen, examined my body for "damage," and internally probed me with his bare hands to detect "disease." When he was satisfied that I was OK, he said I would be sent to Japan.

I was told that I would be working as a waitress in a bar earning approximately $200 per month and that I was not bound to go out with clients but could if I chose to earn more. Agent's fees and other expenses were to be paid after I received my first wage. From the time the agent began working on my travel documents to the time of my departure—which was a little over two weeks—I was kept in a small hotel room and provided with food. The agent said this was necessary in preparation for my departure. I learned later that I traveled to Japan on a tourist visa and someone else's passport affixed with my photograph.

The day before my departure, I was told that I would be escorted from Bangkok airport by a Thai family—a man, his wife, their son, and daughter. I was to pretend that they were my parents and siblings, and I was instructed by the agent to address them as mom and dad and not to talk too much to them. I was specifically instructed not to talk to the Thai and Japanese immigration officials or to any authorities. My "father" would take care of everything. I had to demonstrate to the agent how I would behave with my family, to assure him I had understood his instructions.

I was introduced to my "family" at the airport. The man seemed to be a technician with Thai Airways. I don't know if those were really his wife and children, but they were all fair and well dressed and seemed to know what to do. My "father" kept my passport with him. The agent gave me 30,000 yen [$250] for my expenses before we left. At Narita airport in Japan, my "father" took care of the immigration procedures. After we collected our baggage, the woman went her own way with the boy and girl, and my "father" led me away in the opposite direction, where we were met by a Japanese man with three young Thai women in his charge. My "father" took the 30,000 yen from me, left me with the Japanese, and disappeared.

We were brought by taxi to a karaoke bar in Shinjuku. The owner was a Japanese, married to a Thai mama-san. The bar owner said that he did not accept girls with big tattoos and body marks and asked us to go one at a time into a cubicle at the back of the bar. I was asked to undress and the owner began pressing and massaging various parts of my body. He examined me vaginally. This was a repeat of the same procedure as in Thailand, but here the owner even slept with me before hiring me. I really felt horrible—like a piece of flesh, being inspected, bought, and sold. I had to take a blood test for HIV/AIDS. I was the only one of the four women bought by the bar. The other girls were taken elsewhere. I later learned that if women tested HIV positive or were found physically unpleasing, they were bought only by lower-grade bars where earnings are less and conditions much worse.

As soon as the others left, the mama-san told me that I had to pay off a debt of over one million yen [$8,000]. My food, rent, and other expenses would be added to this amount. We did not receive commissions on drinks, although we had to persuade clients to buy drinks. Clients paid the mama-san directly for taking the women out during the debt repayment period. The mama-san warned me not to try to run away, as she would be very tough, and that all girls who tried escaping were brought back by the Yakuza and severely beaten or sold to other bars, accumulating double the debt. I was shocked and realized that the only way for me to pay off my debt was to go out with as many clients as possible. Tips from clients were the only liquid cash we earned. Sometimes a generous client helped women pay off their debts.

Our living quarters housed thirty girls between the ages of fourteen and thirty. Most were already in prostitution in Thailand before they came to Japan, but like me did not know they would have to go out with clients, pay off a huge debt, and live in total confinement. A few, however, had no idea at all they were being sold into prostitution and had a much harder time. We were packed into a small room with a bath cum toilet above the mama-san's house, far off from the bar. There was no radio or television, and we were instructed to always talk softly or sleep when not at work. We were warned not to peep out of the window, as we would be arrested by the police who came on their daily rounds. It was very cold, but there was no heater or warm water. I was provided with a sheet, a blanket, a pillow, a pair of socks and had to sleep on the ground. We used to hold each other tight and sleep to keep warm. We generally worked through the night, slept in the morning, and woke up in the early evening. We showered in batches to save time and water. We cooked and ate a routine meal of rice with raw, boiled, or fried eggs or omelettes mixed with fish sauce and chilies, and sometimes fried vegetables. I hated this food, but this was what we were given. It was also cheaper and that meant we could work our debts off faster. Other meals at the bar were ordered through the mama-san from an adjoining Thai restaurant and added to our debts. We were never allowed direct communication with the restaurant workers or anyone else. Even our letters were censored.

By 6:30 P.M. we were ready to be escorted to the bar. Most of us consumed drugs or gulped down alcohol before leaving for work. Our regular supply came from the mama-san and was added to our debts. I used a drug called Domikum, which made me feel happy, funny, and carefree. It helped me lose all inhibitions and I never felt intense pain when on it. Most of us didn't know Japanese and were forced to engage in body communication with clients. We had to sit very close to clients, touch and be touched by them, wear short dresses with spaghetti straps without any underwear, or walk around the bar stark naked to attract customers. I could only do this when high.

We could never refuse a client who wanted to go out with us, even if he was dirty, smelly, or absolutely drunk. If a girl resisted being prostituted or accepting a specific client, she was badly beaten. Girls have been raped publicly in front of all of us by the Yakuza, who are especially called in to season them. This terrorizes other girls. Some girls were burned with cigarette butts and their nails hammered with bottles. If a girl was really unmanageable, she was sold by the owner to the Yakuza and we never saw or heard of her again, or she was sold to another bar with double the debt to repay. Also our mama-san would send us out with known sadistic clients when we disobeyed her, and girls came back very traumatized. Some behaved as if they were raving mad. In the one year that I stayed in the bar I never saw a girl being murdered but heard of incidents from friends. I decided it was better to obey the mama-san and pay off my debt as fast as I could than suffer this fate.

On an average, I entertained about three or four clients a night, depending on the number of clients in the bar. Our clients were all Japanese between the ages of twenty and seventy, but the majority were over forty. They liked young girls. Often the younger men swore love to us, but we knew it was only lust. They would soon drop us. Most of my young clients were very insensitive and rough. The older men tended to be gentler. Most of our clients thought that we had come to Japan because Thai women love sex. There were two girls out of the thirty in our bar who said they didn't mind sex, provided it was not violent, but the rest of us drugged ourselves or drank to go through with it. We often got sadistic and kinky clients who were unknown to the bar owner—much more than I got in Bangkok. They would beat us before intercourse with sticks, belts, or chains till we bled. One of my clients wanted me to scream loud while beating me before sex, but he didn't draw blood. Some impotent men used fake penises. There were some clients who inserted coke bottles into the girls' vaginas, lit candles and dropped hot wax over our bodies and into the women's vaginas, stared into a woman's vagina and poured boiling water into it, gave the nipples electric shocks for a few seconds, or demanded oral or anal sex. If girls came back traumatized after going out with a sadistic client, or reacted hysterically or had nightmares, they would be beaten by the mama-san and told that they must have provoked the client to be violent. The mama-san never brought sadistic clients to book. If we cried on the job or resisted a client, we were beaten even more. That is why we routinely used drugs before sex, because then we didn't feel the pain that much.

We had to work even when we were ill or menstruating. We used to insert sponges during menstruation, to prevent clients from knowing that we were menstruating. The mama-san instructed us to tell our clients to use condoms. Some men would, but most would not. As I could not speak Japanese, I could not ask them to use condoms, so I would excite them and slip it on without them knowing. If clients refused to use condoms, we had to give in. The mama-san never asked them to use one.

We used to have a pill a day supplied by the mama-san to avoid pregnancy. Of the thirty girls in the bar, while I was there, two got pregnant. They consumed some medicine and one of them aborted. The other got the girls to stamp on her stomach till she aborted. Generally, abortions were self-induced and facilitated by the girls in the bar. Letting the mama-san know that we were pregnant would get her angry, and seeking her help or going to a doctor would add to our debts. The abortifacient was secretly supplied by Thai restaurant workers, and the women were reported to consume five or six bottles before they aborted. The women complained of fatigue, abdominal pain, and bleeding after that.

We didn't know much about STDs [sexually transmitted diseases] or AIDS, except the names of these ailments. Those of us who visited STD clinics had seen pictures of STD-affected body parts. We were only taken to the doctor when we were unable to stand. The owner was afraid that his illegal operations and our illegal status would come to light if we were exposed to outsiders. Those who were taken to doctors had stiff fees added to their debts.

Many of the girls complained either of a burning sensation or pain while urinating. We were told by the Thai restaurant owners that this was syphilis and were supplied with orange tablets at a price. We did not know what the drug was, but it made us feel better. Other health problems were stomachaches, fevers, injuries, nervousness, hysteria, emotional disturbances, mental breakdowns, including suicides. Some girls got drunk and urinated and vomited all over, and the mama-san increased their debts as a penalty. Others who took drugs got aggressive. We were under constant pressure and we often fought, screamed, and punched one another. There was also a lot of peer bonding as we had only one another to depend on.

One of the girls who was depressed and drunk once slashed her wrists with a broken bottle but fortunately did not cut herself deeply. She was going crazy in controlled conditions, got few clients, and felt she would have to work in the bar forever to pay off her debts. She would often get hysterical. We would try and calm her with medication, get her food, and use the little Japanese we knew to get her clients. A girl in the next building jumped out of the window and died instantly. The mama-san and the girls left the premises, and we don't know what happened after that.

Sometimes the police would come in to check if there were visa over-stayers. The owner was mostly warned in advance by informants. Over-stayers would be concealed or heaped into a bus and hidden in a hotel close by in the mountains till the police left. At other times the bar would be closed for a day or two. There was also a time when only those with valid visas were produced before the police and the police bribed.

Of the thirty women in the bar, four tried to escape, two successfully with the help of clients. The other two were caught and returned to the bar by the police only to be mercilessly beaten up by the owner. The mama-san told us that the girls who escaped would be tracked down and killed. Every single one of us dreamed about escaping. Several of us made plans but were too afraid to act on them.

When debts were paid off, the mama-san returned our passports, and we were free to either leave or stay for a month or two and earn something. Most women in our bar wanted to return to Thailand immediately but had to stay back and earn some money to buy their return tickets and save a little before returning. Thai dealers in restaurants fixed our papers and return tickets for a fee. We were too afraid to go to the Thai embassy because we were told that the embassy officials would cut our hair and throw us into jail, as we were illegal residents. Many girls who dared to leave the bar to work independently after repaying their debts were ar-rested by the police, fined, imprisoned, forced to provide sexual favors to the police, and deported. It's funny because we are punished for no fault of our own, but the bar owners, the corrupt police, and even clients who abuse us badly are never punished.

I finished repaying my debt in ten months. I had some money from tips, but not at all enough to buy my return ticket. I worked for two months more in the bar. With the Japanese I picked up in a year, I then began to solicit clients in front of one of the motels close by. I had a boyfriend whom I lived with. I realized he was not serious about me and was not going to marry me. I had no education, no job, no accommodation, was an illegal resident, and could not return to Thailand immediately without earning something reasonable. So I stayed on with my boyfriend and went out with clients to save some money.

One day I happened to walk into a Thai restaurant and found a pam-phlet that said, "If you need a Thai friend to talk to, contact this number." I rang the number and found myself talking to a Japanese nun. I told her my story and requested her to help me get back to Thailand. She made the necessary arrangements and sent me to an NGO in Thailand. I returned with a saving of 30,000 baht [$685] after five years of struggle.

No one in the world can get over sleeping with one man after another who does not love you. These men want to come to us but don't love us or don't want to marry us. They only use us. The bar owners, recruiters, or clients are never blamed for what they do to us. I don't trust the police or the embassy. In Japan I hated to be so controlled. I feel ashamed about being in prostitution, but I can't change my past. I haven't told my present boyfriend about Japan. I feel embarrassed when people look at me. I think they do so because they know I was a prostitute. I talk loud and rudely. I must take drugs even now, after being so long in prostitution. It makes me feel strong. Society does not accept us. Only women in prostitution won't look down on me and can understand me.

DOMESTIC SLAVERY IN EUROPE

The vast majority of domestic slaves are girls aged between twelve and seventeen. Globally, domestic work is rarely scrutinized or legislated, and statistics are hard to obtain. But the International Labor Organization estimates that at least ten million children, some as young as eight, are trapped in domestic labor around the world. There are two million child domestics in South Africa, 700,000 in Indonesia, 559,000 in Brazil, 200,000 in Kenya, millions more in India and Pakistan. The trafficking into domestic labor of children—mainly girls—is estimated to be worth $7 billion per year.

Seba was one of these domestic slaves. She left her home country of Mali for France at the age of eight. A West African couple took her to Paris, promising her parents that they would educate and care for her, in return for work as a nanny. But Seba was enslaved as a household servant, beaten, tortured, and forced to do domestic chores. She was freed when a neighbor heard the sounds of abuse and beating and managed to talk to her. Seeing her scars, the neighbor called the police and the French Committee against Modern Slavery (CCEM), which was founded by journalists and lawyers in 1994 to assist enslaved domestic workers. Medical examinations confirmed that Seba had been tortured.

In her narrative, which she told at the age of twenty-two, Seba focuses on her mistreatment at the hands of a "mistress." Though she does describe an occasion when the husband joined in a beating, most of the narrative is devoted to the starvation, beatings, and torture by the wife. As well, while Seba terms the woman "mistress," she never refers to the man as "master," only as "[the mistress's] husband." Showing a woman wholly invested in the institution of slavery, this narrative challenges the equation of mastery and manhood.

Seba (FRANCE, 1996)

I was raised by my grandmother in Mali, and when I was still a little girl, a woman my family knew came and asked her if she could take me to Paris to care for her children. She told my grandmother that she would put me in school and that I would learn French. But when I came to Paris I was not sent to school, I had to work every day in their house. I did all the work. I cleaned the house, cooked the meals, cared for the children, and washed and fed the baby. Every day I started work before 7 A.M. and finished about 11 P.M. I never had a day off. My mistress did nothing. She slept late and then watched television or went out.

One day I told her that I wanted to go to school. She replied that she had not brought me to France to go to school but to take care of her children. I was so tired and run down. I had problems with my teeth. Sometimes my cheek would swell and the pain would be terrible. Sometimes I had stomachaches, but I still had to work. Sometimes when I was in pain I would cry, but my mistress would shout at me.

I slept on the floor in one of the children's bedrooms. My food was their leftovers. I was not allowed to take food from the refrigerator like the children. If I took food she would beat me. She often beat me. She would slap me all the time. She beat me with the broom, with kitchen tools, or whipped me with an electric cable. Sometimes I would bleed; I still have marks on my body.

Once in 1992 I was late going to get the children from school, my mistress and her husband were furious with me and beat and then threw me out on the street. I had nowhere to go, I didn't understand anything, and I wandered on the streets. After some time her husband found me and took me back to their house. Then they beat me again with a wire attached to a broomstick until I lost consciousness.

Sometime later one of the children came and untied me. I lay on the floor where they had left me for several days. The pain was terrible, but no one treated my wounds. When I was able to stand I had to start work again, but after this I was always locked in the apartment. They continued to beat me.

SEX SLAVERY IN THE UNITED STATES

Though most of the forty thousand slaves in the United States have been trafficked from thirty-five or more countries (the greatest numbers from China, Mexico, and Vietnam), some are U.S. citizens. Christine Stark, of European and American Indian ancestry, was born and trafficked in Minnesota, which is currently a sex trafficking pipeline to larger cities such as Chicago. In fact, incidents of sex trafficking have been discovered in ninety U.S. cities and in all fifty states, involving victims born and raised in the United States, as well as those trafficked from abroad. Girls as young as twelve years old are forced to have sex seven days a week, with ten to fifteen people a day and to meet a quota of $500–1,000 a night. Some NGOs estimate that there are 4,600 women currently held in the United States as sex slaves; others estimate that 10,000 women are brought into the country as sex slaves each year. Most likely, almost half of the people currently enslaved in the United States are in the sex industry.

As Christine notes, she was "one such girl"—trafficked by her family as a child. Her narrative lays out the gender dynamics of slavery, whereby traffickers and pimps attempt to divide and conquer women: "They rape us in front of our mothers and grandmothers; they rape our grandmothers and mothers in front of us.... They want us to dislike and distrust other women and girls." But Christine counters this attempt at division with her assertion of "a bond deeper than blood to the very women and girls they tried to make you hate," and with her first-person plural voice: "We endure.... We are women in search of freedom."

Christine (UNITED STATES, 1997)

I was born a slave. I was born into sexual slavery in the state of Minnesota in the United States of America twenty-nine years ago. I was born into a prostitution ring, a family of pimps and pornographers and prostitutes. The men pimped the women and girls and sometimes the boys. They made pornography. They sold us in whorehouses and at live sex shows. The men used me in pornography in basements, barns, houses, warehouses, isolated wooded areas, and public buildings.

I come from the farms and suburbs and cities of the United States of America. I come from the strangled, suffocated, mangled voices of the raped, beaten, and starved. I was trafficked throughout the country, from state to state by car, by bus, and by plane. I am not alone standing here before you today. I am not alone in my testimony, and I am not alone in spirit. I have many friends and acquaintances who have endured the tortures, rapes, beatings, and degradations that pimps and johns hand out like candy.

In prostitution rings women and girls are taught to be sexually submissive by men who refer to themselves as masters, by men who are so

Christine Stark
(photograph by
Donna Aase, 2006)

cowardly as to rape, beat, and starve women and girls. Women and girls raised in prostitution rings are sexually abused and otherwise tortured beginning in infancy. They are trained to be prostitutes, to sexually service men. The men are masters of torture and terror who are highly trained in torture techniques. Sometimes these pimp masters are doctors and dentists in the outside world. They rape girls as young as one and two years old.

I was one such girl. I can tell you some of the things they did to me and other girls and women, but there is still much that I cannot speak of. These men gang rape us. They rape us with dogs. They rape us with knives and guns and beer bottles. They tie us down, chain us to bedposts and basement poles and each other. They make us eat shit and maggots and urine. They rape us with masks on their faces. They rape us in the name of Satan and Hitler and De Sade. They rape us in front of our mothers and grandmothers; they rape our grandmothers and mothers in front of us. They play games with us. They force us to choose who will live, which child or aunt or grandmother will live and which one will die. They hold mock executions.

But sometimes they do kill us. You never know when they're only joking, having some fun, or when they will pull the trigger. These men want us, the women and girls being raped, to feel responsible for their actions. They want us to feel like it is our fault that our mother, sister, daughter, grandmother is being destroyed in front of our eyes. They want us to dislike and distrust other women and girls. They want us to feel utterly powerless to stop them. They want us to feel dead, look dead, be dead. Above all else, they want us immobilized. They want to consume our lives, take our freedom with no resistance whatsoever....

It is no small achievement to survive sexual slavery. Survivors are split into pieces, fragmented, broken, filled with despair, pain, rage, and sorrow. We have been hurt beyond belief. We are silent; we are numb. Our eyes see, our ears hear, but we do not tell. Our voices are nonexistent, but even if they did exist, who would believe what we have to say? Who would listen? Who would care? We are dirty, ruined, despised, the whores of the earth. The men who use us throw us away. We are their garbage to piss on, to pile up in the corner. We are their property, they own us. The rest of you turn your backs, avert your eyes, pretend not to see, go on your way. You leave us to the predators.

But we endure. We survive. It should be asked, "Why do these women stay alive?" Sometimes, maybe much of the time, we don't even know. Sometimes we do wish we were dead; we wish they would kill us; we can't take it anymore. So why do we stay alive? We stay alive because we do not want them, the masters, to win. We stay alive because there is something we want, something we seek. We may not even know exactly what it is; we may not have ever experienced it. Or we may have known it only for a moment when something deep inside, deeper than even they can penetrate, stirred, and we felt alive, joyous, loved, at peace. We stay alive because we are women in search of our lives; we are women in search of freedom.

I stayed alive because my belief in something better than what they offered was greater than their hatred and destruction. I stayed alive because I wanted to be free—more than anything, I wanted to be free. I wanted to live in a world of respect. I wanted to be free from them. I wanted their hands off me; I wanted their bodies off me and their dicks out of me. I wanted to not be sold. I wanted to not be bought. I wanted to not be raped and filmed and forced to smile and beg and plead for mercy. I wanted them to stop telling me who and what I was. I wanted to decide how I felt, what I thought, what I believed, and who I loved. I wanted to eat the foods that I wanted to eat, run the way I wanted, be silly or thoughtful or serious. Quite simply, I wanted a life of autonomy and agency....

It is only recently that I have been free from their sexual and physical abuse, and to be honest, I don't always know what to do with myself. I was beaten and raped, or at least verbally assaulted, virtually every day of my life. The intensity of my emotions doesn't match up to a normal life. Other survivors talk about this, too. Even though we have escaped, we live in the pimp's world. We have flashbacks and night tremors. The pimps harass us, so we spend much of our time waiting, wondering when they're going to hurt us again. Our worldview is one of war, constant rapes, and beatings. We may escape, but we will always be isolated, we will never be part of society. We know too much, we have seen too much. The world does not want to acknowledge the truth of women's lives....

I escaped the pimps. It took me more than twenty years to do it, but I did it....I want to be free, and I want my sisters to be free. And I will be free, and I will help women and girls escape, or I will die trying. I have been in a sort of exile myself, on the run, surviving, remembering, waiting for them to kill me, gathering my strength. I have been outsmarting them, outfighting them, and speaking out to help other women and girls....

It is difficult to know what to do with yourself when all you have known is chaos and destruction and the streets. You're not good company, you're not polite or talking or thinking about socially acceptable things. You're talking about your life. You're talking about the lives of other women and girls who are still held captive, who are still being hurt, who may not survive. You feel an urgency, a bond deeper than blood to the very women and girls they tried to make you hate....

There are many women, strong women, brave women all across the world who are rising up to meet and to end the tidal wave of male violence against women. We escape and we organize and we educate and we go back down into the trenches to pull out our sisters. This is war, a battle of life and death. A battle that women must win....The pimps do not know state or national boundaries; women in battle must not know them either. We must be on the lookout for each other. The brothels of the world house all the women of the world. We must go into those brothels, search one another out. We must break down the doors, beat back the pimps, and get out the women and girls held in cages. As I go back, back into the brothels and porn houses, I will be on the lookout for you. I hope I will never find you there, but if I do, you have my word that I will lend you my hand.

CAMBODIAN SEX SLAVERY

Prostitution escalated in Cambodia when the United Nations Transitional Authority forces arrived in 1991. The number of prostitutes in the cities rose from six thousand in 1991 to twenty thousand in 1992, and the Cambodian Women's Development Association claims that half of these women were trafficking victims. Women continue to be internally trafficked for sexual exploitation, usually from rural areas to the country's capital, Phnom Penh, and other secondary cities. Cambodian women are also sent to Thailand and Malaysia for commercial sexual exploitation.

In 1993, Dina Chan found herself "owned" by a pimp in northern Cambodia. An orphan who got into debt for overdue rent payments and tuition fees, Dina was trafficked from Phnom Penh to Stroeung Treng at the age of seventeen. Her narrative describes police corruption, starvation, and gang rape. She points out the irony that she fought for others' freedoms as a soldier, "only to become enslaved," and rejects the response of "pity" to her story. As a member of the Sex Workers Union of Toul Kork, she also issues a call for prostitutes to unionize—and "fight for basic rights." On behalf of herself and her "sisters," Dina demands recognition of her humanity: "We are people, we are women, and we want to be treated with respect."

Dina (CAMBODIA, 1999)

I came here today as a woman, a Khmer woman. I came here today to tell you my story, in the hope that after you listen to me you can understand my situation and the situation of thousands of Khmer women and other women around the world. It is very difficult for me to come here and speak to you. But I am doing this because I want you to listen to me, the real person. And I want you to remember me and what I say to you today when you are in your offices talking about policies and strategies that affect me and my sisters. I want you to remember we are not "problems," we are not animals, we are not viruses, we are not garbage. We are flesh, skin and bones; we have a heart, and we have feelings. We are a sister to someone, a daughter, a granddaughter. We are people, we are women, and we want to be treated with respect, dignity. And we want rights like the rest of you enjoy.

I was trafficked—I was raped, beaten, and forced to accept men. I was humiliated and forced to be an object so men, yes men, could take their pleasure; I brought profit to many and brought pleasure to others. And for myself I brought shame, pain, and humiliation. But worst of all I receive demeaning comments from you; you discriminate against me, you give yourselves a job because of me, and you are busy thinking about the best way to protect the community from me.

The police come to Toul Kork almost every day. They always have a reason to come, but they come more frequently before festivals like Pchum Ben, because we are an easy target to extract money from. In a public forum the chief of these police stands up and states, "We do not arrest the girls"—lies and more lies. They arrest us and take our money, our jewelry, sometimes even our few possessions we have in our room like our bedcovers. If we cannot pay, then they detain us for a day or two; they give us no water. When they are convinced we simply have no money to pay, they take us to another brothel and sell us to a new pimp, usually for $100 for one girl. Then we become indebted once again and have to pay off that debt to the new pimp.

This is trafficking. The police, yes the police, sell us for another cycle of slavery. Do you think it is in their interests to see my occupation decriminalized? Of course not—then they lose their share of the money. In one day we pay almost 15,000 riel [$3] in bribes to the district police, to the municipal authorities and the local authorities. Then another group of police come and arrest us. If we do not run and hide we are resold into slavery. Your solution is to ask these people to protect us. Think again. They live off our blood. Money is too important to everyone, money and more money. It is not enough to eat; people demand more because they want nice things.

I come from a poor family; they sent me to study at a cultural school in Phnom Penh. I was living with a family, but I could not contribute to my living, so they helped me find a job in a nearby hotel washing dishes. This hotel had many sex workers. But I just washed dishes and went to school. One night a man followed me when I was on my way home and raped me. I was only seventeen years of age. You cannot imagine how I felt and what impact this had on me. But after that, I was lured to becoming a sex worker under false promises. I was sent to Stung Treng; I was beaten when I refused to accept men. Shortly after I was taken to Stung Treng a man came to pay for me to go with him. He paid my *maebon* [pimp].

He took me to the pig slaughter house where he worked and locked me in a dirty smelly cell. Then he came back with six other men. They all, one by one, raped me; one man raped me twice. After a whole night of gang rape I was faint with pain. When the morning came I heard the workers preparing to start their work. I heard the pigs being pushed into the pens, they were screaming. I knew what that feeling was like—I was no better than the pigs to these men; they could have killed me. Something inside me did die, and I will never be the same. I am twenty-four years old and my life has been like this since 1993. I did not know the Khmer Rouge years, but I have heard the stories of suffering. People say they were slaves.

Compared to my life for the last five years I think I and my sisters have suffered and are suffering more than you have. I know starvation, I know slavery, I know being forced to work all day. But I also know physical violation and torture every day. I know discrimination and hatred from my compatriots; I know not being wanted and accepted from my society, the society that put me in this condition. I know fear—I feel it every day, even now that I dare speak, my life is in danger.

This is a crime, but no one is punished. I fought the Khmer Rouge, I was a soldier fighting to protect you from the Khmer Rouge and risking my life. I fought for the freedom of the Cambodian people; this is what the commander told us we were to do, and I was proud I was fighting for freedom. I fought for your freedom—only to become enslaved and abused by you.

After all these years I now work as a sex worker. I also run a union to unite sex workers to fight for basic rights and for freedom. We bring our voices to forums like this to educate people like you, with the hope you can learn from us. Many of my sisters are scared to join our struggle because they live in constant fear of abuse and threats.

Some of you think that I am bad because I choose to remain a sex worker. My answer to those people is: I think your society, my society, my motherland, Cambodia, is bad because it does not give girls like me choices, choices that I see are better for me. I think it is bad that my country allows men to rape young women like me and my sisters and go unpunished. I think it is bad that my society lets men seek and demand the services of women like me. I think it is criminal that we are enslaved to make money for the powerful. I think it is bad that my family are so poor and getting poorer because they cannot survive as farmers with little resources, which are getting smaller because more powerful people move them off their land. I think it is bad the police treat me and my sisters like we are criminals, but those who exploit us and take our dignity, our money, and sometimes our lives live in freedom, enjoying their lives with their families. Because why? Because they have a powerful relative, because they have money.

Is this right? Is this justice? My sisters and I, we do not create the demand, we are the objects; the demand comes from the men, the men come to us. We are cheated, deceived, trafficked, humiliated, and tortured. Why? Because men want us, and we bring money to the powerful. But we are the powerless.

You give us AIDS; when we are no longer profitable you leave us to die, but we do not die in peace—you point your finger and you blame us. You, the development organizations, give us condoms and teach us all the time about AIDS. We do not want your words, we do not want your judgment, we do not want you to tell us what is better for us. We know about AIDS; we watch our sisters die from the disease. Ask us if we have the power to demand condom use from our clients. Look at me: you see a woman, but my boss sees dollars. An extra payment to my boss and the client does not wear a condom. If I protest I receive a beating. If I die tomorrow no one cares; there are many other girls who will be tricked and trafficked like me, because we feed many people.

I do not want to go to your shelter and learn to sew so you can get me work in a factory. This is not what I want. If I tell you that, you will call me a prostitute. But those words are easy for you because you have easy solutions to difficult problems you do not understand, and you do not understand because you do not listen.

My life has become this way now; for me there is no turning back, so let me continue to practice my occupation. But recognize my occupation and give me my rights, so I am protected and I can have power to demand justice.

> I am a post Khmer Rouge child
> But was a slave
> I was forced to work against my choice
> My body is tortured
> I am full of pain
> I am not a citizen
> I am not a person
> You see me as a virus
> I am invisible
> Your eyes do not see me
> You hate me
> You blame me
> Some of you pity me
> I do not want your pity

NEPALESE SEX TRAFFICKING

These narratives by Nepalese individuals are narratives of women from beginning to end. Anita, who was trafficked from Nepal to India in 1998 at the age of twenty-seven, describes her husband taking another wife and her pain as a mother separated from her children. She mentions the idea that the women in the brothel are her "sisters," seeks escape by offering an earring to one woman, and finally escapes when another woman accidentally leaves a gate open. She gains empathy from a client by telling him, "I am like your daughter." Even Anita's psychological turning point from freedom to slavery is female specific. "They cut off my hair," she remembers. "I could not leave the brothel without everyone identifying me as a prostitute…short hair is the sign of a wild woman."

Equally, Rita, who was drugged and trafficked from Nepal to India in 1998 at the age of nineteen and was later helped by the Nepalese NGO Maiti Nepal, which runs a rehabilitation center in Kathmandu, narrates a series of experiences that are rooted in her identity as a woman. The traffickers tricked her by explaining that they needed her to help smuggle diamonds—because "girls were not checked as thoroughly as men" by border guards. One of the first incidents in India is the replacement of her trousers with a long skirt. Like Anita, she notes that when women are enslaved they are "made 'sisters.'" She goes on to observe the psychology of women who refuse to leave because they "will not be accepted by society." She describes the horror of public questioning about trafficking experiences. And she focuses, with sustained empathy, on the stories of two other women—Vidhya and Maili.

Between seven thousand and twelve thousand Nepali women and children are trafficked every year across the border to Indian brothels (one NGO puts this number at seventeen thousand), and Nepal has an unknown number of internal sex trafficking victims as well. In response to a dowry practice where they must offer gifts that may be worth several years' income, some parents sell their daughters rather than have them married. Other women are drugged and taken across the border, like Anita and Rita. Once enslaved, Nepali girls and women are more likely to be arrested than rescued by the police, and most Nepalese victims never leave India, even after liberation. Those who do are often shunned by their families and remain in Kathmandu at shelters. Anita describes such familial rejection in the wake of her experience. Another aspect of this enslavement is HIV and AIDS. Some 50 percent of those who return to Nepal are positive for HIV, and Rita makes reference to these "girls with AIDS."

Anita (INDIA, 1999)

My name is Anita Sharma Bhattarai. I am twenty-eight years old. I am from Nepal. Last year, my husband took another wife. Soon after, he began to beat me, torment me, and disregard my children. I decided it would be best if I and my children moved out of our home. I made money by buying vegetables from farmers and selling them in the village market. On November 22 last year I boarded the bus in order to go pay for my vegetables. I sat next to a Nepali man and woman. They offered me a banana to eat and I took it. Soon after I ate the banana, while I was still on the bus, I got a very bad headache. I told the man and woman that I had a headache and they offered me a pill and a bottle of mineral water to help me swallow the medicine. Immediately, I felt myself becoming groggy, and then I fell unconscious.

The next thing that I remember is waking up in the train station in Gorakhpur, India. I am from a mountain village. I did not know what a train was and, of course, I had never been to India. I asked the man where I was. I was confused by the long cars that I was riding and the strange surroundings. The man told me not to cry out. He informed me that there were drugs tied around my waist and that I had just smuggled them across an international border. He told me that if I brought the attention of the police, I would be in trouble for smuggling the drugs. I did not remember the drugs being tied around my waist but I could feel plastic bags under my dress. The man also told me that if I stayed with him, I would receive 20,000 rupees [$400] from the sale of the drugs when we arrived in Bombay. I did not know how to get back to Nepal, I do not speak any of the Indian languages, and I believed that I was already in trouble for carrying drugs. The man told me he was my friend and that I could refer to him as my brother. I decided to stay with him. It was a five-day journey to Bombay by train.

When we got to Bombay, he told me to wait at the train station while he went to sell the drugs. When he returned, he told me that the police had confiscated his drugs and that he did not have any money. He said that I would have to go to his friend's house and wait while he got us some money. He called his friend on the phone from the train station, and she came to meet us there. She was a Nepali woman. She said her name was Renu Lama. I left the train station with Renu Lama. My "brother" told me that he would meet me at her house at 4 P.M. that afternoon.

As I walked with Renu Lama, she told me not to look at people because she lived in a very dangerous neighborhood and there were some bad people that I should not make eye contact with. When we arrived at her house, Renu Lama told me that I should take a bath. I told her that I would wait until 4 p.m. when my "brother" came because he was carrying my clothes. She told me my "brother" was not coming. I waited until evening but he never came. Finally, I took a bath and Renu Lama gave me some of her old clothes to wear.

Renu Lama then asked if I could write a letter for her. I did. She dictated what she wanted to say to her family, and I wrote the letter. When I had finished writing the letter, Renu Lama took away the ink pen. She went to my room and took away all of the pens, pencils, and paper that I could possibly write with. I realized that the writing of the letter had been a test. Now that they knew I was literate, they were keen to keep me from communicating with anyone outside.

I felt very scared that evening and I refused to eat anything. I soon noticed that many men were coming in and out of the house and I realized it was a brothel. I began howling and shouting. I said that I wanted to leave. Renu Lama told me that I was ignorant. She said that I did not just come easily and I could not go easily. She said that I had been bought and I would have to work as a prostitute in order to pay them back. I was never told how much they had paid for me. Renu Lama and two of her associates told me that all the women in the house were "sisters" and that we had to support each other. I cried a lot, but they comforted me and brought me a fine dinner, complete with chutney and a pickle.

The next day, though, I insisted that I wanted to leave. The women began to slap me on the face. They cut off my hair. It was shoulder length in the back with short bangs in the front. Now that I had short hair, I knew that I could not leave the brothel without everyone identifying me as a prostitute. In my culture, short hair is the sign of a wild woman. Then, I was told that all of the women in the brothel had to bathe three or four times each day. The women all bathe nude and they bathed together— four or five girls at a time. I had never bathed nude before and I had never bathed with other naked women. When I expressed my shyness, the other women mocked me. They grabbed me and stripped off my clothes. They forced me to bathe with them.

For the next couple of days the women beat me often. They slapped me on the face and head with their hands and hit me about the waist and thighs with metal rods. I begged to be let go. I said that I wanted to return to my children in time for the biggest holiday of our culture. The women mocked me. They told me that if I worked with them for a couple of days, they would send me home with three bricks of gold and 30,000–40,000 rupees [$600–850] for the festival. I was also forced to learn Hindi—the language of most of the customers. When I couldn't speak enough Hindi, I was beaten about the waist and thighs with iron rods. When I was alone with one of the other women, I offered her my gold earring if she would let me go. She said no.

Later I learned that three of the women were in the brothel voluntarily and they were in charge. The six other women in the brothel, I learned, had all been tricked and forced like me. Renu Lama and the woman to whom I had offered my earring were in the brothel voluntarily. All of the women in the brothel were from Nepal. The six who were forced had all been brought from Nepal but under different pretenses. One girl married a man who said he was taking her to Bombay to buy gold. He then left her in a brothel. None of the other girls could read or write. I am literate because I am Brahmin and the women in my community are educated.

The women tried to reassure me that being a prostitute was not that bad. All of my food, housing, and clothes were provided. All I would have to do, they said, was sell my body. On the fourth day that I was in the brothel, my first client came to me. I refused to have sex with him. He had already paid so he grabbed me and tried to rape me. I fought him off. He had managed to get my clothes off, but he was very frustrated because I was resisting him so much. He stormed out and asked for his money back. A couple of the brothel owners came in and beat me. When they were done, the same man came back in. I then said that I would have sex with him only if he wore a condom. I knew about the need for condoms since I had learned that some of the other victims had very bad diseases. At first he refused but after another fight he finally agreed. By the time he left he had used three condoms.

I only had one client my first day. But the next day, and every day after, I had three or four clients each day. I managed to get an ink pen. I would write messages to the police on the inside of cigarette boxes and send them out with my clients. Many clients promised to help but none did.

Still, I was not able to go out to buy the condoms myself. In fact, for the entire month and a half that I was in the brothel, I was never allowed to go out into the sun. Some of the other girls got to go to the hospital when they fell ill. But I never got sick, so I could never leave. I lived on the second floor of the brothel. The six of us who had been brought there against our will were kept on the second floor. There were no windows on our floor. The three who ran the brothel lived downstairs.

Downstairs there was a door that led outside. Several iron rods used for beating were leaned against the wall beside the door. One of the owners always guarded the door. Outside the door was a metal gate. When customers were not coming in and out, the gate was closed. The gate was held by a heavy chain that was locked by a large padlock. One night I tried to run away with one of my associates. We were caught by the brothel owners before we even made it to the gate. My friend was sold to another brothel in Sarat where the brothels are said to be even more tortuous than the ones in Colaba, Bombay, where I was held.

After I had been serving clients for about eight days, an elderly man came to me as a client. When I was alone with him in the room, I told him that he was old enough to be my father. I told him, "I am like your daughter." I told him my story. He said that he had plenty of money and a Nepali friend. He promised to help me escape. He spent the entire night with me. That was the first time I had been with a client for more than an hour. I cried on him all night long. The next morning, he left with a promise that he would send his Nepali friend to help me. He said that I would know his friend had come when a Nepali man came to the brothel, asking to be with Anita and carrying a gift of candies.

A few days later, a young Nepali man came to see me. He brought a gift of candy. I told him my story. He promised to help me escape. I told him that I did not trust anyone. In order for me to trust him, he would have to go to Nepal, report about me to my father and brother, and bring back some of my personal photographs as a result. The elderly client paid for him to go to Nepal. Before he left, the boy gave me his address in Bombay.

Some of my associates overheard the owners saying that they were also planning to sell me to a brothel in Sarat because I was too much trouble. I decided that I could not wait until the boy returned from Nepal. I had to try again to run away. I asked some of the other girls to run with me, but they were too afraid. We had been told that we would be killed if we tried to run away. But I had determined that I would rather die than stay in the brothel. The other girls pooled their money together and came up with 200 rupees [$4]. In exchange for the 200 rupees, I promised that if I made it out alive, I would get help for them.

A couple of days later, I had a perfect opportunity. Renu Lama was out of town again. The owner who was watching the gate was drunk. A new maid had just been hired to clean and cook in the brothel. The new maid was doing chores and had left the gate open just a little bit. In the middle of the night, I would guess about 4 A.M., I ran out of the brothel. I was wearing only my nightgown and carrying my slip in my hand. I ran down the street as fast as I could.

As I was running I saw two police officers. There were in civilian clothes, but I knew they were police officers by the belts they were wearing. I ran to them, told them my story, and handed them the address of the Nepali boy. They took 100 rupees [$2] from me in order to pay for a taxi. They put me in a taxi that took me to the Nepali boy's house. When I arrived at the house, the Nepali boy was not there. But another Nepali man and his wife were. They were friends of the Nepali boy and they agreed to take me in. The police left me with that family. I did not know it at that time, but that same day, the Nepali boy had met Bob—Robert Mosier, director of investigations at the International Justice Mission. He told Bob my story. Soon after I ran away from the brothel, Bob and the police raided the brothel where I had been. After searching the brothel, they learned that I had run away earlier that night. They came with Bob and met me at the house where I was staying.

Bob told me that I could go back to the brothel to get my things. I was too scared to go back because I thought I might be forced to be a prostitute again. But Bob assured me that I was safe. I went back to the brothel with Bob. I showed him hiding places where they found the other girls. All of the girls who were forced were released from the brothel and a way was provided for them to go back home. The two owners who were there that night are now in jail. Bob also arranged for me to return home to my family in Nepal.

When I first went home to my family, it was very uncomfortable. The people in the village laughed at me. In my culture, a woman is scorned if she is missing for just one night. I had been missing for two months. It was very hard for my family, especially since we are members of the Brahmin caste. So, today I live in Kathmandu. I work as a domestic servant in the city. I am still without my children since they went to live with their father when I was taken away. I am told that my husband's new wife is very cruel to my children, but my husband does not want my children to be with me because of where I have been.

I know that my story will help other women who are forced into prostitution. I am proud that I was able to help Bob free the other girls in the brothel where I worked. Though I am grateful to be here to share my story, I am sad that I am not with my children—that my children cannot be here with me.

Rita (INDIA, 2002)

My home in the hills is in Gorkha. My father died when I was two years old. After that my mother kept me at my aunt's place and got married again. I was fine at my aunt's place. A foreigner sent money for my education. I was studying in a government school at the beginning. Later, I was admitted into an English school in class eight. I had difficulty adjusting and failed. My sponsor stopped sending money. I discontinued my studies because of financial hardship.

A few months later my uncle remarried. I went back to my mother because it was very difficult staying there. I thought of looking for a job, and I told the neighborhood *elders* that I was interested in working if I could get a job. Then one man arranged a job for me in a hotel. There in the hotel I got acquainted with a friend. We came to know each other because she was a dancer and I a waitress. Some months later my friend said, "Look, how long am I going to be dancer in this dance restaurant and how long are you going to be a waitress here? Let us look for some other work or business." I was attracted by the idea because of the greed to earn more and because of poverty. Then I asked my friend what kind of business she was talking about. She said she knew some young men. My friend said they were really good people and that they dealt in diamonds.

Two days later two men came and my friend introduced me to them, saying these were "the brothers." The friend said that these brothers would give us diamonds and we had to carry them to India. I asked the brothers why they needed to take us girls. Because men wouldn't go, they said. They said they had to take girls because girls were not checked as thoroughly as men. Mainly because I trusted my friend and because she said the men were really good and she knew them well, I agreed. So I said, "Fine!"

We went to Manakamana before going to India. After performing prayers we came and sat down to have tea. While waiting for something to eat they gave us soda. We never thought about what might happen to us, whether those men could be trusted, and after drinking it, we felt very sleepy and sick. I remember getting into a truck. After that, where they took us, what they did … I don't know anything. We were taken to a very quiet place through some internal routes.

After crossing into India they kept us in a hotel. Then the main man took us to a big house. We hadn't even climbed the stairs and there was a fat woman sitting there. They said she was the owner. We greeted her and they took us into a room and kept us there. Then the main man said they were going to get money and we were to stay there. I was a bit frightened and held on to the hand of one of the boys. I asked him why we were being kept in the room like this and what was really happening. "It's nothing," he said, "you two shouldn't panic. Stay calm here, the brothers will come back with the money and then we can all return to Kathmandu." And so we stayed inside.

In the adjoining room we heard a boy and a girl talking. There was a place from where one could peek in, and so I looked and said to that boy, "There is a boy and a girl in there. What's going on in this hotel?" "It's nothing, this is a hotel and these things happen," the boy said. And after that, all of a sudden I suspected that we are being sold, and I asked the boy. It wasn't like that and I shouldn't worry, he said.

Shortly after that, the fat woman came. She told the two of us to wait in the room and left with the boy. "The brothers are going to come back with money," she said and locked us from the outside. And we kept on sitting there. We felt like crying, for this had never happened to us before. Then around evening, they sent us off to freshen up and have a bath saying, "You must be tired." Then they took us to another room and said, "Wait here, the brothers will come."

A woman entered at one o'clock in the morning. "The brothers have come, let's go," she said. We were so happy then. But the woman said, "The two of you shouldn't go together, you must go one at a time else the police will suspect." She left my friend there and took me alone to another house. I asked her where the brothers were. She said, "They will never come back again. They have sold you and left." I felt as if I had fallen off a cliff. I just couldn't believe it. I collapsed when that woman said I had been sold.

I still find it difficult to talk about this matter. And I found it extremely difficult at that time. All I could think of was, what am I to do, and how do I escape? I had no interest in the food they served. There were many Nepali girls, sisters, in another big room. On the other side, some were watching a movie, some were sleeping. I was kept in a separate room. Then they snatched my citizenship papers. I had gone wearing a T-shirt and trousers and I was asked to remove them. They made me wear a long skirt.

I was trying to run away. There was only netting on the window, no windowpanes. At times like that one seems to gain strength. I had managed to take out half the netting after locking the room from inside. Somebody knocked and asked who was inside. "I am here, didi, I am here didi, I am going to sleep here. I don't like sleeping outside, I will sleep here," I said. I was frightened. "Come outside fast, my customer has come," she said. After that I had to open the door. They realized I was trying to run away. Two, three of them beat me very badly—all were women. And the madam to whom the boys had sold me first sold me to a second madam the next day. She beat me with this big stick. I was beaten until that stick broke. My condition was really bad. They banged my head on the wall. I can't tell you now how I felt then. I told them, "I won't do such work. Please, let me go from here." I pleaded with them. They told me people who come here can never return. They said, "You work hard, and if you work well we will send you back in two years." I didn't even eat for two or three days.

I suffered a lot and was forced by circumstances to do that work. Once you come to a house like that, you can forget about not wanting to do bad things. They tell you what to do. They force us when the man is sent for the first time. In the beginning a Muslim man came and told me to go with him. And I went. I felt like crying, and I cried. He asked me why I was crying, what had happened. And I had to talk, though it was frightening. I told him how I was sold. I told him to take me away from there: "I want to go, and don't want to work like this." I spoke to him like that. Some men are gentlemen. I told the first man everything. He said, "You are a beginner, you are new. Since somebody has sold you, I will not do this to you." The man who came some days later did it. When I didn't agree he went to tell the madam, and I was frightened. He asked me to remove my clothes and I removed them. If I didn't agree I would be beaten. Whether we could or not, whether it was painful or not, we had to do it. And if we complained of pain they would give us medicine.

You sit all by yourself. They put on the television, and if a customer comes we have to go with the customer. We are sitting there and they say, "Let's go." Inside, there are rooms. There were thirteen small rooms in that place. A big room is partitioned into smaller rooms...girls are made up and kept here. They also provide cosmetics. The boys come themselves, it's not like other places where old women sit and call, not like that. The customers come, and if they like, they take the girls. When a man comes there once, he tells his friends about it. That friend comes, and he tells his friend. Like this, the number of customers increases.

I stayed there for about four months. Customers do not like old workers, and there are many customers when new recruits arrive. I had to service twenty to thirty customers in a day. A customer is charged 75 rupees [$1.50] during the day, and it takes about five minutes, ten minutes. The madam tells us not give too much time to men who pay 75. But if the person books for three, four hours, then you have to stay for three, four hours. If I have five, six customers, I have to service them one by one. They wait. We don't get a single paisa [0.1 rupee].

It is very difficult. Customers come even when we are sleeping. We had to service customers from five o'clock till one o'clock in the morning. I can't describe how we felt....It was very painful for me down there, but when I couldn't service customers, they would ask for the reason. If they found out about my pain, they would immediately take me for injections. Everybody used to go. And for new girls, on the way we used to be accompanied by two people—one on each side. They used to do that to me.

We never knew anything about HIV/AIDS. We knew that we could get pregnant having sex without a condom. We didn't know about other things....I asked two, three friends of mine what happens to girls with AIDS. "They are not kept here," they said. "They are sent home." And if somebody gets pregnant after having been careless, they will keep that girl also, the mother in one place and the child in another. Or they make them abort the baby. If the girls don't say anything even after conception, signs of pregnancy show up after three, four months. When abortion becomes difficult they are allowed to deliver the baby.

They pretend to love us because we bring them money. The more customers serviced the more money earned. They coaxed me to work when I was new by pretending to love me. We were coaxed all the time. "We were also sold like you," they used to say. "We are doing this kind of work because we were not able to return to Nepal. You shouldn't have come, but you have. Now do your work well, pay back the money, then if you feel like going home, you can go. If you don't want to go, you stay back here. If you insist on going back, you will be sent back in two years time." But from top to bottom, there wasn't a place where I was not beaten. I had blue marks all over my body. And after a beating we were forbidden to tell the customer. If they asked, we have to say we fell down the stairs. There was an ointment available to remove the marks, and they would themselves apply that ointment on me. Two or three days after the application of medicine the marks would disappear.

The windows and doors there have steel grills. The windows have grills. There is one door to come in and go out of and male guards on both sides. The madam sits outside twenty-four hours a day. The old girls are sitting outside twenty-four hours. Twenty-four hours, the guards are sitting outside. There is absolutely no chance of getting out. When they were first taking me to give me an injection I tried to escape on the way. But when you try to escape, no matter from which direction you go, you are still in the same place. It looks the same. After that I thought, "Even if I run away from this place, I will probably reach the same type of place." So I didn't run away. Suppose somebody is kept in a tank full of water—how suffocating it would be. Just like that, I also felt absolutely suffocated and longed to escape from there. You couldn't speak to anyone, couldn't make friends with anyone.

There was this younger sister, Maili, in the place I was staying. Poor thing, she didn't have customers coming to her. She was abused verbally, and she tried to run away one day. That time I was sick and sleeping. She tried to run away, and succeeded, too. But she was caught and brought back by the people who bring the tea. A person went to grind salt and chili. The paste was applied to the girl's genitals. That girl was beaten so badly. I was sleeping. She was beaten black and blue all over the body and hands, and on top of that, chili was put inside her. The madam told everyone not to give her water even if she asked for it. That poor girl got up, crying, and came to me. She asked me what to do and said, "This is what they have done to me." There was talk going around about selling her to another place.

Three months after that one Indian man came. I had asked many men who came there to help me get out. "I want to get away from here," I had said. Most of the men were too frightened to help me get out of there. It was a very dangerous place. There were thugs, and if anybody came to help girls escape, they would kill the helpers. That's the kind of place it was. But I told him everything. He said he would help me and asked me for my home address. After that he went to Maiti Nepal, which has an office in Bombay. And they came to get us out.

There are so many other sisters in the place where I was sold. I told them we shouldn't stay there. "Let's go! We will go to Nepal instead. We shouldn't do this kind of work, let's go," I begged. The newcomers agreed to come, but the girls who had been there for fifteen to sixteen years didn't want to come. When the police arrived I begged them to leave the place. "Let's go, let's not stay here," I said. But they said they wouldn't go. "What will we get if we go to Nepal? We'll get nothing but misery. We've been sold like this, we've become prostitutes. We will not be accepted by society. We won't go," they said. "Even if we go, we will go only with money." And even the policemen who came to raid said they will take only those who wish to go.

Vidhya, the friend who had gone with me from Kathmandu, was in another house. I told them that my friend was in that house and to go get her too. But they couldn't find my friend. The madam found out the police was coming and hid her elsewhere. When they have information about the arrival of police, the girls are immediately shifted to another place. In the beginning I was shifted to another house when the police came. And later I was hidden in the interiors inside the cupboard on the wall. When it's time for the police to come we are hidden deep inside as if we are buried in the earth. They have made such places to hide the girls. Somehow they get information even before the police arrive. They don't call the police "police" but call them "uncle."... I think the police of the lower ranks provide information. That's how it was with them. We would be hidden inside, and the police would go back with nothing.

Vidhya was left behind. I still feel sad thinking about her. I couldn't help set her free. They didn't find her. And I found out from other friends later that she was sold to some other place. If they find that someone is trying to run away then that's what they do, it seems.

We were harassed by lawyers and police after we come back to Nepal. The way they question—it is like scratching a wound. They question us as if we went knowingly. "They have done this willingly," that's what they think. We have come back from that sort of place with all the pain and suffering, and even then we have to file a complaint with the police. The men there question us and ask, "How many did you sleep with?" After I came back from there, when I went to the Jawalakhel police station and a man was writing down the complaint, there were many boys and other men present. Those policemen should have thought about how awkward it would be for this girl, being questioned like that in the presence of everyone, but they don't. Forget about giving us justice—instead, in front of everyone they ask us questions. They shame us in public. It's more painful because of this.

I had suffered as much as I could take. But thanks to the support of Maiti Nepal we were able to come here to Kathmandu. I work as a counselor. Those who have been sold and have returned are suffering lots of pain and grief. They aren't able to tell others or share this with anybody. We go to them and talk to them, hoping to lessen their grief, and we give them advice. People may detest me, but I always wished to return to Nepal. That wish of mine has been fulfilled. When I arrived at Maiti Nepal the brothers and sisters here gave me encouragement.

I had come to totally detest Nepalis because I was taken to India and sold by a Nepali. After coming back from there I used to get angry just looking at Nepali people. But there is training at Maiti Nepal for up to six months. As one by one the days passed by, I felt like making friends. After that, slowly, I got used to it. Or, after coming out of that place in India, I used to be afraid of talking to important people at first. Now I am not frightened to talk. I wasn't able to study earlier; now what I feel is that since I can read a little, now I wish to do something in life. And my pain, my past, if somebody understands, if he is willing to accept me even after knowing everything, I will get married.

This happened to me because I trusted my good friend. To say that only the uneducated are sold is wrong. Because even many educated ones are being sold. There are many educated girls, too; they are coaxed, misled, and taken. Many are taken away with the promise of marriage and later sold. We were made "sisters" and taken.

From very young I never got my own mother's affection nor a father's love. If anyone had given me a little bit of affection probably I, too, might have become something. That's how I feel. Even at Auntie's I couldn't get much affection, couldn't get a mother's love, either—forget about getting that of a father. Since I was very young, I was running about in search of affection. I wished somebody would give me a little love. I went, trusting a friend, and it's turned out like this now.

You have to try and compare yourself with others. I consider myself lucky. The way others have contracted HIV has not happened to me. I was able to come back fast. That is what makes me very happy. But I don't like to remember the days I spent there. I want to forget the things that happened.

RUSSIAN SEX TRAFFICKING

Olga was lured to Israel from Russia by a female acquaintance in 1998. After socialism was dismantled in the USSR in 1991, "transition countries"—nations that moved from socialism to capitalism—saw an explosion in the export of men, women, and children as slaves. The U.S. government believes that annually as many as one hundred thousand women are trafficked from the fifteen former constituent countries of the Soviet Union to international destinations for prostitution. Russian women are trafficked to over fifty countries for commercial sexual exploitation, including countries in central and western Europe and the Middle East. In Israel, where Olga was sold into sex slavery, women are trafficked from Russia, Ukraine, Moldova, Uzbekistan, and Belarus. NGOs estimate that in 2005 between one thousand and three thousand women were trafficked to Israel for sexual servitude.

Olga's narrative recounts the experience of forced drug addiction. This is one of several control mechanisms used by traffickers, along with intimidation and threats, violence, torture, rape, starvation, blackmail, debt bondage, and social isolation. Another control mechanism is identity control: victims of sex trafficking are often given new names and appearances to demonstrate that the traffickers not only own them but have created a new person for sexual exploitation. Olga's narrative includes details of this particular control mechanism, describing the loss of her name. One final moment of identity loss comes toward the end of her narrative, with her pretence of being Muslim.

Olga (ISRAEL, 2000)

My name is Olga. I am from Siberia in Russia. In December of 1998, a female acquaintance of mine returned from a trip to Israel with a lot of money. She told me that she had worked as a housemaid, in shops, and in bars, and that I could go and find a job, too. I asked her, how could she do this work without knowing the language? She told me that there were many Russian immigrants in Israel who wanted to hire Russian women so their children would not forget their heritage and original language.

I had no money for a ticket to Israel, but the woman said, "Don't worry, I'll buy your ticket. You'll make so much money that you'll be able to pay me back in no time." I decided to go, and got a visa to travel. She went on to Israel before me, telling me she would meet me at the airport.

When I arrived, she was waiting with two big Israeli men. We went to a small city in Israel, where they showed me around, introducing me to many people but speaking in Hebrew so I could not understand. They told me they were people who might hire me. For a few days, it was as if I was a tourist just visiting. Then the men came back and told me that they had a job for me, but because I did not have a visa to work in Israel, I would have to give them my passport. A couple days later, they gave me a false passport, with my picture but the name of an Israeli woman.

Then another Israeli man came, and my friend told me to put my things in his car, that he would take care of everything. He took me to Tel Aviv. He told me then that I had been sold to him for $10,000 and that I would have to pay him back. He told me I would have to prostitute myself. I was angry and disruptive, screaming and fighting every time he tried to take me from the apartment where I stayed. Because of this, he separated me from the other Russian women he owned. Every day I was taken to a brothel where all the other women were Israeli.

I was still resistant, so I wasn't making much money for my captor. He then told me that I had earned $8,000 of my debt and that he would find me another job to make the rest of it quickly. He promised I would not have to be a prostitute anymore. He took me to a hotel and told me to wait for my new employer. Two men came to meet me there. They gave me something to drink, which was drugged. I lost consciousness. When I woke up, I was locked in a dark room with no furniture. I could hear people speaking Arabic, but I could not understand them.

I tried to escape, but the men there caught me quickly and again gave me some kind of drug to calm me. They told me just to sit down, that I had not been sold to them and that if I behaved well, everything would be OK. A Russian-speaking Arab told me that I had been kidnapped and was in Palestine. I began to fear that they would sell me to a harem in Iraq, or some place worse.

The men there didn't tell me what I was to do. I told them that I was Muslim, hoping that would give me some kind of protection. Several days later, they sold me back to another brothel in Israel.

I told the brothel owners there that I would never work for them, so they locked me in an apartment and sent clients in anyway. If I refused to work, they would not feed me. They beat me, but only across the back near my kidneys, so it would not hurt my appearance. It was very painful. I saw only clients who spoke no Russian, so I couldn't tell them my story. I saw fifteen to twenty customers a day, and the brothel owners gave me drugs so that I would work. I began to feel crazy and sick, so he gave me some kind of pills, which he told me were for headaches. I found out later that it was Ecstasy, a drug that makes you relax and more willing to be intimate. After three weeks, I was dependent on the pills and asked for it every day. I began to try and learn some Hebrew from my clients so I could explain what had happened to me. Those customers never came back. But finally I told a Polish Jew, who contacted the police. The brothel was raided in May of 1999, and I was deported back to Russia.

ARMENIAN SEX TRAFFICKING

Most of these narratives by Armenian women describe the involvement of other women in the trafficking process. This is an increasingly common aspect of the slave experience in eastern Europe. Between 50 and 60 percent of all traffickers in Ukraine and Moldova are now women. Amasya and Farida were trafficked to Turkey, where victims also arrive from Ukraine and Moldova. Alina, Iliona, Shahnara, and Tamara were trafficked to the United Arab Emirates (UAE), where an estimated ten thousand women from sub-Saharan Africa, eastern Europe, South Asia, East Asia, Iraq, Iran, and Morocco are victims of sex trafficking. In addition, victims of child camel jockey trafficking still remain in the UAE. Thousands of young boys have been trafficked from Pakistan, Bangladesh, Sudan, and Mauritania to work as camel jockeys, and though the UAE enacted a law banning the practice in July 2005, questions persist as to the effectiveness of the ban. As well as Turkey and the UAE, Armenian women and girls are trafficked for sexual exploitation to Russia, Greece, and other European countries.

The narrators describe public discrimination and the change in their social status as women. They also discuss familial rejection after liberation.

For example, Alina came out of slavery through a police raid, but the rejection of her relatives and friends after her return to Armenia made her a "real prostitute."

Amasya (TURKEY, 2000)

When the war started I decided to go to Karabakh to help wounded soldiers. I was there during the whole period of military activities. After the cease-fire I came to Armenia, but there was no work and no means to live. My neighbor was going to Turkey to do trade. She said that the Turkish agency could help us in getting a job that would allow us to earn some money to buy products to sell in Armenia. This was a very good way out for me; at least I thought so. We went to the Turkish bus agency and bought tickets. The bus operator said that it was always possible to get a job in Turkey and their agency could help us there. Everything was going very well. In Istanbul the agency recommended us to a man who introduced himself as an owner of a sewing factory. He said that that even if we did not know how to sew clothing he could still arrange a job there. He always needed helping hands. He also advised us to rent a small apartment from somebody he knew well. That day he asked us to give him our passports for registering us as temporary residents. We did not object.

The next day he took us to his "factory." It was not a factory at all, it was a massage parlor or brothel; we could not understand. He told us that we should clean up there and prepare coffee and drinks to serve to customers. He told us that we should wear short dresses and other pieces of very vulgar clothing. We did not want to do that, but we realized that we had no choice. At the end of the month we asked for the salary, but he said that we had not earned the promised amount of $400, but that he could give us only $100 to cover the rent for the flat. We could earn the rest by providing sexual services to men. If we did not agree we would never receive our passports. As our visas had already expired and we were staying illegally in Turkey they could send us to prison. I could not believe that it was happening to me, that somebody could use my vulnerable situation and threaten me.

Next day I went to him and said that I would agree to his proposal if he gave back my money and passport. He agreed to give me money, but he said that he needed my passport to extend the visa. Two weeks later he gave me only $200 instead of $700 and explained that it was due to costs related to food and expenses for visa extension. We worked twelve to fourteen hours instead of the agreed ten. He said that he had also bribed the police to leave me unpunished for working illegally in Turkey. I realized that this man was going to create big problems for me if I did not take some steps. The next day we told him that we would go to the police if he did not pay us and give back our passports. He said that the next day he would have the passport and money ready. When we came home that night our landlord said that he could not let us in anymore because we were illegal. He refused to let us in and we could not even take our belongings.

We had no other choice than go to the police department. We were unable to make ourselves understood, nor did we have any documents, so they kept us one night at the police station. The next day we were taken to the immigration police for deportation. Thank God our stay was not long; we had to stay there for one night, as the bus to Armenia was leaving in the morning and the drivers agreed to take us to Armenia on the condition that we would pay them in Yerevan. I do not want to remember again the night that we spent in the immigration police. Even though I have seen the horrors of war, that night was unimaginable.

Farida (TURKEY, 2000)

When my husband died I was left alone with my four children. I did not have money and the children's needs were increasing; they needed education, clothing and so on. I could not find a job in Armenia. My neighbor, who was also looking for a job, told me that many of her friends had found work in Turkey through bus operators. We went there together and were very happy when the agency told us that on arrival in Turkey people would be meeting us at the office of the travel agency. When we arrived in Turkey we went directly to the office and found a man waiting for us. He proposed us a job at the canteen of a factory he owned. We agreed that he would pay us $200 a week for ten hours of work per day. We also rented a room in a three-room apartment that we shared with two other groups—one group of three young men, the other three women from Russia.

A week passed, and when we asked for the salaries the man said that we had to work more and that he had to reconsider our salaries. We worked for a month and got no salary. We found another job in order to cover our accommodation. Every night we worked for four additional hours to get some more dollars to cover accommodation, food expenses, and the delay in our salaries. At the end of the second month he told us that he didn't need both of us anymore and that he was going to keep only me. At the beginning of the third month he gave me $100, but only when I asked him. I needed to send money to my son. He was serving in the army at the border of Armenia. My neighbors informed me that he was sick and that my children did not have money to buy medicines. I sent the money through a Turkish bus agency to Yerevan. Later when I asked for my pay he threatened to report me to immigration police about my expired visa. I was scared.

Everybody knew what Yabanja Shube, the immigration detention center, meant. One of my friends was there. Later in Yerevan she told me what had happened to her. A group of policemen raped, beat, and humiliated her for four days in a row. She said that there were three more women at the immigration prison who shared the same fate. She was deported in an almost unconscious state. We agreed to everything, every kind of humiliation, but not to go to this place.

Every day when I came to work asking for the money the man requested additional favors from me—to serve in his family, to clean his house. I was doing all the work hoping that at last he would pay me. Once he told me that he would be very favorable to me if I agreed to have sexual relations with him. The next day he was more persistent. When I asked again about the money he said that he would immediately call the immigration police and imprison me for violation of the visa regime. I did not know what to do. I could not go back home because I had no documents and was afraid of the immigration police. So I had to accept his rules in order to get my passport. As soon as I received it I immediately bought a bus ticket to Yerevan. I heard from my roommates many similar stories. None of the migrant workers who lived in the apartment with me were satisfied with the working conditions, payment, and attitude. None of them had a contract and none of the bosses wanted to legalize their work and stay.

I do not know what to do now. When I heard about jobs in Turkey it seemed to me the best solution. Now I am back. I have the same debts, the same problems, and four children to take care of.

Alina (UNITED ARAB EMIRATES, 2000)

I met my boyfriend at my girlfriend's house. He had been dating me for a month already when he told me he was going to marry me. My boyfriend told me we could earn some money for our wedding if we went to work in Greece at his friend's company. We would stay for three months there to earn enough money and come back. I was extremely happy. I could not believe all that was happening to me. He took my passport and all necessary papers and said that he would take care of visa and travel arrangements. I was so happy and careless that I did not even ask to see the tickets or documents.

The day of departure came. We took the plane, and instead of Greece we landed in Dubai. As I had not been abroad before, I could not really understand where I was. I could only recognize the Arabic signs and people dressed in Arabic robes. When I asked why we landed in Dubai he said we would have to stay for a couple of days in Dubai, and then later we would go to Greece. He took me to a hotel and said that he was going to see his friend and would be back soon. Two hours later a man came to take me to another hotel saying that I was his property. I could not understand; I kept saying that it was a misunderstanding and that my friend would come soon. I had come to Dubai for another purpose. The man told me that my friend had sold me to him, that from now on he would have my documents and I had to do whatever he told me to. He said that the next day I had to move to another place and serve all the clients he would send to me. I was shocked by what was happening. The next day he came and took me to another hotel. He said that every day I had to give him $500, no matter how many clients I would serve. He was so violent. It was a continuous hell. Each day I served around thirty to forty clients. I was not able to move or think. It went on for weeks. I was living between clients and tears. That was the rhythm of my life. I could not even realize what they wanted from me. The intensity of the process lasted for a couple of weeks. One day I got terribly sick. He left me alone and sent another Armenian woman to visit me. That day I understood that it was an organized enterprise and that there were many women from many countries who shared the same fate.

Meanwhile the pimp refused to give back my passport because of the debts he said he had incurred on account of me. I had to work and earn money if I wanted to go back home. Then he introduced me to another man telling me that he had sold me to him and that I had to take my passport from him. The next day I was beaten like for the first time. He was an extremely cruel man. He came every morning to pick up his money and beat me terribly. I had no right to speak or express my concern, everybody knew him well for his cruelty. I did not receive any money from him. He did not even buy food. It all depended on the client's will. I was resold four times.

One of my clients was trying to kill me. If it were not for the women in the next room I would have been killed. In his frenzy the man was beating me. He squeezed my throat. Luckily enough there was a police raid in the hotel where I was working and I was taken together with other women to a police station and detained. My pimp did not do anything to release me from prison. I spent four months there. Though it was prison and the conditions were terrible, it was incomparable with what I had gone through before that. Nobody was cruel or rude to me there and I had to wait while my temporary documents from Armenia and the ticket for deportation were arranged. I came back without any money. All I had before remained with the pimp, I could not pick up anything. The most shameful thing happened at Yerevan airport. Everybody was treating me as if I were a prostitute, saying bad words. My life has changed since that time. Now you see me here in the street. I have become a real prostitute.

Iliona (UNITED ARAB EMIRATES, 2000)

My friend told me that we could earn money by doing trade in Dubai. I sold my house to get money for the trip and to buy some stuff from Dubai to sell in Armenia. I had done the same before, in Turkey. This time I was cheated. We traveled with my friend. Her friend from Dubai sent us an invitation. When we came to Dubai we were immediately taken to a hotel. Our friend who was married to a local Arab man told us that they had sent us the invitation not for shopping but for doing sex work. She also said that we had to serve as many men as they would propose and pay her a daily rate. I had been involved in sex work for many years; nevertheless I could not stand the pressure. They were forcing us to have sex with at least forty men a day, sometimes even more. You had no right to reject the customer, even when he did not want to use condoms. Of course I understood that I was at risk to contract a disease, but I had no right to turn the client down. They were beating us awfully and we could not refuse a client even if we were feeling terribly sick.

If someone spent more on food than we were supposed to (food is expensive in Dubai and in many cases we were hungry and thirsty), the Arab partner of our pimp would beat us with a belt. It was so painful. There were many cases when the clients were also violent. You were between two extremes—the violent client and the more violent pimp, who would terribly beat you or refuse to pay out if you disobeyed. The younger ones were crying all the time; they could not get used to all they were forced to do. They were like senseless objects after almost twenty-four hours of work.

There are many Armenian women in Dubai, including my friends from Echmiadzin and Hrazdan. They are still coming. I am sorry for the young girls; they cannot stand this. They get sick quickly and are sent back home.

It depends on the pimp; there are ones that never pay even one dollar to children, but I have heard of those also who gave $1,000 when a child was returning home.

As I did not have any documents and knew very well how corrupt the police were all over the world and their attitude to prostitutes, I did not even think of running away. I had no money and was collecting the few dollars she gave to me to bring home for my son. He needs money to go to college. I want him to be an educated person and hold a high position in society. I got sick in Dubai and she had to send me back. Now I am here and do not even have a cent to buy bread. We live here from hand to mouth. I'll try to get some money to do trade in Turkey.

Shahnara (UNITED ARAB EMIRATES, 2000)

I was twelve when my mother died. My father and my uncle had been using drugs for many years. Soon my father was imprisoned; I do not know for what offense. My uncle sold everything in our house to buy drugs. When I was thirteen he forced me out to the street. I was living in the streets, sleeping under benches in the park. He told me to sell myself if I was not able to find money in another way. I went to the police and they sent me to Vartashen orphanage. Once my classmate told me that there was a woman in her neighborhood helping young pretty girls to go to Germany to work for a fashion magazine. I could not believe it. I was so happy. Later the woman told me that after she had arranged documents for me and other persons we would all travel together to Germany. After a short while the papers were ready and we could to start off. There were fourteen of us, girls of different ages between thirteen and twenty-three. We went by taxi to Tbilisi. From there we traveled to Moscow and from Moscow to Dubai, as we found out later. The woman who had recruited me had twenty-seven children employed, mostly from orphanages or from the streets. She deals in this business for twelve years already.

The hell I lived through at home continued in Dubai. They placed us in a hotel. They had special interest in young virgins. They were selling them at enormous prices to rich Arab sheikhs for one night, after which they were working with clients like other ordinary girls. We received only a fraction of what the sheikhs gave to the pimp. In some cases the girls received some special presents from the sheikhs. My friend who was thirteen was taken to a wealthy man. In the end the man asked her what she wanted from him as a present. The girl asked for two sacks of flour. Even the money given to the girls as a gift was confiscated by the pimps.

Two days later they took us to a nightclub and explained the nature of our work and the amount that we should pay them every day. They explained that they had paid a lot of money for our passports and travel, in total $6,000 for permission to fly and tickets. They were also paying for our room and food. Almost all the children were crying. They could not understand what was expected from them and how they were going to do it. The Arab partner of our pimp was getting angry when he was not getting the amount of money they were expecting us to provide. He was beating children with a belt and was very violent. I was also crying at the very beginning, but what could I do?

Sometimes there were rich businessmen who hired us every time they came to Dubai. I was very happy when one businessman called me and said he was coming to Dubai. He spent his time only with me. He rented a room for me where I stayed and sometimes we went shopping together. The pimp also placed children with us when they were not able to earn enough money and requested the businessman to pay for them too, although at a somewhat cheaper price.

After nights of work we were getting so tired that we could not do anything else but sleep. We did not communicate with each other. We were living in different hotels, even though we were from the same country and were together on the same flight. When our visas expired we traveled with our pimp to Iran to extend the visas. We stayed there for no more than two hours. Our passports were usually given to us at the airport and taken away after passport control. We could not run away or complain to the police since they assured us that they were bribed.

One of my clients who was working for the immigration police threatened my pimp and took my passport back. Later on, I was caught by the police again and deported through Moscow. As I was deported I could not even bring the small things that the clients had given to me. My Arab client promised to send those presents to me.

I have twice been in UAE. As soon as I came back home, I decided to buy a small one-room flat because I had spent most of my life in the streets and I wanted to have my own home. As I was under eighteen I could not register property on my name, so I did it under my uncle's name. A month later he needed money for drugs, so he sold my flat and everything I had in it.

Tamara (UNITED ARAB EMIRATES, 2000)

I was working as a waitress in a café. When the café closed one of the regular clients saw me in the street and said that she was going to Dubai. She said there was a lot of work in cafés, bars, and restaurants where I could get a better job and salary. The proposal seemed very attractive and I agreed to go. When I went to her house I met another woman there. The woman told me that she was taking a group of women as it was easier to arrange. As I did not have money she paid the ticket for me and gave me $200 to leave behind for my family. She also took me to the hairdresser and dentist and bought me a dress. She said that I needed to look good in order to get a high salary.

We traveled directly from Yerevan. All our documents had been changed. She paid the officials at the passport agency to get new passports for us, because all of us were younger than thirty. One was even seventeen. At the airport everybody knew her—the police, customs, and border guards.

When we arrived in Dubai, one of the women had a problem with her documents. After a conversation of ten minutes and a phone call to some place all problems were settled and they let us out of the airport. She took us to Sharjah to a small hotel that allegedly she had completely reserved for us. We stayed there for three days. Our documents were given to the receptionist at the hotel. On the fourth day she said that she could not keep us in this hotel, as it was too expensive. She moved us to a very cheap hotel and told us to stay there and receive our clients. When I heard the word "clients" I was so surprised. I was prepared to work as a waitress. I asked the other woman what they thought about it. Nobody wanted to talk.

The next day our "organizer" came accompanied by an Arab man. They explained to us that we had been sold to him and if we did not do what we were told he could do with us whatever he wished. It is his country and everybody would believe him. Police or immigration officials would not accept complaints. Everybody used his services and they were all his friends. From that day on my misery started. He was sending around fifty clients a day, sometimes even more. I did not understand what was happening. I had no right to be sick, I had no right to refuse or choose. I do not know how he had established the terrible conveyor, but the line did not stop. Though we lived in the same hotel with other women from Armenia who had come at the same time, we almost did not communicate. When we had couple of minutes in the morning everyone was telling the horrible situation they went through and more horrible stories of other women, especially those from Russia. They told that they had found one young beautiful girl who had committed suicide in her room. The body disappeared the same day. No police came.

Next day another woman was living in her room. Nothing happened. Later our "boss" always presented her example to us, telling us that other pimps were so merciless. Once I got so sick that I could not even move, but the pimp wouldn't pay attention to me and kept on sending clients to me. I do not know how I got through that day. I was feeling so hopeless that I decided to die. I thought that whatever I would tell at home, whatever kind of excuses I would offer to my parents and son, nobody would believe and forgive me. I went to the balcony, thinking that throwing myself out would solve all problems. Immediately, I was called in as the next client came. If I did not get terribly sick I would never see my home. I told the pimp that I needed to see a doctor, but she said that it was very expensive and I could not afford it. The next day I was so weak that I could not even stand. I asked the receptionist to call the pimp. She came with a doctor, who said that I needed some medicines for the moment and an operation later on. I asked for my documents to go home, but the pimp said that I could not go and she would take care of me there.

Time passed by and she kept sending more and more clients to me, so that my health condition became worse. I had no choice, I called my mother and told her to go to the house of the pimp together with police, and tell her relatives that if she did not give my passport to me in Dubai the Yerevan police would put her relatives in jail. That threat worked out; she gave me my passport and a ticket and I came back home.

Once I heard that my child in Yerevan was sick. I tried to hide $100 in a piece of chocolate butter. Somebody reported me to the pimp. I was terribly beaten and my money was taken away. I thought of going again to earn some money to do an operation. I would be clever this time and would not be trapped. I have no right to be deceived again, I have a child and need to take care of him.

MOLDOVAN TRAFFICKING FOR DOMESTIC AND SEX SLAVERY

None of these Moldovan women had fathers while growing up. The narratives are stories of mothers, daughters, and sisters. Alana remembers crying when her sister was raped and concludes with a description of the rape of her mother; Milena and Bahar try to keep the truth of their experiences from their mothers on their return, but cannot; several of the women explain their decision to seek work outside Moldova as attempts to help sick or poor mothers; and Maria prays to her dead mother during enslavement. The narratives are stories of women in another sense—they explain the involvement of female traffickers, like the woman who locked Alana inside a house or the gypsy woman who trafficked and then rescued Milena.

All the women except Maria were trafficked into sex slavery. Maria was trafficked into domestic servitude in her late thirties. Along with Albania, Moldova is one of the main countries of origin for the trafficking of women and children into European sex slavery. Moldova's economic conditions fuel this trafficking. In 2000 the country's GDP was 40 percent of its level in 1990. Moldova has the lowest average salary level of countries in the former Soviet Union, and women's salaries are 70–80 percent that of men's. Unemployment remains extremely high, especially among women, and 80 percent of people live below the poverty line. As Maria explains, "In Moldova there is no work for us." Consequently, people are forced to look outside of the country for work, and pimps take advantage. Some victims are kidnapped, but more often they answer job advertisements promising work and then are forced into sex slavery. An estimated ten thousand women have been trafficked out of the country in recent years. Most Moldovan trafficking victims are taken to the Balkan countries, though other destinations include Asia, Turkey, western Europe, and the Middle East. Bahar was trafficked to Turkey and Maria to Ukraine. Alana and Milena were trafficked to Russia, where men and women are also trafficked in from Central Asia and North Korea for forced labor and sexual exploitation.

Alana (RUSSIA, 2005)

I was born in Costesti. I have one older sister. My father died when I was young and we were always very poor. In November 2003 a gypsy man in the village offered for me and my sister to work in Russia. He told us he buys goods from Moldova and we can sell them in a market in Moscow. He paid 6,000 lei [$470] for two passports and bought us train tickets. My mother was very sick at that time, so I prayed we could send her money for heating wood and medicine.

When we came to Moscow, the man's wife picked us from the train station. She took us to a small house where there were four other Moldovan girls. She told us we would go to the market in the morning, and she locked us inside. The other girls asked if we knew why we were there. We saw clothes hanging on the wall for nuns. There was the name of a church written on them, but I could not read it in Russian. The other girls told us we would dress like nuns and beg for money.

In the morning when the wife returned, my sister told her we would not do this kind of work. She told us it was better than selling goods and we would make more money. We worked like this for two weeks from eight in the morning until late at night, but we could not keep any money. After two weeks they moved us to another apartment with other girls. There were three gypsy men here who beat us badly and told us we must have sex with clients. I panicked and told them I would not do this work, but they raped me and said, "If you behave well, you can go back to Moldova in one year. If you do not, we will kill you and no one will look for you." Every day many clients came for sex, and every day these men beat us. They punched our ribs and our back, but not our face. I cried when I watched them rape my sister. I wished they would kill me.

The men moved us to many apartments for two years. We could never escape because they always locked us inside. One day they moved us to the street and we tried to escape, but the men caught us and beat us badly. We tried a second time and we made it to the train station. The police asked for our passport, and we explained what happened. They took us to detention for one week and deported us to Moldova.

When we came back to Costesti, my mother thought we had been dead. One week later, the same gypsy man who first took us to Moscow came to our home at five in the morning. He had other gypsy men with him, and he said we must return to Moscow and pay off our debt. He tried to take us, but my sister and I ran. My mother could not run, so they raped her. We told the police the next day, but the gypsies were gone, and they never found the man who did this to us.

Milena (RUSSIA, 2005)

I grew up with my mother in the village of Costesti. I never knew my father. In 2003 Roma gypsies came to our village. A woman and daughter moved into a small house near mine. I was seventeen at that time. I became friends with the gypsy girl, Dolina. My mother worked as a waitress in Chisinau, but I did not have a job and I was not in school at that time. One day Dolina asked me if I wanted to go for work abroad as a nanny. She told me we could make $400 or $500 each month and the work was not very difficult. I told her I would think about it. I did not tell my mother because I thought, "If I go, I can make more money than my mother and come back and surprise her." Also, I thought my mother would not let me go abroad. A few days later I decided to go.

The next morning when my mother left for work, I dressed up nice and left a note telling my mother I was going for work and would be back in a few weeks. Dolina took me to Chisinau on a bus and we stayed with her relatives there for a few days. They treated me very nice. Then Dolina, me, and a two gypsy men went in a car to Moscow. They spoke their language, so I could not understand what they were saying. At the border, they showed the guards documents and we passed through.

In Moscow, we went to an apartment building. Inside the apartment, there was one sofa, one table, and calendars of naked girls on the walls. The calendars were not written in Russian or Moldovan. I asked Dolina, "Will I babysit here?" She told me, "Yes, in this place." "Where is the little girl," I asked. "Where is the mother?" "They are visiting the neighbors," Dolina told me. "They will be here in a minute." At that time the men were looking at many documents. They told me, "A man will come soon. Do not be afraid if you see many men."

I was alone in the apartment for a few hours and became afraid. Soon two Russian men came. They were friendly with me and asked me questions. They asked me how old I was and if I had had sex with men before. I asked them why they needed to know this, and they laughed. Then three other Russian men came with vodka and food. They put plastic on the sofa and we ate from it. I was very hungry, and I ate one sausage and bread. They made me get drunk, even though I had never had alcohol before. The room went spinning around me and I was very dizzy. The men laughed. One of the men touched my legs and breasts. I objected, but he hit me and said, "You will do what I say!"

They told me to undress. I refused, but they punched my ribs and undressed me. All five men raped me again and again. Two of the men forced themselves inside me at once, and I bled very badly. They said they were teaching me to be a prostitute. I cried, but they did not stop. When they finally left, the room was messy with empty bottles and smoke in the air. I felt very ill and wanted to go home.

In the morning, another man came and raped me. He told me, whoever comes I must have sex with them. I asked him where was Dolina. He said he did not know. He left me food and told me to shower. That day five men raped me. Each day a man gave me breakfast and dinner. Sometimes he brought me new clothes to wear. Every day I was alone, except when the men came to rape me. Eight, ten, sometimes fifteen men in a day. I do not know how long I was in that apartment. There was one small window, which was always locked. I could see from it that I came in the spring and left in winter.

One day, Dolina and the same two men who first brought me to Moscow came to the apartment. I could not believe it. I asked Dolina, "Why did you do this to me? Don't you know these men sold me and raped me?" "I did not do this to you," Dolina told me. "When we came I was told they only needed one girl for a nanny and you would be sent back." Dolina and the gypsy men drove me back to Moldova. We stayed in Chisinau for a few days with her relatives. This time they made me live separately. I ate alone, slept on the floor, and they made me wash myself separately. Dolina asked me, "Would you like to go home?" I said, "Yes." She told me my mother had alerted the police I was missing, and she made me promise that I must say I was working with a friend in Chisinau this entire time.

Dolina took me home, but my mother was at work. I climbed in through the window, and when my mother returned, she could not believe I was back. She asked me where I had been for so long. I tried to lie, but I could not. I told her the truth. We went straight to the police and told them everything, but they said the gypsies had moved from Costesti long before. No one ever found Dolina or the other gypsy men.

Bahar (TURKEY, 2005)

I live with my mother. I never knew my father. We make handiwork for money and live in a small village outside Comrat with other Romas. It is very hard for us because we do not have a man in our home, and every winter we do not have enough food to eat or wood for heating. In 2003, Turk men came to our community and told many girls they can work in a hotel in Istanbul for $500 per month, but we must go next week to get the jobs. They said they will pay for our passport and transportation.

I went for this job with five other girls. I thought, "I will make so much money that my mother will never be cold in the winter again." They took our picture for the passport and gave us a visa. We went by minibus and ferry to Turkey. It was no problem to cross the border. In Istanbul we were taken to an apartment. These men left us there and said other men will take us to the hotel. They did not leave us any food for four hours. The other men came late that night when we were asleep. They gave us food and alcohol, and then they raped us. One girl shouted, and they whipped her on the back with leather belts. They said if we want to live we must have sex with any man who comes to this apartment. If we do not, they said they will kill our families in Comrat. They took three girls from the apartment and left me and two others.

Many Turkish men came every day for sex. They didn't care about having sex with all three of us at once in the same room. After a few weeks, one of the girls bit a client who was hurting her. The client beat her very badly and broke her jaw. The pimps took her from the apartment, and a few days later another girl came. She was very young. She was also from my village in Moldova. There was no electricity or phone in the room and no windows. I think one man was always in the apartment next to us, and if we made too much noise, he threatened to beat us. Sometimes the police came and had sex with us. Sometimes the men who first brought me to Istanbul came for sex.

After one year, the men from the apartment sent me home. I saw my mother and burst into tears. I tried to lie to her that I had done cleaning work in a hotel, but I could not. She asked why I had never written to her, and I told her the truth. She told the police, but they could do nothing. Those men had left long ago from Comrat, but they took thirty girls from our village in one year since I was gone.

Maria (UKRAINE, 2005)

I was born in Costesti and have only lived here and in Chisinau. My father left when I was young, and my mother died when I was twenty. I did not attend school and worked odd jobs since that time. One year ago I saw a job listing for a nanny and cleaning person in Ukraine. The job said it will pay $400 each month. I called the number and took the job.

A Ukrainian lady named Olga arranged my job. She made for me a passport and bought me a bus ticket. When I traveled to Ukraine, a man named Stephan met me at the bus station. He took me to the home of a man and woman near the Black Sea. They were maybe forty years old and had three children. Their home was very big and they forced me to cook and clean from very early in the morning until late at night. They did not give me a break, and when I asked to go back to Moldova, they beat me. They kept my passport and locked me in a small room at night. I slept on a mat on the floor and they only let me eat the food they did not finish.

I was very sad those days, but I did their work so the man would not beat me. His name was Victor, and he was very big. Sometimes if he did not like the food I cooked, he removed his belt and beat me with it. If I was bleeding or very ill, he would not call a doctor and made me keep working. In my room at night I cried often and prayed to my mother to send help.

One day, after ten months, the family sent me back to Moldova. I asked them for money for my work, but they paid me nothing. I have been in Costesti four months since then and cannot find work. In Moldova there is no work for us, but I will never again take a job from Makler.

THE TURNING POINT

Liberation from Bondage

You shall see how a slave was made a man...the turning-point.
    Frederick Douglass, *Narrative of the Life of Frederick Douglass, an American Slave,* 1845

The day they told me that I was going to be free, a bird came.
    Maria Suarez, a former domestic slave, United States, 2005

CHILD DOMESTIC SLAVERY IN INDIA

Kavita's psychological turning point from slavery to freedom came some months after her escape from domestic slavery. As she explains, there was no turning point on her initial arrival at a shelter: "I was very scared. I refused to speak for the first two days. I just cried and cried." It was only when she reversed the most traumatic aspect of her experience in slavery that Kavita reached a turning point. Trafficked with her younger sister into domestic servitude within India in 2002, at the age of twelve, Kavita was forced to watch her sister "beaten up, tortured, made to work every day." She recalls "sitting in a corner, tied, a witness to the beating of my younger sister...unable to protect her....Each time I think about that, I just stagnate." But when she was encouraged to "help out the tiny ones" at the shelter, Kavita was able to counter this trauma. She began to gain confidence to "start my life afresh."

There are millions of enslaved domestics in India, and a further 264,000 child domestics in Pakistan. Children are often sent away from their villages to work in order to clear a family debt. These loans have immensely high rates of interest, and in many cases no remuneration is given at all. The debt is often passed on to a younger sibling or on to the domestic's own children. The children work fifteen or more hours a day, seven days a week, for little or no pay under abusive conditions, generally have little or no freedom of movement, are denied schooling, and are often sexually exploited. Consequently, domestic work is often a precursor to commercial sex work. Many domestics in India—some as young as seven or eight—are on duty around the clock, sleep on the kitchen floor, eat leftovers, and have no holidays or rest breaks.

Kavita (INDIA, 2004)

My sister and I were living in a village. We were happy. We were poor and our parents had to struggle to give us a daily existence, but there was a bond. There was love, there was affection. I'm fourteen now, so when I left home I was about twelve. But even though I was twelve, I was still very innocent. I hadn't seen life beyond my home.

When we came to the house in Allahabad, they made every single effort to break my bond with my sister. I was tied and thrown into a room like a piece of furniture. I had clear instructions not to talk to my sister or to speak with her, to have no contact with her—almost like I didn't exist. I was nothing. In front of me, my sister was beaten up, tortured, made to work every day. I couldn't console her. It was crazy. This was my sister, someone I shared every single moment of my life with. There was no bond. Think about it. I am sitting in a corner, tied, a witness to the beating of my younger sister. Even being elder, I'm unable to protect her. I can only hear her cries of pain. I can't talk to her. Nothing. Each time I think about that, I just stagnate. My thoughts become still. I can't think beyond the fact that there's a possibility I will never meet her again. The pain is so deep. I'm alone. Pretty much at a loss for words.

When I left that house, I had no idea about anything—where I would land up, what I would do. I was just so scared. I didn't know anything. When I was waiting at the station, fear crept into my heart. I kept thinking, "Where will I go from here? What will I do?" Even when I came to the shelter, I was very scared. I refused to speak for the first two days. I just cried and cried. I would sleep uncontrollably for days. Ravatni helped me a lot. She talked to me and would console me: "I understand that you have a ten-year-old sister who's been left behind. I understand that your parents are dead. But you must also understand the fact that there's nothing you can do about this at this point in time. You're in a new place, a place that can teach you a lot. So maybe it's possible for you to try forgetting the past and move on." Something went down, registered, slowly. But even then, I was just so emotional I did not want to study. I would see others around me opening their books, studying. But even though my mind was in it, my heart wasn't.

So Ravatni encouraged me with this thought—that I would help out the tiny ones. Any younger child I would see, I would help them out with the homework, with little lessons that I could do. And then there was a friend of mine, Sonia. I would steal her books and read from them. So my interest developed. I began to read little by little, and now each time I see a book I want to devour it. So my interest in studies is definitely increased. It's a lot to do with Ravatni—her encouragement, her wisdom, her knowledge, and the confidence that she gave me to start my life afresh.

Now I'm happy, very, very happy—happy with the life I'm leading over here and happy when I think where I could be, in the place where my sister is right now. But even though I am happy at the life and the activities that I do here, each time I think about my sister and what she has to go through in her daily life, I am just so hurt, so resentful, and so angry. I am happy about my luck and my fortune, that I am where I am, but still angry at what she is suffering. When I ran away from that place, it was the very first time I had come to Allahabad, so I was not familiar with the names of the places or where her house is. I have descriptions, I know the village setup. The house where she was working was a big house. There was a shop close by and that's what all I remember. I remember what it looked like but not the exact location of it or the name of the place.

People who do such things must understand that we are children. We are so innocent, so vulnerable. They must understand they must not do this to anyone, anywhere. What I would like to say to the world is when it comes to children, they're small, they're innocent, they're vulnerable. They just like playing, laughing, having fun, and very often they are unable to comprehend the repercussions of what the elders are doing to them. I believed them, and I went with them to that house.

What I've learned from this shelter is how to become a better human being. I learned the values of empathy, the values of sympathy, the values of sincerity. To deal with not only my pain but that of somebody else. How to respect emotions; how to know when to give people space; how to talk to the person who's tormenting me, to explain what they're doing is wrong in a polite yet effective manner. I've learned how to deal with myself and with others. I want to grow up and I want to study to become a nurse. I want to become a nurse so I can help other people and look after them in their hour of need.

AGRICULTURAL TRAFFICKING IN THE UNITED STATES

Miguel's narrative marks a clear turning point when he knew he could remain in bondage no longer: "A week before Easter it happened." He told other workers, "Now is our time to leave." Miguel had arrived in the United States from Mexico in 2001, and became a slave in a labor camp run by the Ramos family in Lake Placid, Florida, after being recruited in Arizona. He and several others were transported to Florida and then told they owed $1,000 each for transportation. The Ramoses also deducted from their weekly pay for food, rent for substandard camp housing, and work equipment. Miguel sometimes ended up with only $20 a day and had no control over records of payment and credit. His employers were armed with guns, watched for workers trying to escape, and cut off access to the outside world. Relatives of the Ramoses owned the stores where workers were taken to shop.

The U.S. Department of Justice estimates that between 14,500 and 17,500 foreign-born individuals are trafficked into the United States annually: 5,000–7,000 from East Asia and the Pacific, 3,500–5,500 from Europe and Eurasia, 3,500–5,500 from South America, 200–700 from Africa, 200–600 from South Asia, and up to 200 from the Near East. Mexico accounts for the majority of federal trafficking cases. The United States has strengthened its border patrols in recent years, forcing many migrants from Mexico to rely on underground channels, and smugglers charge exorbitant fees, to be repaid through indentured servitude, as in the case of Miguel. The CIA declared that in 2004 it detected 16,000 undocumented Mexicans and Central Americans subjected to sex and labor slavery after being trafficked to the United States. But, while Miguel entered the country illegally, not all victims of human trafficking are illegal immigrants. Many enter the United States legally, but because of their poverty or inability to speak English they are exploited by traffickers. Florida is one of the top four destinations for people trafficked to the United States, along with New York, California, and Texas.

Miguel reached the turning point from slavery to freedom in 2001 with the help of the Coalition of Immokalee Workers (CIW), a community-based worker organization of over two thousand members in Immokalee, Florida's largest farmworker community. Between 1997 and 2000, CIW helped end three modern-day slavery operations, resulting in freedom for over five hundred workers, and in 2001 it began investigating the Ramoses. In November 2002, three members of the Ramos family were convicted of conspiracy to hold seven hundred workers in involuntary servitude. In May 2004 they were sentenced to a total of thirty-one years and nine months in federal prison.

Miguel (UNITED STATES, 2005)

I come from Mexico. I have one son and he has cancer. It costs a lot for the medicine and treatment, and the government helps out, but they can only give so much treatment and it still costs a lot. The wages in Mexico are so low and I wasn't earning enough there. It's maybe $40–60 for a whole week of work. I thought if I could go to the United States and earn $6–7 an hour, maybe in a whole day I can earn $48–50. And with that, I could be earning in three or four days more than I can earn in a whole month in Mexico. I could be sending that home. It would help sustain the family and help pay for my son's sickness. My dream was to work like in Mexico but not with the same wage that I get there. In Mexico if you don't like working with one guy you can change. When I came to the United States, I thought I could change jobs if I didn't like one.

"Miguel" (photograph by Peggy Callahan, Free the Slaves, 2005)

But it was a really tough decision to come to the United States, because you have to cross the desert and I heard that they kill people there. I gathered together some money, and borrowed maybe 3,000 pesos. Here that is not much money—$300. We decided together that we'd go, five or six of us. We had more courage to go as five or six together. In a larger group we had the strength to say, "Yeah, we're going to do this."

I went to the border of Mexico and the United States and into Arizona, walking. We really had no idea where we were going or how to get there, we were just kind of walking in the direction of the house of the guy who gives rides to Florida. In the desert we spent about eight days looking for the house, and we looked for a boss who could send money to the guy who would drive us. Then we could pay him back by working. From the 21st of February to the 14th of March was the time that it took to get from Mexico to the border, to cross the border, to wait around in Arizona, to get a ride, and then to come here. Ramiro Ramos is the one who sent the money and arranged for us to come here. We didn't know of him, but we just asked around for somebody who would give us a ride across and who we could work for; someone who could pay for our ride and then we could pay them back. Supposedly, you can find these people. If you just ask around people will know them, and so that's what we did. It wasn't a direct way to get to Florida. We had to stop and wait and change.

When we arrived, we hadn't eaten for three days. We arrived in front of a shop, fourteen of us. The driver said, "You wait here, I'm going to look for the boss." He went off, but he didn't find him. He came back and said, "Uh, don't move, you just stay here. There's no problem with Immigration or Border Patrol. You just wait here." This was my first time in the United States and I was afraid of Immigration [U.S. Immigration and Naturalization Service, INS]. Then the guy spoke on the phone—it was hard to talk to this guy cause he was always on the phone.

Another guy came up to us and said, "OK, OK, so we're all here to work, right? You're all here to work." He told us about the jobs. He was one of the Ramos family. He said, "Do you have any money to pay me for the ride? Here's the telephone, call your family members in the United States and tell them to pay me for the ride." I knew I didn't have any family here. "If I had family here," I said, "I would have come with them. I wouldn't have taken your ride, and I wouldn't have to owe any money." That's when he first threatened us. He said, "Look, you're going to work here, and it's hard work. You've got to work hard; you've got to be motivated. You've got to cut oranges and you've got to harvest those oranges, you've got to use a big, heavy knife. If any of you assholes try to leave without paying back your ride, that's when I'm going to really fuck you up." He said that we can take something to eat, but whatever we took we would have to pay for. Then Ramiro Ramos came and said, "Don't take much food, and hurry up because we've got to get to work tomorrow." He took us to a little ranch and we started to get more threats. I was with a friend and he asked about a television. Ramos said, "Shut up and don't talk about TV. This isn't a place to watch TV. This is a place to work, and if you're going to complain about it we're going to kill you and throw your ass into the pond." We had to work, but we didn't have any social security cards or insurance, so we weren't really sure what this work was going to be like.

We didn't work for money by the hour but by the bucket. It wasn't really a bucket, it was a really large container that we had to fill with oranges and carry over to a large bin. We had to fill one of those bathtub-size things at least ten times, and this took at least an hour. There were so many oranges and we had to pick up only the really nice ones. I was working from really early in the morning to really late at night. We could only fill maybe three or four tubs and that that would get us maybe $28. We had to pay not just the ride money but rent and some taxes. They took it from our check and charged us money at the shop for cashing the check. He would never take us to another bank. There was almost nothing left after they took out everything. One day it was only $20 and what am I supposed to do with $20? How can I send that when they charge money to send it? We started talking to each other about what to do and decided we were not earning anything. It was a misery wage—the same as it would be in Mexico.

There was this time when a guy was talking about going. We saw him go toward the Kash 'n Karry supermarket, and they saw him too. We heard one of them outside of our apartment talking on the telephone, saying, "We're going to get that motherfucker. We're going to get him and we're going to throw him into the pond with the alligators and kill him." There were about eight of us in the house and we knew he meant what he said. Those words are serious because that's how they work. The words have meaning. We knew that they can hit us hard or shoot us with a gun. Around forty guys who were working for Ramoses were there watching us. They were everywhere.

Four of us tended work in the same place in the fields, and we started noticing this new guy. He came in fifteen days after we arrived. He was an older guy, maybe forty-seven years old. He was always tired and always threatened by them. He said he wanted to sit down and take a rest and asked one of the guys watching if he could just take one day off. The guy said, "We don't want any fucking assholes to be resting here. This is a place of work, and if you want to go rest you can get the hell out of here." It made me feel so sad to see this old man so tired. He wanted to rest and he was being forced to work. We had to take all these threats and we couldn't say anything against them.

I felt like a slave from the moment I arrived. We couldn't pay for the ride and they started to threaten us. It was horrible. We were piled in a dorm, three beds on top of each other, six in a room. The person on top had to jump over all of us just to get to the floor. From the 14th of March to the 14th of April we hadn't had a single day of rest. Even when it was raining we had to work. We had to work every Saturday and Sunday. We were afraid because the bosses kept threatening us, but we still had to endure all this stuff. We were talking about getting out somehow but we couldn't do it in the middle of the night or even in the morning because they get up really early to start working and could easily find us down the road in the car. When they found us they were sure to kill us. I was thinking about my family—that's why I came here, to send them money. So I said, "One day we're going to have the opportunity."

Around that time a couple of people arrived. One was a Mexican. His name was Lucas Benitez. And the other was an American. Her name was Laura Jamino. They asked us, "How are y'all doing here? What's the situation like here?" And none of us wanted to say because we thought maybe they're spies of the boss. In Mexico you learn from your parents to kind of lay low and assess the situation because otherwise you end up dead. But there was another group who were there before we arrived, and they called out to them that we were getting threats, they're not paying us wages, we don't have papers. They started to open up, saying things like, "I've been here for six months, but they're not even paying me enough for the ride that I have to repay." I didn't say anything to Lucas and Laura because I didn't really trust them, but I did say, "Give me your card." I was the only one who took a card.

A week before Easter it happened. I said, "This is the day we've got to leave. We're working here and we're not earning anything and they keep threatening us." I was really scared because that same day two people had disappeared. I said, "Why don't two of us try to go and two stay behind? Then two can give a shout out to the others if something happens, like Ramos comes." Two of the other guys went to make a phone call to Laura, who decided to try to meet us at a hotel across the street. But the brother of Ramos came in and said, "I don't want any of this shit going on. If I catch any of you motherfuckers messing around I'm going to kick all your asses." We were all scared and thinking about what to do. I said,

"I can't take it this. I've got to go. Now is our time to leave. I can't take this slavery anymore." I was scared and surprised at the same time.

I grabbed some scissors and stuck them in my boot. I thought, if any of them come I'm going to stick those scissors right in his neck and they're going to have to call the police. And that's it. We were all really scared, and then a car pulled up and I saw Lucas in there. I said, "I'm going to get in that car. I'm going to get the hell out of here." I knew I had to jump in that car. I knew that this was my chance to leave. As soon as I jumped in, he drove off in a big circle really fast.

I was afraid, but I knew that in Mexico there's a lot of violence but we still live in a free society there. So if there are rights that we have there then we must have those rights here too. He brought us all the way here to Immokalee. The coalition was the one that freed us. If it wasn't for that, who knows what would've happened? Maybe we would've been killed or left there stranded, away from our families.

Now things are different. I have permission to work, and I'm working eight hours a day but for a boss who pays me. I work eight hours, no more, no less, and it's my own will. I know if I want a day off he's going to give it to me. And I know if I want to work ten hours I can work ten hours, but not because I'm being forced to. My wage is really satisfying, and my son is doing really well. He's getting his medicine, and I send what I can. It's still not a lot, but I send what I can. I'm still afraid for my family. It's been four years since I saw them. America is beautiful, but it's not with my family. It's a scary thing if you come here illegally. If you try to work you could end up in the same situation as a slave. I think the world should know that these things happen.

DOMESTIC SLAVERY IN THE UNITED STATES

In 1999 Roseline Odine reached the turning point where she could be a slave no longer. "That's it. That's it," she said. Shortly afterward, Christina Elangwe decided "it was about time" and escaped too—noting in her narrative that when Roseline "ran she opened the door for all of us." Roseline's narrative features a long escape sequence as she moved through the turning point from slavery to freedom.

Roseline and Christina spent two and a half years and five years, respectively, as domestic slaves in Washington, D.C., held by fellow Cameroonians. Promised American educations and babysitting jobs, they were tricked into leaving their families in Cameroon at the ages of fourteen and seventeen. On arrival in the United States they worked long hours for no money, weren't sent to school, and were beaten and verbally abused. Roseline was sexually harassed. The women also recount a process of indoctrination and mind control. This eventually meant that Roseline "didn't want to talk to the cop because of what she had told me in the house—that America's no good."

After escaping, Roseline met Louis Etongwe, a cousin of the man who drove her to safety. She told him that there were two more Cameroonian slaves in the area, including Christina and a young woman who had spent three years in bondage from the age of fifteen. Louis helped them to escape, then took tapes of all three girls to Cameroon to show their parents and gather evidence against the traffickers. Roseline's captors, Louisa and Kevin, were eventually convicted, sentenced to nine years in prison, and told to pay her $100,000 in restitution. Kevin was also convicted of attempted sexual assault. Christina's captors received five years of probation and were ordered to pay her $180,000 in back wages. So far she has received about $2,000.

Roseline (UNITED STATES, 2005)

I grew up in Cameroon. I always wanted to be a designer. I was in school back then and I always liked to make a little skirt, a little blouse, and do knitting—just trying to create something. I was fourteen years old when I came to this country. I wanted to help my family. I was so close with my family, especially my sisters. We did so many fun things together. When we get off school we did each other's homework. When I came here my sisters didn't want me to go. But I had to do it because I was told that I was coming here to go to school. It was hard leaving them. If I could wish for anything, I would wish to be with my sisters. I've talked to them once in a while, but since I came here I've never seen them.

Unfortunately, when I got here it didn't happen the way it was supposed to. Things changed a little bit...well a lot. I never went to school when I was living with them and I wasn't getting paid. She told me that she would send money back home to my parents, but I've never talked to my parents so I don't know if they sent any money. If you don't know somebody, don't send your kids out to them. Don't just hear that your kid is going to go to school, because they will make that promise but it will never be fulfilled. They won't do it.

I would get up in the morning around 5:30 A.M. and at 6 A.M. make breakfast and get the kids up and have them ready for school. And once they went to school I would stay home and clean and cook and do their

Roseline Odine
(photograph by Peggy
Callahan, Free the
Slaves, 2005)

laundry. When she wasn't home I tried to finish my work so I could relax a little bit. But when she was there I had to make sure that I'm doing something so I wouldn't get yelled at or hit. Even if I had to sweep the floor three times, I just had to do something. It was actually pretty hard, because I had nobody to talk to. I used to take care of two kids and sometimes the sister's kids as well. That's all I used to do.

I had been in the States for a week when I started getting abused—hitting, yelling, cursing. One day I got up around 8 A.M. and she hit me and yelled at me that I can't get up that late; I was supposed to be up before the kids get up and they were already up at 6 A.M. I lived with them for two and a half years and the abuse continued until the day I decided to run away. I couldn't go for a whole week without getting hit. I really didn't know what to do. I was just hoping that one day it would stop. I did everything that she wanted me to do. I tried to make sure that everything was right so I wouldn't get yelled at or beaten up, but everything I was doing wasn't right so I still got beaten by her or her sister. She would use her hand or anything that she had. One day, I was cleaning using Windex and she got upset with somebody outside and started yelling at me. She pulled the Windex away from me and sprayed it on my face. I had real long hair and she said she would cut it off. Her and her sister held me and tied me down and put scissors on my hair. One time, her and her sister were beating me up at the same time and I tried to open the door so that I could run out. She dragged me back and started hitting me.

When I came my bed was in the kitchen. It was actually a couch. And when I was in the kitchen sleeping, the husband, who always liked to go to bed really late at night, 2 A.M. or 3 A.M. sometimes, started approaching me, trying to sleep with me. I was fighting, and he would say: "I'm just trying to make you feel like a woman. I'm not going to get you pregnant." It didn't just stop there; he continuously did that until it got to the point where I started going to bed in double clothing. Whether it was hot or cold I had to put on jeans and sweatshirts and pants in case I fell asleep and he came without me hearing. It was a couple of months before I was sent to the kids' room to sleep. They had a bunk bed so I slept on one of those together with the kids.

One time, one of her friends had a little boy who I babysat, and she gave money to Louisa to give to me but I never got it. At Christmas her friend bought me a Christmas present and a birthday present, because I have my birthday on Christmas Day. It was a set of makeup, and I kept it in the closet and used it just once. I don't know what I did to her one day, but she just got really upset and sent her kids to the closet to pull out those things her friend bought. She messed them up in front of my face and made her kids step on them. When they finished I just picked it all up and put it together. Then I called her friend and let her know what had just happened. She said that it was OK and that she couldn't do much about it because she didn't want to get involved.

I never went to the doctor when I was with them. One time I was really, really sick. I had a terrible back pain and couldn't even walk. I couldn't breathe properly. I was sweeping the living room and I just fell down and started crying. I couldn't stand up any more. I said, "I can't breathe, I can't breathe," and they had to rush me to the Holy Cross emergency room. They did an X-ray. I never knew what actually happened to me, they didn't give me the results. I was just taking pills. The same illness came back again while I was at her sister's place where Christina used to live. We were all together with the kids because sometimes they went there for weekends. I was crying, rolling on the ground, and she said I was a "witch" and she was going to send me back to my parents so I wouldn't die in her house. Christina had a cloth and I put it in hot water and put pressure on. So that day they didn't take me to the hospital.

I didn't have phone contact with my parents, but I wrote letters to them. There was a point when she was hitting me and said my dad had written to her to let her know that any time I did something wrong, she could hit me. She said he gave her the right to hit me any time. I wrote a letter about this to my parents, asking if is was true, and they replied that it was a lie. When I was still living with her my mom had a stroke. She said she was going to buy a wheelchair and send it to my mom, but she was lying. She never did. I know.

I think I was a slave. Because if I sit back sometimes and think about it and have a flashback, it was terrible. There were several nights and days and nights that I would sit all by myself and think about things I could do with my sisters. How we used to play together. I would cry because I missed them, hoping that one day I would get to see them again. Everything, my dreams, just crushed down and I wasn't going to get it. I wasn't going to reach it.

I never thought of running away until when we moved down to Post Gate Terrace. That's when running away started coming into my head. But I never knew how to do it because I knew nobody. I didn't know where to go. She told me that America is not a place to walk around on your own. Whatever opportunity we had, Christina and I got together and talked about running. But we didn't know where to go and how to do it.

One day I had taken their daughter to school earlier in the morning, and the little boy had to go in the middle of the day, around 11:45 A.M. When I went to drop him off at the bus stop I met a friend who used to live in the next building and we talked. Then I went back to the house and changed clothes. I knew I was going to be doing house chores so I put on a short skirt and a little T-shirt. I went inside and grabbed the trash and I was heading to the trash can, and I met the guy I was talking to at the bus stop. I asked him what he was doing, and he said he was cleaning his car.

While I was talking to him, she was driving right behind me. When she saw me she started shaking her head. She parked and started cursing at me. She called me a prostitute, a whore, said all I wanted to do was to have sex, that I'm planning to have sex with that guy, that before I become pregnant she was going to pack my things and send me back to my parents. She called me all the nasty names you can think of. I just walked inside the apartment and she fell on me, still calling me names and cursing me. I kept on doing what I was doing, and she kept on yelling.

For some reason I wasn't thinking anymore—it was like my blood pressure was rising, my head was pumping inside. I had no shoes on, no jacket. I didn't think of anything, I just opened the door and ran out. I had a blackout and fell down and hit my head on somebody else's door. I can remember somebody asking me if I was OK. I told them I was fine, and he asked, "Do you need help? Do you want me to help you?" I said I was fine, that I didn't need help, and he went back inside and locked his door. I laid there for a couple of minutes and I didn't know where I was going. I ran upstairs to the building's hallway and sat in the window, looking down and thinking about what to do next. I kept telling myself, "That's it. That's it. I'm not going back in there. I'm not going back. That's it. I have nowhere to go, but one thing's for sure, I'm not going back."

I sat up there from noon to 3 P.M. When the kids got back from school, she realized that they had walked home by themselves. That's when she came out looking for me. I remembered one of her friends, and I ran up the hill to her house. Her back door was open, so I went right through. I was crying and I told her, "I don't want to go back there. Please don't take me back to her. I don't want to go back to her place." She said it was OK, and that I should stop crying. She asked me what happened. I didn't tell her. I just cried.

Louisa came and told me to go back home. I ran out of the front door and she followed me. So I went upstairs in her friend's building and hid on the fourth floor. I locked the door and prayed that she wouldn't come in there. I don't know what I would have done if she had. She came upstairs. I could hear her climbing the stairs, looking for me. She didn't find me and went back down. I left, and when she saw me run out, she started chasing me. We were running around the building and the neighborhood until I lost her somewhere round the front.

I told myself, "I guess this is it. I guess I have to go." But I didn't know where I was going. Her friend saw me and she called to me, "We should go inside and talk about this. We shouldn't get the cops involved." So I went into her place. She sent me to get her a pen and then she picked up the phone, called Louisa, and told her that I was there. When I heard that I dropped the pen and went straight out the front door.

I went up to the townhouses where we used to live before we moved, and I was just crying and walking around. I saw this lady and I stopped her to beg for shoes, because I didn't have any on and it was really cold.

She asked what size shoes I wore, and I said seven and a half. She wore size nine, but I said, "It doesn't really matter. Whatever you have I will take." She said: "Stay right here, I'm going to get you some shoes." But I followed her and she went home and down to her basement. I sat down on the stairs waiting for her and she got a pair of flip flops and gave them to me. I thanked her and ran out.

I saw a cop coming and I acted like everything was OK, like I'm a totally normal person, because I was afraid. I didn't want him to take me back to where I just left. Of course, I knew that she had called the cops and they were looking for me. I also didn't want to talk to the cop because of what she had told me in the house—that America's no good. She told me that the cops are not friendly. When he had driven by I ran down to the big K-Mart and walked around there doing nothing.

Around 5 P.M. I saw a cop in front of K-Mart asking questions and I ran to the ladies' room and sat there waiting for him to leave. I remembered that her husband's friend had given me his number a long time ago. He said if I had any problems I could always call him and he'd be willing to help me. I had his number in my head, but I didn't have any change to call, so I begged thirty-five cents. I made a phone call to his work, and they told me that he had gone out of town but would back that same day. I called again around 8:30 P.M. and they passed me to him. I was really afraid and was crying and begging him, "Please come and get me; I've run away from home." He laughed, thinking that I was joking, but I was crying, and he said, "Oh my God, are you serious?" He said he couldn't leave work right now, but that if I could wait for him he would pick me up at 11:30 P.M.

K-Mart closed and everybody had to leave. I had no jacket, just flip flops and a little short skirt. This was in November. I stood outside and I told myself, "I really give up. I don't care what happens with my life. I've tried my best, running away, and now I won't do it again." I sat down somewhere dark and put my hands inside the T-shirt because I was really cold.

A man came and told me, "You can't sit there. You could get raped. Go and stand in front of the light where somebody can see you." I said, "I'm really sorry, I'm fine right here. I don't really care right now." He left. At that point I wasn't thinking about being alive at all. I didn't care what happened to me. I had fought enough and I had given up. All I was thinking was that I was really sorry for my parents to lose a daughter.

Then a woman came and talked to me. I said, "I can't leave this place. I really want to be here." She said, "OK, if you're not leaving this place, I'm going to sit with you. Why don't you come with me and get in my car, and get in my car and stay warm? We're going to wait for whoever you're waiting for." She asked who it was, and I lied to her and said I was waiting for my daddy. I said I couldn't sit in her car because I didn't know her. I didn't trust nobody at that point. She said, "OK, I'm going to get in my car and you're going to sit here, and I'm going to wait until your dad comes. And when your dad comes, then I'm going to leave." So she sat and waited until 11:30 P.M. The guy came and picked me up and I thanked her. She drove away and the guy took me to his place. He turned on the heat to keep me warm and started making some phone calls to see who could help me out, because he couldn't keep me.

I was living with Louis's cousin then. I didn't want anybody to know where I was. I didn't want to get involved with anybody. I just wanted to stay somewhere with nobody disturbing me. When it was Thanksgiving time and they were taking pictures, all I was doing was hiding, trying to stay away from the cameras and the videos, in case somebody looked at those pictures and said, "Oh, I know that girl; she used to live here." I was trying to hide away and I was dragging Louis's attention. That's how he started asking questions about me.

I really appreciate what Louis did for us. It took a lot of guts and a lot of courage for somebody like him to do what he did. People are afraid to do such a thing because that's how we Africans are—trying so much to not have our names out there. He really took a risk. Hopefully, somebody out there will do the same thing that he did for somebody else.

Louisa and Kevin had a trial and they pleaded guilty and got nine years in jail. Whatever punishment they gave them actually won't do me any good. It's not taking away what they did to me. What they did to me, that's part of me. It's going to stay in me, so why don't they stay in jail for thirty years? It really doesn't take away my pain. I don't look at it like, "Oh my God, they're in jail, I'm OK now." No, I'm still not OK. The clock can't turn back, it can't change, it can't rewind. Whatever damage it did to me is something that will stay with me for the rest of my life. Even if I say something to them it won't change what they did to me. Even if they have to say "Sorry," it still won't heal the pain that they did to me. I will take it to my grave with me. I can't forget even if I get married tomorrow and have my own kids. I can never forget, because that's actually the whole part of me, that's my whole life. I didn't get to spend my teenage life like other teenage kids did, so mine was a total waste.

I can't sleep; it's really scary. I couldn't sleep even when I ran away. I had a room on my own yet it was very difficult. I couldn't trust nobody. I could go to bed, but I won't be comfortable, even though they tell me a hundred times, "You're safe here, nobody will touch you here, nobody will do anything to you here." It's going to take a very long time for me to trust anybody. To be comfortable on my own, it took me a long time.

I haven't seen my mom and dad ever since I came to the States, and both of them passed away in 2002. My dad passed away on February 9 and my Mom on Thanksgiving Day. They didn't really know the things that happened to me, because I never got that chance to tell them. I'm scared because back home we don't have lawyers like they have here. You can take somebody's life away and get away with it. Over here you can get away with it for a couple of months, but not forever. They will get you regardless. I'm actually really afraid for my sisters. I don't want anything to happen to them while I'm here and they're over there, because I'm going to be alone without seeing them again. I don't think I would want to live a life like that with no family.

I want to get my education finished and hopefully one day with God's help I will get to see my sisters again. I hope to get married and have my own kids. I want to be a registered nurse, and right now I'm working as a geriatric nursing assistant. I think it's good, after all, that everything happened. It actually made me strong so I can face anything that comes to me—anything. No matter how big or how small it is, I think I can handle it. I don't think anything can make me fear anymore.

If there's anybody in a similar or the same situation as I was, get out. If you know of any opportunity, use it. Don't think and don't wait, because that is the mistake I made. I waited too long. If you know you can do it, just get out. There are so many things you can do with your life than sitting in one spot and being abused all day. Find help—people will help you out there.

Christina (UNITED STATES, 2005)

My name is Christina Elangwe. I was born in a village in Cameroon, Southwest Province. I have four older sisters and three brothers. I grew up. I went to elementary school. I finished elementary school. My dream was to go to high school, and my parents didn't have enough money to send me to high school right away. I didn't want to wait for the whole semester, and an opportunity came. An old lady from another city came to the village looking for somebody to come live with her. She was going to put me in school, so I accepted and went to a city to live with her. But I didn't go to school right away, though I was there for maybe a year. Then the old lady told me that they would like me to go the United States to

Christina Elangwe
(photograph by Peggy
Callahan, Free the
Slaves, 2005)

take care of kids. I said OK, and they sent me back to the village to inform
my parents. At first my dad refused—he said it was too far away. But we
convinced him. I said, "This is my dream—America."

I always dreamed of this and watched movies back home. America was
like heaven. Sometimes I would sit and talk to myself about how I would
like to go to America, because back home it was like America was like gold
and silver. I wanted to go there to further my education, so when the opportunity came I thought, "OK this is it."

The agreement was that as soon as I came here I would start school.
I came in the month of February, and they told me that the semester would
soon be over and that next semester I was going to start school. The agreement was that I'm going to babysit and while I'm babysitting continue my
education and go to school. That whole year passed and they didn't send
me to school. They only sent me for two days a week to the GED [general
equivalency diploma] class, and it was free too. The following year came

and I asked them. They said they were still thinking about it and they're going to send me. I should wait.

Days go by, years go by. You start figuring that these people are not going to do anything. Maybe their kids will grow up and go to college before they even start thinking about it. Or maybe they will never think of doing anything. When I asked her one time, the lady told me that just bringing me into America is more than good enough—they don't have to do anything with me. Just to come here I should feel lucky—there are other people dying to come here and they can't. I should be happy that I'm here.

It was seven days a week. I did everything from five in the morning until maybe midnight or 1 A.M. I had to get up, get the kids ready, give them showers, make their breakfast, keep on doing household jobs like cleaning, cooking, everybody's laundry, ironing, and when the kids came back from school I gave them lunch. Sometimes when there was an occasion coming up I would stay up until 4 A.M. or 5 A.M. to braid their kids' hair. Sometimes I felt sorry for myself—sad. Just hoping one day everything is going to be OK, or one day it's going to be over.

Nobody was allowed to call me and I wasn't allowed to call anybody. The five years I was with them I never talked to my parents. They would tell me that they're trying to get hold of my parents, but they were lying. They always talked to their own parents, but when it was time for me to talk with my parents, the line didn't go through. I never received any letters. I wrote letters and I don't know whether my parents received them or not. I never wrote letters when they're around, but when the kids were in school and I was home cleaning, things were going through my mind.

They never paid me anything while I was there. When I asked them, they said they didn't have to. I asked them for something after I was there for about three or four years, and they told me they were not paying me but they were paying my parents. I knew they were lying to me, but I never talked to my parents while I was there. I think they were just telling me that so that I would feel better. I was thinking about getting out, but there was no way. I didn't know anybody, but I was just praying for one day to come when I could be free. I never knew when the day would be. I was just hoping and praying, and I was mad. I should have just stayed back home. I should have listened to my dad. I should have continued my education back home.

I talked to Roseline on the phone and cried and tried to figure out what to do. But there was no means. If we leave, where are we going to go? We didn't know anybody, so just had to stay there. Until one day she couldn't take it in there anymore, she had to run away. When she ran she opened the door for all of us. She took a big step.

After she ran away, she and Mr. Louis Etongwe contacted me. Roseline told me that I have to get out of there, and that there was somebody who is going to help us to be free. At first I didn't know. It took me a while to trust Mr. Louis Etongwe. I talked to him and I thought, I have to do it. I have to do something for myself and my family. It took me a month or two for me to make the decision to leave though.

I'm sure around that time, when Roseline went, they knew that I knew something about it, because they were asking me where she was and whether she would contact me or not. I said, no, I won't hear from her. Their eyes went wide open; they were thinking maybe I'll be the next person. So they had tape recorders around the house, just in case anybody called me. They told me even if I wanted to run away I shouldn't do it the way Roseline did.

I finally realized that there was no hope if I continued living with this family. So I'd better do something. It was about time. I'd already given them five years of my life, now it was my turn. I had to do something for myself. So I told Mr. Louis that I was ready. When the employer dropped me off where I used to take the GED classes, I asked a few people for change to catch the bus and they gave it to me. I asked how to get to Silver Springs metro station. They told me, and I took the bus and went there. Mr. Louis Etongwe came and picked me up.

He's a very nice man. He's the one who helped us get out of this situation. He really helped us after we left. I wouldn't have left otherwise, and I actually lived in his house until I was able to take care of myself. I'm very grateful for that too. When I didn't trust him it was because I didn't know him. The only people I knew were my employers and their sisters and friends. And they were treating me like ruined stock, saying, "America is a bad place," "You can go out there and get killed," "You can't make it in America."

Afterwards, I used to think a lot about the kids, especially the youngest one. I was really, really close with her. But then I thought, they have their parents and I'm here by myself. I'd helped them enough already and I have to think about myself now. My parents heard about it because Mr. Louis Etongwe took a tape back home and put it on for them to watch. They were really, really sad and said, "They should send my child back home."

I consider myself a slave because I worked for so many hours without getting paid and without going to school. And I couldn't leave. I feel like they stole my life from me. We didn't know anything like this happened.

Roseline Odine and
Christina Elangwe
(photograph by Peggy
Callahan, Free the
Slaves, 2005)

It's like we were brainwashed so we didn't know the laws, we didn't know
the rules. All we knew was what they were telling us. And we believed all
that they were saying. We were blind then. Anybody in my situation
shouldn't take that long to get help. There's help out there. They shouldn't
believe it when their employers are telling them it's scary out there. There
are good people out there. They should reach for help immediately if
they're not getting what they were promised. And no matter what, you
shouldn't send your child away, especially with strangers.

The people were found guilty. They pleaded guilty and they did some
community service. They were asked to pay me some money for the years
that I worked for them. They are paying bit by bit, but not that much.
Right now I'm just trying to keep away from them. I just want to live my
life. I don't want to even see them. But if it happens, I would say, look at
me now—here, look at me now.

I work as an agent's assistant. I'm proud of myself now because now I have a job. I have a roof over my head. I have a car. I can do whatever I want. I'm building a house for my parents and I paid my siblings' school tuition. My mom is always sick so I pay her medical fees—send her to a bigger hospital so she can get more tests. What I dream now is to be a registered nurse. I love helping people. With the help of God I'm going to do it and I'll be a registered nurse. Everything is possible. I'm trying to work hard, save some money, go to school. I'm going to do it. I have to do it.

HEREDITARY SLAVERY IN NIGER AND MALI

Tamada was born into slavery in Niger, home to some forty-three thousand hereditary slaves. Found among four of the country's eight ethnic groups, slavery is a centuries-old practice in Niger. Slaves are controlled through violence and indoctrination, and are separated from their parents at a young age. Women and girls perform domestic duties, men tend herds of cattle and goats, and children are often passed from one owner to another. Individuals are also born into slavery in Mauritania, Mali, and Chad.

Slavery was outlawed in Niger in 1960, when the country claimed independence from France, but this remained a theoretical ban. In May 2003 slavery was made punishable by up to thirty years in prison, and that same year Tamada learned that her mother and grandmother had escaped from their master. She decided to do the same. But her turning point took several months; she waited, worried, and thought about running away before seizing her children one evening and beginning her escape. Leaving Mali where her master has moved her, she crossed the border back into Niger with her two children—the first born when Tamada was twelve years old. She was assisted by Timidria—which means fraternity/solidarity in Tamacheq—a human rights organization founded in 1991 to end slavery in Niger.

Tamada concludes with an acknowledgement that life after bondage remains hard. And the 2003 law seems to have made little difference for other slaves. In September 2004, the Tuareg chief Arissal Ag Amdague made a written promise that he would release seven thousand slaves owned by his people. Claiming that his religious beliefs as a Muslim were incompatible with slaveholding, he said he wanted to release the slaves he had inherited. The date was set for this first ever release of slaves in Niger: March 5, 2005, at a ceremony in the village of Inatés, near the border with Mali. But no mass emancipation took place. Instead, on March 5, just a month after Tamada had narrated her story, Amdague stood before the crowd and denied that he owned any slaves.

Tamada (NIGER/MALI, 2005)

My name is Tamada. I don't know my age, but I think I am about twenty years old. The situation of a slave is more than I can say. With all the violence, I lived every day in fear. I was born into slavery, like my mother and grandmother. I was separated from my mother when I was very little. My master took me with him from Niger to Mali and gave me to his eldest son.

I worked every day since I can first remember. I was always moving: pounding millet, washing, cooking. I worked from dawn till late after dark, collecting firewood and fetching water. I was also made to clear up my master's feces. When I was small I looked after the camels, and if they wandered off I would be beaten. As I got older I began to look after my mistress's children, and then I had to do all the household chores.

Tamada (photograph by Romana Cacchioli, Anti-Slavery International, 2005)

I only saw my mother sometimes. When my master's father came with his family, then they would join our encampment.

My master and mistress often insulted and spat at me. I was scared because if I didn't do what they said they would hit me. There was so much violence, verbal insults, spitting. My master used to beat me often. I was so afraid of him.

I heard from other slaves that my mother and grandmother had escaped, and then things got bad for me, as my mistress wouldn't let me out of her sight. But I started thinking about running away. It was hard. I cried a lot. I kept thinking of my mother. I didn't know where to go and kept thinking of the danger. I have two small children and I was very scared. One evening a few months later I grabbed my children and when no one was looking I ran. I carried my children and walked and walked, very far, over thirty kilometers. I walked from encampment to encampment begging for food and shelter, and when I got near Inatés on the border with Niger some people told me about Timidria. I remember being so scared; I thought my master would come after me.

Thanks be to God, some good people took me to the Timidria people. They helped me so much; they helped me find my mother. I cannot find the words to say how life is better, now that I live in Ayorou with my mother and grandmother. I am happy now that I have my own family, and I no longer live in fear; but life is hard, we have very little, sometimes not even enough to eat.

DOMESTIC SLAVERY IN LEBANON

After several months in slavery, Beatrice Fernando reached the point of no return. Standing on a fourth-floor balcony in Beirut, she realized there was "no other way to get home" but to "dive backwards." In a recent interview she explained of her decision to step off the balcony: "When we take a step against slavery, the world will take another step."

In 1980, at the age of twenty-three, Beatrice had responded to an advertisement for work as a housemaid in Lebanon. She left her home country of Sri Lanka, intending to send money to her parents and her three-year-old son. But in Beirut she became a domestic slave. She was locked inside a home, starved, beaten, never paid, and forbidden from communicating with the outside world. Guards were instructed to shoot her if she tried to leave. After she reached a turning point and escaped by jumping from the apartment's fourth floor, she spent twenty-one days in a coma. Doctors told her that she was paralyzed. After fourteen months in the hospital she recovered from the paralysis and returned to Sri Lanka. In 1989 she came to live and work in the United States.

Thousands of Sri Lankan women—as well as women from Malaysia, Indonesia, the Philippines, Somalia, and Ethiopia—have been trafficked to Lebanon for domestic servitude in private households. They often enter Lebanon legally but then find themselves caught in involuntary servitude. In addition, thousands of Ethiopian girls are trafficked to Lebanon each year for sexual exploitation. Sri Lankan women are also trafficked to Saudi Arabia, Kuwait, the United Arab Emirates, Bahrain, and Qatar for the purposes of coerced labor and sexual exploitation; and as many as twelve thousand Sri Lankan children are trafficked into sex slavery each year.

Beatrice uses the present tense in her narrative. This expresses her static, timeless existence in slavery, when chores seemed "unending" and the "daily routine" was unchanging; it also insists that slavery continues for others—like another woman who "was so desperate that she jumped off a fourth-floor balcony." What is past for Beatrice is still present for others. "Two decades after I had to dive off a balcony to save my life, women are still facing the same agonizing situation," she concludes.

Beatrice (LEBANON, 2005)

Thank you for the opportunity to testify before you on the problem of slavery. I cannot believe that I am here, speaking to political leaders of the most powerful country in the world. If I close my eyes, the memories of pain take me back to a time when I felt all alone. It happened two decades ago, but it feels as if it were happening right now.

I am at the airport in Colombo, Sri Lanka, saying good-bye to my three-year-old son. With his eyes filed with tears, he asks, "Can't I come with you, Mom? When you make a lot of money will you buy me a car to play with?" I take him in my arms, my heart breaking, and tell him, "If I have the money, I will buy you the world." My desperation to give him a better life has driven me to leave him with my parents, to go to Lebanon and be a maid.

At the job agent's office in Beirut, my passport is taken away. The agency staff makes me stand in line with a group of women in the same predicament as me. Lebanese men and women pace in front of us, examining our bodies as if we were vacuum cleaners. I am sold to a wealthy woman, who takes me home to her mansion up on the fourth floor of a condo building.

My chores seem unending. I wash the windows, walls, and bathrooms. I shampoo carpets, polish floors, and clean furniture. After twenty hours I am still not done. There's no food on my plate for dinner, so I scavenge through the trash. I try to call the job agency, but the woman who now owns me has locked the telephone. I try to flee the apartment, but she has locked the door.

I can feel the burning on my cheeks as she slaps me. It is night and her kids have gone to sleep. Grasping me by the hair, she bangs my head into the wall and throws me to the floor. She kicks me and hits me with a broom. If I scream or fight back, she will kill me. So I bite my lips to bear the pain and then I pass out. This is my daily routine, the life of a slave.

But now I am standing on the balcony of her condo, four floors up. I am holding on to the railing, staring down at the ground far below. I feel my heart rising. I miss my family, and I know my son is waiting for me. There is no other way to get home. I grasp the railing, close my eyes, and ask God for his forgiveness if I die now. This is no suicide attempt. I am desperate for freedom, not death. With the tiny hope that I might survive, I let go of the railing. I dive backwards into the night air. And I scream.

Dear leaders of Congress, how did a nice Sri Lankan girl like me end up jumping off a balcony in Lebanon? How did I end up in slavery? Could this have been prevented? And how did I survive the leap? . . . Let me make a few observations about the problem of human trafficking from the point of view of someone who experienced it.

1. We need more public awareness campaigns about the dangers of trafficking. I got swept up in human trafficking because I did not understand the risks. I needed to make money, and like many people from South Asia and Southeast Asia, I pursued work in the Middle East. I didn't know my passport would get taken away, and I didn't know that I wouldn't get paid.

We can reduce the power of traffickers by educating at-risk populations. People don't know what can happen to them and can easily be tricked. So here is my suggestion: We need to make sure there are public service announcements and public education campaigns, not just in the United States but around the world. For example, I am ready today to record a message for Sri Lankans, in Singhalese, telling them about what happened to me and warning them to be aware.

2. We need to monitor—and make sure other governments are monitoring—the job agencies that send so many people to work in the Middle East. In my case, there was an office in Sri Lanka and an office in Lebanon. The directors of these offices are both responsible for what happened to me. They did nothing to help me, and they never paid me. These agencies are sending thousands of people to work overseas. In fact,

the population of Kuwait is two-thirds foreign workers. The percent of foreign workers in the United Arab Emirates is even higher. People like me are actually the majority, even though we have no guaranteed rights.

The waves of workers arriving in these countries come through job agencies, but the agencies are not being watched closely enough. One idea is to insist that agencies have registration programs, so relatives of workers can always track them down. My parents back in Sri Lanka were worried sick about me and couldn't understand why I wasn't answering their letters. But they had no way to reach me. We need accountability, and we should pressure governments around the world to monitor job agencies more closely. And job agencies should be made liable if employees' rights are violated by the contracted employers.

3. We need to give survivors of slavery a platform to speak out and help other survivors recover. After I jumped off the balcony, I blacked out. I woke up later in the hospital, paralyzed. Eventually, I got a flight home to Sri Lanka. I didn't speak much about what had happened to me. I was ashamed, and I quietly prayed to God for strength. Only a few years ago, I began to feel I was ready to discuss what had happened to me.

We need to remove the shame from slavery. To do that, survivors need to talk openly about their experience in order to help victims of trafficking recover. Our message is that there is no reason to be ashamed, even though you will at first feel ashamed. Our message is that you have to believe in yourself and hold on to your faith, even if people will treat you like an animal. There is a spiritual and psychological side to the recovery process that should not be neglected.

4. We need to have even tougher monitoring of foreign countries. Every year, the State Department's annual report on trafficking should list the amount of money each country spends on antitrafficking efforts. We need to evaluate if funding matches performance. The report should also document the repression of antislavery groups. For instance, in Mauritania the government still bans the abolitionist group SOS Slaves [SOS Esclaves]. The United States should do more to support antislavery activists in repressive countries where the government doesn't allow free discussion on the issue of slavery. And the United States should fund a commission of government officials and NGO activists to ensure the liberation of all slaves in Sudan.

Dear congressional leaders, I speak before you on behalf of the millions of slaves who could not be here even if you invited them. Just a few weeks ago I read about an Indonesian maid enslaved in Bahrain who, like me, was so desperate that she jumped off a fourth-floor balcony. It pains me to think that two decades after I had to dive off a balcony to save my life, women are still facing the same agonizing situation.

We can be doing much more to help these women—and children and men. We need to educate them about the dangers of slavery before they get caught up. We need to monitor the job agencies that ensnare them. We need to help them overcome their shame after they escape. And we need to hold accountable the repressive governments that are part of the problem rather than part of the solution.

DOMESTIC AND SEX SLAVERY IN THE UNITED STATES

Maria Suarez marks the turning point in her decades-long journey from slavery to freedom as the moment when a bird knocked at her window. She had no idea she about to be freed, but when the bird came she knew that she "was going to have some good news." She waited, and minutes later officials told her she was going to be free.

At the age of fifteen, in 1976, Maria immigrated legally to the United States from Michoacán, Mexico, with her father. She was soon approached on the street in Los Angeles by a woman offering work as a house cleaner. The woman then sold her to sixty-eight-year-old Anselmo Covarrubias for $200, and Covarrubias made her his domestic slave. For five years he held her in bondage in his house in the Los Angeles suburb of Azusa, raped and beat her, and threatened her with black arts wizardry. Maria believed that he read her mind, possessed her soul, and would hurt her family if she told anyone about the abuse.

In August 1981, Covarrubias was bludgeoned to death with a table leg by Pedro Soto, who was renting a converted garage on the property. Maria washed the weapon and hid it under the house, as directed by Soto. She was arrested, along with Soto and his wife. Soto was convicted of first-degree murder, and his wife was convicted of soliciting murder and being an accessory to a felony. Maria was convicted of conspiracy to commit murder, sentenced to twenty-five years to life, and incarcerated at the California Institution for Women in Corona. Officials eventually confirmed that she suffered from battered woman's syndrome—allowed as a legal defense in California after 1992—and she was paroled in 2003, after five years in slavery, and twenty-two years and six months in prison.

But Maria still wasn't free. According to federal law, noncitizens convicted of violent crimes must be deported on their release from prison, and she was taken directly to a federal detention facility. She spent more than five months fighting deportation, then was certified as a trafficking victim eligible for a T visa—a new status for victims of slavery and trafficking in the United States. She was freed in May 2004.

Maria (UNITED STATES, 2005)

I grew up in a village of between five hundred and seven hundred people. Most of the people there were family: cousins, my grandpa, my uncles. Everybody was family. It was a very, very nice life for me, growing up with my parents on the farm with my brothers and sisters. When I was a little girl I saw my parents working hard, and my dream was to one day become somebody, have money, and give them the best in life—treat them like a king and queen. I always wanted to take care of my parents. That was my dream.

I was fifteen, I was going to be sixteen, and my father came to this country. He came to get his residential card, and I came with him. And he left. I stayed here. It wasn't my plan to stay here; I thought I was going to go back with my father. But he left after two weeks and I stayed here with my sister. A month later I got a job offer from this woman I didn't know. She offered me a cleaning job, and coming from my country, it was like, wow! I'm going to get a job! I believed her. I thought it was real. But

Maria Suarez (photograph by Peggy Callahan, Free the Slaves, 2005)

it wasn't a job. It was just a trick, a trap that I fell into. I didn't even ask how much they were going to pay or anything. She told me not to tell my family and that she was coming very soon. It sounded good because I was going to surprise them with the job.

She didn't show up for another week or so. I forgot about it. But then she came and asked me if I still wanted a job, and I said, "Yes. I want the job." She told me to go and meet the people. My sister was working; I was at the house by myself, and my brother-in-law was at work. I was going to go and tell him that I was going to go to this place, but she told me not to do anything—told me, "Just let's go. We're coming back very soon." She took me to the place, and it felt like it took forever. I didn't know the area—I just knew how to get to my niece's school and to the store. She took me all the way to Azusa. I was living in Sierra Madre, so it was a long drive.

When we got there, I met this old man. Probably he was sixty-five or seventy, I don't know. When I met him, he had a big smile. She introduced me to him. It was kind of nice, but at the same time, it was creepy—like, you don't want to be there. But I didn't follow my instinct. I didn't. And I should have. It didn't feel right for me to be there.

They told me to sit on the couch, and I sat down. They went away and talked—I don't know what they talked about. They came back and I told them, "I want to go back to my house." He told me not to go but to stay there and start working. I didn't want to stay there. He kept telling me, "You stay here, you'll meet my wife. And then I'll take you to your house tomorrow." I didn't want to, but between the two of them they convinced me.

They told me to call my sister, but the funny thing was the phone had a lock. He removed it from the phone, and he let me call my sister. When I called my sister, she didn't want me to stay there. She goes, "No, you're coming home." I explained to her that it was an old couple, and she asked me for address, the phone number, the names. She kept telling me to come home. I said, "I'm coming tomorrow." That tomorrow never came, never came until a year ago. A year ago I came home.

The third day in the house he told me that he had bought me, that I was his slave, that he paid $200 for me, that I was there to do whatever he wanted to do to me. I didn't have a mind of my own. I was controlled by his witchcraft. He told me he was a witch. I was afraid of him. I was terrorized by him. He beat me, raped me; every day he abused me mentally, physically, emotionally, spiritually. I was not in touch with my family because I was afraid of saying something to them that he disliked, or making him think that I was going to escape. I lived in fear. When I fell asleep because I was so tired, I'd get woken up by him putting things on my face, and telling me, "You have the curse and you cannot leave this house."

My family reported him to the police, and the police came to the house. I opened the door, because he told me to. The policeman sat on the couch asking me if I'm OK, asking me in front of this man, and how can I say "No I'm not"? I was so afraid of him, because he had threatened to kill my family. And he threatened to kill me. Every time that I did something that he disliked or I didn't want to have anything to do with him, he told me that he was going to kill me. I can actually tell you that I'm a miracle because so many times I was close to dying.

Once in a while I thought, how can I get out of here? But then I changed. I was afraid to think that. He told me that he knew what I thought. He had me believe that he saw everything in his crystal ball. So I believed him. My family suspected that I was not in the right place, that I didn't want to be there, and they did send the police, but I was afraid that he was going to kill my family so I told the police that I was fine. I was afraid. I couldn't allow him to do something to my family.

By then I hadn't seen anything. I didn't know nothing. I was just a teenager, sixteen. I wanted to be with my family the way I was before, and my dreams were crushed, crushed. They never let me bloom, like a rose. They never let the rose grow up to be a rose. That's how I felt.

Ya know, faith is the last string in my life. I can be almost at the edge of falling down, and my faith is going to keep on going. I always dreamed. I dreamed that I was in a tunnel and the little dot of light was freedom to me. Every time that I had that dream, I knew that was my freedom. But I had no way out. I just used to pray a lot. I thought God had forgotten me. I asked him why. I asked him give me a sign, to show me something that I can see, feel, touch. To give me a sign that I'm going to be OK and that my family's going to be OK if I leave this house. I remember spending nights crying and praying on my knees. And I did lose faith in God. I felt like he forgot me, because I was begging for him to show me a sign. I used to ask God, "Why did you forget about me? I'm your child." I kept on like that, day after day, day after day.

After I reached eighteen, he sent me to work in the factory and I brought my check back. A lot of times I wanted to die, just die. That was my only way out. I didn't want to provoke my own death, but I wanted to die. I was just living one more day. Either he was going to kill me or I was going to die.

The way I ended up in prison was that he had another place in back of his house. He rented to a young couple and tried to pursue the wife. He was trying to do witchcraft on them, and one day the young guy killed him. I heard the noise and I came out. The victim was on the ground. The only thing I remember is that he told me to grab the stick and put it under the house. I did that. He put it in my hand and I did it. I put the stick under the house. I didn't know anything else but to follow commands. I don't even know if I called my family or how my family got there, but my sister came and took me with her.

I was like a zombie. I didn't talk. I didn't want to eat. I couldn't sleep, and I was very fearful, thinking that he was coming to get me. I was arrested and I felt that he was going to come and get me. I spent one year fighting my case, but I didn't know what was going on. I didn't understand the law terms. I didn't speak English. I didn't understand what they were saying. My family didn't know anything about laws or attorneys either, so they got ripped off. The attorney who represented me was already disbarred and he was using someone else's bar number to fight my case. He promised my family that I was going to be free by Christmas. I never got free. I was sentenced to twenty-five years to life.

They felt that they needed to blame someone in order for them to be safe. They said whatever they wanted to say. When the parole members used to come they wanted me to say that I was guilty. And I was not going to say anything like that because they asked me to put my hand on the Bible and told me to swear that I was going to tell them the truth. It was not the truth that they wanted to hear from me.

They did an investigation on my case and they found out that I hadn't done it. They went in and interviewed people at my job and asked them if they knew me, how I looked, how I was. They found out that I'd been telling them the truth. I just wanted somebody to listen. To believe in me. And to know that I had been telling the truth—just a little bit of justice. I wanted to get out of there. I felt that I had done more than enough time. I just wanted a chance. I wasn't going to go crazy outside, I was going to be a normal person. I thought I could be an asset to society.

I did a lot of things while I was in prison. I figured, I'm not going to be here one year or two, I'm going to be here longer. I chose to use my time productively and to be a better person. I was going to be a decent human being. And I had a family who every time that I did something good they were very happy. That was my payback. To see how happy they used to get when I got my GED, when they heard me speaking English, when I used to write them in English, even though it was hard for them to understand.

I was going to show them that I was doing something. Professors used to come in there and teach us. So I took classes. I learned a lot of trades. I learned computing, the basics. I learned how to work with people. I got involved in HIV education because people need to be aware of certain things and not put down people with that disease. They need love; they need help; they need care. Not to be put in the corner and forgotten. They are also human beings. And we don't know—I could be the next to have AIDS. We never know. I feel a lot of compassion for people who are ill and elderly people. I work with doctors, with people who are mentally distraught, and I get so much joy from doing that.

I have a lot of people around me who have been supporting me in different ways. They don't know me, they just hear about me, but they believe in me. Their support means a lot to me. I will keep that forever. I'm sitting here today because of all those people. I owe my freedom to them all.

The day they told me that I was going to be free, a bird came and told me at the window. I was very sad that day and the bird came. With his little beak, he knocked on the window and I knew I was going to have some good news. And I told the person that was in with me, "I'm going to have some good news today." I didn't know anything. The bird came and confirmed it. He came and knocked the window again with his beak. I put my plate at the table to eat and they knocked at the window and told me.

NIGERIAN SEX TRAFFICKING

An orphan who was tricked into leaving her village in northern Nigeria in 1998, Joy Ubi-Ubi describes the turning point from freedom to slavery as the moment when she drank blood during a voodoo ritual. Afterward, once Joy was in Europe, her captors said this ritual meant the "juju" would kill her if she tried to escape. As Joy explains, she was thereby "forced to do the work" of a prostitute. She was enslaved for three years in the deprived Bijlmer district of Amsterdam—home to many West African immigrants. But her narrative also includes a parallel turning point from slavery to freedom—the moment when she was asked to drink something again, a liquid that would make *her* bleed and miscarry. This time, she refused to take the drink. Not wanting to abort her pregnancy, she made the decision to escape, then was helped by a West African Pentecostal minister who operates mission houses in Amsterdam.

This use of native West African voodoo is a common feature of the slave experience for Nigerian women held in western Europe (of whom there are around ten thousand). The women and girls undergo an initiation ritual before leaving their country; for Joy this included the marking of her face and hands and laying hands on a "juju" (statue), as well as drinking blood. They are often made to swear to the gods that they will work hard for their employers and will never mention their real names, run away, or contact the police. Captors threaten the women with punishment by the gods for any disobedience and warn that any attempt to escape will awaken a curse on their families. Once in Europe, they are drugged, then resold. Held in brothels, they have sex with customers but are not paid—Joy notes that all money changed hands before the clients reached her room. Any pregnancies are aborted.

Joy (NETHERLANDS, 2006)

I was born in 1972 in Nigeria. In my family we were six, four brothers and two sisters. I didn't go to school. I was working with my brother on the farm. I lost my parents when I was very small. When I was about five or six, I lost my mother, then my father at age ten. They were sick. My brothers and sisters were smaller than me; one brother was nine, another six, another four, and the youngest was two. Sometimes my aunt would come, and at harvest time, friends would sometimes come to help us on the farm. Sometimes neighbors would give us work or food.

When I was twenty-six, I was taking care of the children, and a man came to me in the village and said he wanted to help me. He said it would help me to take care of the little ones if I would go to Europe. I didn't know him, I hadn't seen him before in the village, but he said he knew me. He said he had a lot of work in Europe on a farm with tomatoes and fruit. He had a wife and children there, and he said that maybe I can assist his wife with the children. I said, "OK, why not." He said he would be back in three days time to take my picture to get an international passport for me. Then he came back, took my picture, and said he would be back in a week. When he returned he showed me the passport and said he had to take me somewhere.

We went very far—before, I had only been to the next village or to the market. When we got there I met some men. They had white clothing and a very big place. There was a woman there too, a priestess. They went outside to talk—I don't know what they discussed—and then they asked me to pull off my shoes, and they brought blood for me to drink. They asked me to drink it for my own good and said that it wasn't going to kill me. I drank it, and they marked my body and my hand. Then they gave me a sheep's eye and said I had to eat it. I said, "What do you want me to eat this for? I can't eat it." They said that anybody who was going to Europe had to do this. I didn't want to eat it, but I was desperate. They gave me water to swallow it, and when I was finished, they asked me to put my hand on the juju.

After we finished, they bought me clothes and shoes. Then they took me away in a car, then straight into a ship. In the ship they asked me to hide. They had a cabin and they made me go underneath the bed. One white man took my passport from me and guarded the door. They were all speaking English. All I was thinking was that I found people who were going to help me. We got to Rotterdam, and two boys from Nigeria met us there and asked me to come with them. I followed them, and we arrived at a place. They said I had to stay there and rest. I didn't see the man anymore. They gave me food to eat, and after three days they said I had to go with them to Amsterdam to work. They took me there, to the red-light district and said, "You are one of them, you can also work like them." I said, "What kind of job is this?" They said, "Prostitution."

They said it took a lot of money to bring me to Europe and that this was what I would do to pay back the money. I thought they were joking, but they were very very serious. One man, Johnson, said that if I went to the police, or if the police arrested me, they would deport me to Nigeria, and then he would come to Nigeria by himself to kill me. He said that I have to change my name and that he was going to give me a new passport, British—not a real passport. He said I have to have it in case the police came.

They said to me that because of everything I drank before coming, and because I had put my hand on the juju, if I went to anybody or tried to run away, the juju would kill me. So I was forced to do the work. They said I had to get $60,000. I didn't see the money—when I saw the customers they had already paid. The money was already collected. They used to give me a drink, and they were putting some drugs in it. Even my food had the drug in it. They didn't allow me to talk me to anybody, and they had guns. I did talk to some customers, and they said I had to go to the police, but I was afraid.

The two boys used to sleep with me a lot, and they used no protection. The first time I was pregnant was in 2000. Johnson asked me to abort. I didn't know how to do it, but he gave me something to drink. And when I drank it, I miscarried. Then in February 2001, I was pregnant again. He said I had to do what I did before, but I said, "No, I don't want to do that anymore." It was very painful. He said that if I didn't take the drink he would use a knife to cut my stomach. He was very serious. He said if I didn't want to drink what he gave me before, he would force me to do it.

I said, "OK." I pretended like I'm going to work, and I made up my mind not to drink what he gave me. They dropped me to work, and I knew that they were around the area, watching me. I met a customer and I explained it to him. He said I had to go to the police. But I was afraid at that time—I thought that maybe if I went to the police they will lock me up. I followed the man as if I was following him to a house, and I took the metro.

HEREDITARY SLAVERY IN MAURITANIA

Selek'ha Mint Ahmed Lebeid and Oumoulkhér Mint Mahmoud were born into slavery in Mauritania. Selek'ha escaped in 2000 at the age of twenty after she reached a turning point and realized she *was* a slave: "I felt my situation was wrong. I saw how others lived." One day she started walking and didn't stop until she was free. Then, with the human rights organization SOS Slaves, Selek'ha returned to seek the release of her mother, Oumoulkhér. But for Oumoulkhér, the turning point was harder to find. She initially refused to leave her master, and it was only when Selek'ha began to cry, in response to insults from the master's wives, that she got "angry and...decided to leave." Oumoulkhér's narrative oscillates between assertions that freedom remains out of reach ("I *am still* a slave") and acknowledgment that she is now free ("I *was* a good slave").

Oumoulkhér's initial reluctance to accept her freedom because she is "an old lady" symbolizes the ancient and deeply rooted form of slavery practiced in Mauritania—chattel slavery, more difficult to dislodge than the new slavery of the global economy. The practice of buying, selling, and breeding Africans hasn't stopped in Mauritania since the thirteenth century, when Arab invaders entered the country to convert the Africans to Islam, abducted women and children, and bred a new caste of slaves. Slaves are raised to believe that serving their Arabo-Berber masters is a religious duty, and most remain in bondage their whole lives. Virtually all extended families of the dominant white Moor (Arabo-Berber) caste have owned slaves for generations; slaves are the property of a male family member, and children of slave women become property too. Slave families usually live within their master's household, are not paid for their work, and generally have no freedom of movement. They work as herders of livestock, agricultural workers, and domestic servants. As in the nineteenth-century American South, race matters intensely: most slaveholders are Arab Berbers, and most slaves are black Africans. Estimates of the number of black Africans enslaved in Mauritania range from one hundred thousand to one million, a vast proportion of the country's three million population.

Selek'ha (MAURITANIA, 2006)

I am Selek'ha. I am about twenty-six years old. I was taken from my mother when I was two years old by my first master, Mohamed Salem. Salem was my master and my mother's master, and he inherited us from his father. They belong to the Ehel Hobatt family from the Hyayna clan of the Awlad Gheilan tribe. They live in Tawaz, in the department of Atar, the region of the Adrar, and they are connected to the Ehel Saka family who are in Tidjika, in the region of Tagant.

I was a slave with these people, like my mother and my cousins. We suffered a lot. When I was very small I looked after the goats, and from the age of about seven I looked after the master's children and did the household chores—cooking, collecting water, and washing clothes. Salem wouldn't let me sleep until the children slept. If I did, he would put tobacco in my eyes or sometimes he would whip me. When I was ten years old I was given to a Marabout, who in turn gave me to his daughter as a marriage gift, to be her slave. I was never paid, but I had to do everything, and if I did not do things right I was beaten and insulted. My mistress did nothing.

My life was like this until I was about twenty years old. They kept watch over me and never let me go far from home. But I felt my situation was wrong. I saw how others lived. One day, I was making the tea, and I walked— I walked away, and kept walking until I reached the town and found some help.

My elder brother had been freed by Salem some time ago; he came to see me and told me that I would go to hell for leaving my master. My brother is an ally of my master—because he was freed, and freedom is the greatest gift your master can give you.

Sometime after escaping, I went to SOS Esclaves to ask them for help in freeing my mother, Oumoulkhér Mint Mahmoud, who is fifty years old, and my brothers and sisters, Khaïrat Mint Mahmouda (twenty-seven) and Oume Elbarka Mint Mahmouda (twenty), who were with the Ehel Hobatt family in Tawaz; Bilal Ould Mahmouda (sixteen); El Kheir Ould Mahmouda (thirteen); Abdel Barka Ould Mahmouda (ten years); and El Maimoun Ould Mahmouda (seven). My cousins are with the Ehel Saka family at Tagant and still in slavery.

Oumoulkhér (MAURITANIA, 2006)

I am Oumoulkhér Mint Mahmoud. I have been a slave all my life. I was a good slave. A slave who obeys her master is a good slave. I am still a slave; I am looking for my freedom. Since I have been here, with SOS, I feel peaceful. I don't care what my master thinks—I don't think about my master.

When Selek'ha was taken from me, the master said he would bring her back, but he didn't. I cried and cried. I had three other children at the time; I had nowhere to go. My son Hamit was given to a Marabout in exchange for a remedy to cure my master's son who was sick. Hamit escaped and I have not seen him since. My son Mbarack—the master said he died of thirst while looking after the camels. I don't know if it's true, but they said he was dead. My daughter Behuja Habah was rented out by my master for money. They said she ran away too.

I have spent my life working. I tried to run away when I was younger, but they always found me in the bush and brought me back. When Selek'ha came for me, I refused to go, because I am an old lady and useless, but then the master's wives started to insult her and Selek'ha was crying, so it made me angry and I decided to leave. Selek'ha has promised to look after me. Now I can rest.

NOT YET REALIZED

The Problem of Freedom

The dream of my life is not yet realized.
  Harriet Jacobs, *Incidents in the Life of a Slave Girl,* 1861

I still didn't exist as anything more than a slave.
  Jill Leighton, a former sex slave, United States, 1997

CHILD SEX SLAVERY IN THE UNITED STATES

Born and raised in the United States, Jill Leighton was trafficked into sex slavery from her home state of Ohio in 1981 at the age of fourteen. She made one attempt to escape, which led to punishment so severe that she never tried again. Contacting her family was out of the question, in part because she had left behind a dangerous home environment to become one of between 1.3 and 2.8 million runaway and homeless youth in the United States. These individuals are particularly vulnerable to sexual exploitation by traffickers; the Department of Justice estimates that 293,000 youth are at risk.

Jill notes that, after her liberation from slavery, she "still didn't exist as anything more than a slave, except I was an escaped slave." Jill still felt "less than human" after her three-year captivity ended and struggled to recognize herself as a human individual. But narrating her story, she explains, is "an integral part of my recovery."

Jill (UNITED STATES, 1997)

In 1981 I became a statistic—I became a runaway teen, escaping sexual and physical abuse. When I ran away, I no longer had a place to live with my parents, nor did I have a living relative who would take me in. Filled with a sense of bravado, invincibility, and bravery, I left, figuring that my life couldn't be in any more jeopardy than it already was at what I'd called home. In leaving I hoped there would be no more broken bones, no more sexual abuse, no more rationalizations of molestation and cruelty. When I left that day, I had no more than a change of clothes and under one hundred dollars. No longer did my name, childhood identity, school, or grades matter. All became irrelevant in the world I was about to enter.

As a runaway teen, your old concerns quickly disappear and are replaced by new, life-threatening ones. There were no familiar faces and no one who wanted to talk to a teenage girl who was homeless; even my name became irrelevant. Instead, my concerns were more pragmatic, involving finding food, shelter, water and passing time without the money to financially support these needs. I'd resorted to sleeping in cemeteries and stealing food out of dumpsters and from convenience stores in order to eat. Getting drinking water and a chance to wash my face became quests of endurance. I had to hide from security guards, store and restaurant employees, and others who didn't want a homeless girl "loitering." As a runaway teen, I was viewed as something less than human. Still, it was safer than going home.

Into my hunger, loneliness, and desperation came a man named Bruce. Attractive, well dressed, and very charismatic, he approached me in a suburban mall and offered to "help" me. He could provide me with food, shelter, clothing, work—and I really wanted to work. I wanted desperately to be off the street and to have something to do. In essence he knew exactly how to manipulate a desperate teenage girl with his promises to fulfill all my needs. The manipulation began within minutes of meeting him. When I questioned whether or not this "work" was prostitution, he retracted the offer and began to walk away. Desperate, I ran after him, pleading with him to give me another chance and to forgive my insult.

He brought me into his "office" (which was actually his cellar) blindfolded, under the pretense of not wanting competitors to know his location in case I was a spy for them. I put my fear aside and agreed to being blindfolded because I needed what he was offering. When we went into his "office," he explained that I had to audition for the job and should step on the stage and raise my hands. When I did so, I felt leather straps being put around my wrists but didn't understand what was going on. He pulled my pants down and my shirt up, leaving me virtually naked. When I tried to stop him from undressing me, the reality of what was happening became very clear. He shoved out the wooden box I was standing on, and I was left hanging in midair, naked, suspended by my wrists. It was the beginning of my "training" for a position as a prostitute that catered to "clients" who wanted to act on their violent bondage/torture fantasies. While still hanging from my wrists, I was told that unless I agreed then to sign a contract, I would never be let down. This threat was followed, while I was still hanging, by being hit, punched, whipped, and penetrated with a beer bottle. I could barely breathe, and my arms, wrists, and shoulders were screaming in pain. I gave up and agreed to sign, at which point I was let down, bound behind my back, gagged and blindfolded, thrown into a tiny closet under the cellar stairs without food or water and left there. Bruce did not come back until after what seemed like a couple of days, at which time he freed my hands and told me to sign by his finger while I was still blindfolded. What I signed was what is known in these "rape and snuff" circles as a slave contract. By doing so I was essentially agreeing that I was no longer a human being but, rather, a slave, whose sole purpose in life was the fulfillment of Bruce's desires and those of his "clients." The contract took away my right to feel, to speak without approval, to have emotions. In it, I agreed to do anything that I was told and to accept any punishment or training he determined necessary.

What followed next—the "training"—was months of being tortured, starved, dehydrated, sensory deprived, and raped. I was supposed to learn how to "want" to be a slave and "want" to be punished. To that end, I had to beg for everything, using phrases that Bruce had written. I had to apologize for being alive, had to thank him for each act of torture and beg for more. If I resisted, the punishments got worse, until I gave up and agreed.

Once he was satisfied that my training period was nearing the end he began to refer me to "clients" who would use my body for their fetishes. They paid Bruce to rent my body to rape in as many ways as they could devise without killing me. I was held underwater in toilets or bathtubs, whipped, hung, shocked with electrical current, and paid to have me tell them how much I was enjoying it.

One of my early clients portrayed himself as a nice guy who was going to help me escape, which I agreed to try. It turned out to be a test of my "loyalty," the failure of which resulted in a savage night of gang rape, beating, being hung by my wrists and ankles, and an attempt to hang me by my neck, which left me physically scarred and damaged my vocal chords for life. I nearly died that night and never tried to escape again.

For three years I was forced to let men rape me for Bruce's profit. During that time, I'd nearly been killed several times, including Bruce's failed attempt to perform an abortion on me after I'd become pregnant. In 1982 I entered a suburban Los Angeles hospital bleeding extensively from my vaginal area. On my wrists, ankles, and neck were burns, cuts, and scars. Having been hung from the ceiling by my wrists while my pimp attempted to abort a child that I was pregnant with, I was in shock and nearly unconscious when I was brought into the hospital. A broken, long-neck beer bottle had been shoved into my vagina as the object to remove the fetus. Needless to say, it didn't work out. The fetus remained in my womb, but the abortion attempt nearly killed me.

Fearing retaliation from my pimp, I didn't communicate to the doctors what had actually transpired but, instead, remained silent allowing my pimp's explanation of my abortion attempt to go unchallenged. Had these doctors given any thought to their ethical oaths, it should have occurred to them that the bruises, scars, strangulation marks, and so on were inconsistent with attempting to abort my own child. Exactly how did I destroy my larynx attempting to abort a child? How did I self-inflict leather strap burn marks around my wrists and ankles? Since I was an inpatient for three days, why wasn't a mental health professional sent to talk to me? Why was I questioned only in the presence of my pimp who was masquerading as my older brother, who was pretending to help his psychotic little sister? Had I been questioned alone and placed in the psychiatric ward away from him, perhaps the outcome would have been different.

When we left a Midwestern city, I was thrown into the trunk of a car and taken across country. After being left in the trunk for long periods of time in the Southwest desert in July, I became sick from dehydration. At one point this pimp took me out of the car on a remote road in the desert, handcuffed me, tied me by my neck to the bumper of his car, and told me he was going to drag me until I was nothing but hair and a grease stain. This fate was guaranteed unless I agreed to remain totally compliant.

Arriving at an Arizona truck stop, he pulled me out of the car, took off the blindfold and shackles, and told me to walk with him into the truck stop and get a Pepsi. Weak from fatigue, dehydration, and exhaustion, I couldn't walk. I became violently ill on the brick patio of the truck stop. EMS [emergency medical service] was called to the scene. I was violently ill, dirty from head to toe, and had sores on both my wrists from the handcuffs and the corners of my mouth from being gagged for days. Did they call the police?

No. They accepted his explanation of the death of "our parents" and his caretaking of his schizophrenic little sister. Why didn't they ask questions? Why did they only treat the symptoms of heat exhaustion and not ask how I got to that point? Why did the lady getting into her Cadillac with her husband not help me as the pimp was tying my hands behind my back and putting me back into the trunk in plain view?

These incidents are not meant to shock but to illustrate the reality of my day-to-day life. Bruce and his "clients" inflicted every torture imaginable on me, forcing me to do disgusting, humiliating things that have had a devastating effect on my mind, my body, and my soul.

In 1984 my captivity came to an abrupt end. Bruce was arrested on unrelated charges, and I was able to escape after he'd been handcuffed and taken away. The police who arrested Bruce offered me no support, despite finding a young girl locked in a closet, bound, gagged, and blindfolded. Even my request for a female officer to speak to was denied. The police told me that they were there to execute a warrant and that I'd better shut up or I was going to be arrested, too. I wasn't even eighteen yet.

Taking whatever money I could find in the house, I left immediately, taking a taxi to the airport and flying to the first destination available with the amount of money I had. After arriving in the new city, I found a cheap hotel and literally slept for days. The face I saw in the mirror when I awoke was hardly like the one I'd seen at age fourteen. I'd lost a third of my body weight. My once thick, long hair had fallen out in clumps and was now thin, fragile, and lifeless. Emotionally, I was still stunned, lost in my own world, trying to readjust to a life that suddenly left me free but with no place to go and no one to turn to. Sleep was filled with nightmares, daytime with flashbacks and raging paranoia of being located by Bruce. After three years of eating dog food and being forced to beg for it, I was unaccustomed to eating anything normal and struggled with anorexia. In essence, I still didn't exist as anything more than a slave, except I was an escaped slave.

It has been more than a decade since then. In many ways, I've recovered, having eventually regained enough sanity to get a job and hold it. The physical injuries either healed or scarred, and I learned to compensate. But having survived this experience doesn't mean I've become safe from it.

Depression is still part of my life, as is shame, fear, and a strong drive for self-destruction. I still feel like I'm crazy and fear that I'm a burden to my friends, a failure as an employee, and that I'm destined to again be homeless, vulnerable, and alone.

There are issues on which I'm working toward recovery—an integral part of my recovery is speaking out about what happened to me, what

I faced as a runaway teen, and what I face even to this day trying to live with the memory of what I survived. I write this story so that maybe someone who hears it will somehow be able to avoid the pain that was forced on me, and for others to know that things like I experienced really do happen—and they can happen to anyone's daughter, sister, girlfriend, niece, or wife.

Through whatever fluke, I escaped without having any sexually transmitted diseases, but there were other serious consequences. My ability to have children was destroyed; my voice is a raspy shell of its former self from being choked with ropes, belts, hands. There are extensive and deep scars many places on my body. Emotionally, the effects were worse. Flashbacks, nightmares, and depression have been constant battles since my escape. It has taken a great deal of therapy and support from friends for me to evolve to a point where I'm able to move on. It has also seriously impacted my ability to have and maintain relationships. Until recently, my relationships were dominated by failure. Many "romantic" relationships turned out to be with abusive men. In the rare instances that I found a quality person who did love me, I usually destroyed the relationship with my actions. It took many years for me to deprogram the need to self-destruct. Recently, I've evolved to the point where I'm no longer seeking suicide through self-destruction. Instead, I'm working on living…on maintaining the friendships and relationships with the really awesome people who are in my life now. I have some really wonderful, supportive friends who I love and who I believe love me. A great deal of therapy has gone into believing that I'm worth these quality friends and can maintain the relationships. I've hurt too many people in the past through my low self-esteem and self-destruction. But going forward, it's my goal to see beyond the horrors of the past and fatalistic programming and, instead, focus on the future and on being authentic to myself…and on a commitment to living.

EGYPTIAN SEX SLAVERY

Egypt is a transit country for women trafficked from sub-Saharan Africa, eastern Europe, and the countries of the former Soviet Union to Europe and Israel for sexual exploitation. Internal trafficking occurs as well. Ragaa is an Egyptian woman trafficked into sex slavery within Egypt in 1995. In addition to sexual slavery, in Egypt, children are trafficked from rural areas to work as laborers in the agriculture industry. Each year over one million children between the ages of seven and twelve work eleven hours a day for Egypt's agricultural cooperatives in cotton pest management.

They face routine beatings by their foremen and exposure to heat and pesticides.

Ragaa's experience included the offer of a "pleasure marriage," which is a temporary arrangement to permit sexual intercourse, and a "temporary marriage," because brothels are illegal and forbidden under sharia (Islamic law based on the Koran) in Egypt. She explains that her escape brought no sense that the experience was over. The problem of freedom after bondage was an ongoing fear of her traffickers.

Ragaa (EGYPT, 1997)

In 1995 there were no job opportunities, so I worked on commission selling goods in the street markets for a man named Mr. Asam Abass Mohamed. I had been working for only five days with some other people, when, on the sixth day, Mr. Mohamed ordered me to stay and guard the goods while everybody else went out. He then offered me some juice with breakfast. I drank it and afterward lost consciousness.

When I awoke I had been raped and was locked in a hotel room. I didn't know where I was. Then some strange people came and took me to a train station. They took me to a small village called Nga Wansy in the Aswan governorate in southern Egypt. There they threatened me, locked me up, and beat me, until I became very ill. They tried to rape me in spite of my sickness. When I protested, they offered me a pleasure marriage, but I refused. They locked me up again for a long time, leaving me alone in my room. They told me that if I tried to go back to my family, my parents would blame me and kill me for running away.

They moved me all across the country to different places, torturing me and trying to have sex with me. In the town of Adko in Bihera governorate the people who were keeping me tried to force me to accept other temporary marriages. I refused again.

By chance, my family—my mother, my sister and her husband—found me in a city near Zakazik. They helped me to escape and I went to my father's house, where I stay now. I am living in terror of those people who kept me for so long. The police refuse to protect me.

MEXICAN SEX TRAFFICKING

The U.S. Department of Justice estimates that of those 14,500 to 17,500 foreign-born individuals trafficked to the United States annually, some 80 percent are female, and 70 percent of these women end up as sex slaves. Feeder countries include Albania, the Philippines, Thailand, Mexico (many from the central region of Tlaxcala, a haven for modern-day slave traders), Nigeria, and Ukraine. Often the women are forced to work to pay off the debts imposed by their smugglers—debts ranging from $40,000 to $60,000 per person. They might perform four thousand acts of sexual intercourse each year to meet their quota, at $10 to $25 per act.

In 1997 Inez, Maria, and Rosa were trafficked from Mexico into sex slavery in the United States. Inez and Maria were eighteen, and Rosa was fourteen. They were transported to Texas, then to a trailer in Florida. Up to four young women worked in the same trailer, each of them having sex with up to thirty-five men a day, for twelve hours a day. They were constantly guarded and beaten and raped by their bosses. After they had been enslaved for several months, FBI agents, along with agents from the Immigration and Naturalization Service and local law offices, raided their brothels. Some of their captors were tried, others escaped and returned to Mexico. Inez now observes that she cannot "seem to get past the ordeal" of slavery, Maria that she is "in fear for my life more than ever," and Rosa that she "can't put it behind me." The turning point from slavery to freedom has not occurred. Inez's narrative is filled with phrases like "I will never forget," "I try to act like a normal girl, but it is not always easy," and "I lack confidence and never feel secure."

Inez (UNITED STATES, 2000)

Before I came to the United States, I lived in a small town near Veracruz, Mexico. I helped support my family by working in the fields harvesting lemons. Although I did not mind the work, I wished I could earn more money to help my family.

Sometime in 1997, a woman named Maria Elena approached me and told me about opportunities for work in the United States. She told me she had worked there at a restaurant and had made good money. When I told my mother about the offer, she was skeptical. Since I was interested in helping my family out, I decided to learn more about this opportunity. Maria Elena set up a meeting with two men named Abel Cadena-Sosa and Patricio Sosa. At the meeting, the men confirmed that they had job openings for women like myself in American restaurants. They told me that they would take care of my immigration papers and that I would be free to change jobs if I did not like working at the restaurants.

I decided to accept the offer. In 1997 I was brought into the United States through Brownsville, Texas. Maria Elena traveled with me. We were both transported to Houston, Texas, where a man named Rogerio Cadena picked us up and took us to a trailer in Avon Park, Florida. In Avon Park, I met a girl named Sue who lived in the trailer. She asked me if I knew why I had come to Avon Park. I said I was going to work in a restaurant. She told me that I was actually going to be selling my body to men. I looked at Maria Elena in utter horror, but she did not appear surprised. Maria Elena admitted that she had already worked in trailer brothels in the past. She said it would not do anybody any good to complain. I was going to have to do the work anyway, since I had a smuggling debt to pay off. Maria Elena also warned me, "If you escape, Abel Cadena will go after your family because you owe him money." Some of the other girls in the house also warned me that if I tried to escape, the men would find me and beat me up or abuse me. Rogerio Cadena said I had no place to run anyway, because my family was very far away and each trailer was located in a very isolated area.

Rogerio then bought some tight clothes for me to wear when I worked, and I was subsequently transported to a trailer in Fort Pierce, Florida. A man named Jose Cuevas-Ataxca (known as "Lupito") told me he was in charge of selling "tickets" to customers so they could go into the sitting room and pick a girl to have sexual relations with. I learned that the tickets were condoms. I was told that each customer would pay around $22 and that, in turn, each girl would be paid about $3 per customer. The rest of the money would go to pay our smuggling fee, our rent, and water. I also learned that every fifteen days I would be transported to a different trailer to keep working.

I did not understand what happened to me. There was no way out. I began "working" in the trailers. The work was demeaning and frightening. I never had a moment's rest. On the weekends, I would often have to see around thirty-two or thirty-four men, for $15 each. I would get myself drunk before the men arrived, so that I could stand the work. At the end of the shift, I would fill a bathtub with hot water and lay in it, drinking and crying. I would smoke one cigarette after another, and then go to bed drunk because it was the only way I could fall asleep.

The bosses had no mercy. I felt terrible pain in my vagina, and I asked repeatedly to be taken to the doctor. No one ever took me. But they did take the girls who became pregnant to a doctor where they performed forced abortions. Several of the young women and girls in the brothel had had these abortions.

Many of the men were violent. I will never forget a night in Avon Park. Rogerio Cadena had thrown a party in the trailer. I went outside for air.

He thought I was trying to escape and he ran out after me and told me, "You don't know what I'm capable of." He hit me on the mouth, broke my lip, and began to beat me on the chest. I stumbled back to the trailer. I knew I could not take this anymore. I went to my room, put some clothes in a bag, and jumped out of the window. One of the other girls came with me and we ran to a house nearby where she said she knew someone. We spent the night there. The next morning, the bosses arrived at the house. Somehow, they knew we were there. They took us back to the trailer, and we began another day of work.

Although it has been more than a year since all of this occurred, I cannot seem to get past the ordeal. I am dating a young man now, and I try to act like a normal girl, but it is not always easy. I also have a steady job and will soon be promoted, but I lack confidence and never feel secure. Once in a while, I still have anxiety attacks. I still remember the horrible beatings, the constant threats, and the drunk and pushy customers.

I am trying hard to be the person I was before I came to the United States.

Maria (UNITED STATES, 2000)

My name is Maria. I am in disguise today because I am in fear that my captors would recognize me and thus place my life and that of my family in danger. My story begins in May of 1997 in Veracruz, Mexico. I was approached in Mexico by an acquaintance about some jobs in the United States. She told me that there were jobs available in restaurants or bars. I was working as a domestic helper in Mexico and had a job at a general retail store. This seemed like a great opportunity for me to earn more money for my daughter and family. I accepted the job and soon was brought by a coyote to Texas.

Once over the border, I was kept at a safe house. Then, I was transported to Florida. Once in Florida, Abel Cadena, one of the ringleaders, told me I would be working at a brothel as a prostitute. I told him he was mistaken and that I was going to be working in a restaurant not a brothel. He then ordered me to work in a brothel. He said I owed him a smuggling debt of approximately $2,200 and the sooner I paid it off the sooner I could leave. I was eighteen years old and had never been far from home and had no money or way to get home.

Next, I was given tight clothes to wear and was told what I must do. There would be armed men selling tickets to customers in the trailer. Tickets were condoms. Each ticket would be sold for $22 to $25 each. The client would then point at the girl he wanted and the girl would take him to one of the bedrooms. At the end of the night, I turned in the condom wrappers. Each wrapper represented a supposed deduction to my smuggling fee. We tried to keep our own records, but the bosses would destroy them. We were never sure what we owed.

There were up to four girls kept at each brothel. We were constantly guarded and abused. If anyone refused to be with a customer, we were beaten. If we adamantly refused, the bosses would show us a lesson by raping us brutally. They told us if we refused again it would be even worse the next time. We were transported every fifteen days to another trailer in a nearby city. This was to give the customers a variety of girls and so we never knew where we were in case we tried to escape. I could not believe this was happening to me.

We worked six days a week and twelve-hour days. We mostly had to serve thirty-two to thirty-five clients a day. Weekends were worse. Our bodies were utterly sore and swollen. The bosses did not care. We worked no matter what. This included during menstruation. Clients would become enraged if they found out. The bosses instructed us to place a piece of clothing over the lamps to darken the room. This, however, did not protect us from client beatings. Also, at the end of the night our work did not end. It was now the bosses' turn with us. If anyone became pregnant we were forced to have abortions. The cost of the abortion would then be added to our smuggling debt.

The bosses carried weapons. They scared me. The brothels were often in isolated areas. I never knew where I was. It was all so strange to me. We were not allowed to go outside of the brothels. I knew if I tried to escape I would not get far because everything was so unfamiliar. The bosses told me that if I escaped, the INS would catch me, beat me, and tie me up. This frightened me. I did know of one girl who escaped. The bosses searched for her and said they were going to get the money she owed them from their family. They said they would get their money one way or another.

I know of another girl that escaped and was hunted down. The bosses found her and beat her severely. The bosses would show the girl that they meant business by beating and raping her brutally. All I could do is stand there and watch. I was too afraid to try to escape. I also did not want my family put in danger.

I was enslaved for several months; other women were enslaved for up to a year. Our enslavement finally ended when the INS, FBI, and local law enforcement raided the brothels and rescued us. We weren't sure what was happening on the day of the raids. Our captors had told us over and over never to tell the police of our conditions. They told us that if we told we would find ourselves in prison for the rest of our lives. They told us that the INS would rape us and kill us. But we learned to trust the INS and FBI and assisted them in the prosecution of our enslavers.

Unfortunately, this was difficult. After the INS and FBI freed us from the brothels we were put in a detention center for many months. Our captors were correct. We thought we would be imprisoned for the rest of our lives. Later, our attorneys were able to get us released to a women's domestic violence center where we received comprehensive medical attention, including gynecological exams and mental health counseling.

Thanks to the United States government some of our captors were brought to justice and were sent to prison. Unfortunately, not all. Some of them are living in Mexico in our hometown of Veracruz. They have threatened some of our families. They have even threatened to bring our younger sisters to the United States and force them to work in brothels as well. I would never ever have done this work. No one I know would have done this work. I am speaking out today because I never want this to happen to anyone else. However, in order to accomplish this goal women like me need your help. We need the law to protect us from this horror. We need the immigration law to provide victims of this horror with permanent legal residence. We came to the United States to find a better future, not to be prostitutes. If anyone thinks that providing protection to trafficking survivors by affording them permanent residency status is a magnet for other immigrants like myself; they are wrong. No woman or child would want to be a sex slave and endure the evil that I have gone through. I am in fear for my life more than ever. I helped put these evil men in jail. Please help me. Please help us. Please do not let this happen to anyone else. Thank you.

Rosa (UNITED STATES, 2000)

When I was fourteen, a man came to my parents' house in Veracruz, Mexico, and asked me if I was interested in making money in the United States. He said I could make many times as much money doing the same things that I was doing in Mexico. At the time, I was working in a hotel, cleaning rooms, and I also helped around my house by watching my brothers and sisters. He said I would be in good hands and would meet many other Mexican girls who had taken advantage of this great opportunity. My parents didn't want me to go, but I persuaded them.

A week later, I was smuggled into the United States through Texas to Orlando, Florida. It was then the men told me that my employment would consist of having sex with men for money. I had never had sex before, and I had never imagined selling my body. And so my nightmare began. Because I was a virgin, the men decided to initiate me by raping me again and again, to teach me how to have sex. Over the next three months, I was taken to a different trailer every fifteen days. Every night I had to sleep in the same bed in which I had been forced to service customers all day.

I couldn't do anything to stop it. I wasn't allowed to go outside without a guard. Many of the bosses had guns. I was constantly afraid. One of the bosses carried me off to a hotel one night, where he raped me. I could do nothing to stop him.

Because I was so young, I was always in demand with the customers. It was awful. Although the men were supposed to wear condoms, some didn't, so eventually I became pregnant and was forced to have an abortion. They sent me back to the brothel almost immediately.

I cannot forget what has happened. I can't put it behind me. I find it nearly impossible to trust people. I still feel shame. I was a decent girl in Mexico. I used to go to church with my family. I only wish none of this had ever happened.

CHILD SOLDIERS IN THE PHILIPPINES, SRI LANKA, AND COLOMBIA

Aida was recruited as a child soldier by a militia group in the Philippines at the age of fourteen and then prevented from leaving. She now imagines "many untoward things that might happen" and feels like she is "dying inside" when she remembers her experiences. Similarly, Manju, who was abducted and forced to work as a child soldier in Sri Lanka at the age of seventeen, begins to imagine "my future" but shifts to a description of her "fever," states that she wants to "study" but doesn't know "how to fit in," and concludes with an assertion that the abduction "changed my life entirely." Only one of these former child soldiers, Dia, who "had to join" a guerilla group in Colombia at the age of fifteen, sees a partial transition from slavery to freedom.

Aida was engaged in armed conflict for six months, Dia for nine months, and Manju for a year. They are three of around three hundred thousand children who participate in armies and armed groups in more than thirty countries around the world. The problem is most critical in Africa, where up to one hundred thousand children are estimated to be involved in armed conflict. Child soldiers also exist in Afghanistan, Burma, India, Indonesia, Iran, Iraq, Israel, and the Occupied Palestinian Territories, though international law sets eighteen as the minimum age for all participation in hostilities.

In the Philippines, where three major insurgent groups have fought the Philippine military since the 1960s, there are an estimated two thousand child soldiers. The communist-oriented New People's Army, established in 1968, began an intense recruitment of children in the 1990s. By 2000, some 25 percent of new recruits were children, and more than 10 percent of its regular combatants are now under eighteen. Parents volunteer children to serve as combatants and camp guards. The Moro Islamic Liberation Front allows the training of children as young as twelve. Parents volunteer their children, seeing it as an observation of Islamic teaching, and Muslim youth organizations recruit students from schools and colleges. The Abu Sayyaf ("Bearer of the Sword"), a Muslim separatist group that appeared in the late 1980s, uses Islamic religion to draw minors into the movement for use as combatants, human shields, and hostages.

In Colombia, both sides engaged in the country's forty-year-old conflict have used children: the government-backed paramilitary Autodefensas Unidas de Colombia, and the left-wing guerrilla groups Fuerzas Armadas Revolucionarias de Colombia (FARC) and Ejército de Liberación Nacional. Estimates of the total number of children fighting in paramilitaries and urban militias range from eleven thousand to fourteen thousand. FARC has the largest number of minors, including several thousand under the age of fifteen. Women and girls constitute up to half of all recruits to the armed opposition groups and face pressure to enter relationships with male commanders. Children take part in combat, act as messengers, and lay explosives. Most are denied contact with their families.

In Sri Lanka, children as young as nine have been abducted and used in combat by the Liberation Tigers of Tamil Eelam (LTTE). The LTTE used children as soldiers throughout its conflict with the Sri Lankan government between 1983 and 2002. Children—most aged fourteen or fifteen and over 40 percent girls—were used for massed frontal attacks in major battles, and some between the ages of twelve and fourteen were used to massacre women and children in rural villages. Others were used as human mine detectors, assassins, and suicide bombers. A cease-fire was implemented in February 2002, but a final peace agreement has not been reached, and the cease-fire didn't halt the LTTE's use of child soldiers. Children are now more likely to be *forcibly* recruited; people see no reason to give their children to the LTTE if they don't perceive themselves at risk from the government, and so the LTTE resorts to abduction. In 1994, one in nineteen child recruits was abducted. In 2004, only one in nineteen was a volunteer.

Aida (PHILIPPINES, 2001)

The problem was at first we were happy, but then there were times that we could not buy rice because we didn't have money. My mother would then be very worried about what we are going to eat; in fact it was not only our mother who thought about this, even us! I would do what I could so that my mother could eat, so that my mother wouldn't feel so troubled. It's all right that I experience difficulty, as long as I could help my mother. When I was small, I wanted to do the laundry, so that I could help my mother. I would give my earnings to my mother. My employer would give a loan to my mother, and then I would work to pay for that. My father wasn't earning much during this time. My mother is really more progressive or more knowledgeable than my father—in almost all aspects. Instead of buying my materials for the school project, the first thing that comes into my mind is to give the money to my mother, to buy food, just so I could help. If I have money I spend it all to buy food.

I was in grade two then. I thought that I would not be able to pass with a score of 85 in the card. I was so worried because I really thought I wouldn't pass. But it turned out that I had the highest grade. I said to myself I could really make it. But I stopped schooling after that. What a pity.

My employers said that they might go back to Sugbu and they had been thinking what would happen to me if they left. Maybe they thought that I wouldn't be able to find work without them. I took care of their children; I did the housekeeping and I would have to feed the pigs. Her husband worked in the rice field. That's why I couldn't go to school, because I had so many house chores. I had to wash the clothes and then take care of the child. I would wash the clothes at night, so that when I woke up there would be less work to do. I would start at six o'clock to cook, then wash and then clean the house. I would wonder how long I could stand the work because I was still a child. When I was already busy with a task, then she would ask me to do something more.

My second employer was the daughter of a teacher I used to work for. When she gave birth, my first employer asked me to work for her daughter. She was also a teacher. There was no one else who could help my parents then, and I wanted to be able to help my parents. I was so exhausted while working there. They wanted me to go to work for their son who had gotten married there. But this was so far, so I didn't want to go because I would like to see my mother often. That's what I wanted, to see my mother often. I would cry then because I felt pity for my mother.

I was still small, so when I joined the movement, the people would point out how small I was. There were thirty people, all of them armed. They spoke with me and convinced me to go with them. They told me that I should join them, that I should be on the side of the farmers. They explained to me that there should be equality, that when the farmers sell their products, they should get a fair price for their products, these were the things that they were explaining to me. They told me that if I was inside the movement, then I would be able to help more people. So I thought about it. After they spoke to me, that very night, we left. When I arrived to meet them that day, they politicized me. They told me that even if I was still young, I could be a big help. My mother wouldn't agree to let me go with them.

When I first joined I felt no fear and I asked so many questions, like what was the life of the masses, why is there war. I asked them what we do with the masses. They said that we should help the masses and make them understand our principles. We had education meetings. At first there were thirty in our group. We were reduced to five people. The others formed other groups. We had to undergo education first. That's how it is in the movement—study first. They did not give me any task until I had undergone some studies. Only then did they give me some tasks.

You must shed your bourgeois ways that still come from outside the movement. For example, you were a teacher and you still carry on some of the privileged attitude, like asking people to bring you food. You must change that. If you want to join the movement you must change your ways. You must be advanced in your character because you are given tasks. You educate the new recruits; you have to be calm in the face of many things. You have to make people understand many things. That's what I learned in the movement. And if you have proven yourself as advanced, you are given many tasks.

In fact, they did not want to release me because they said I am a big help in educating the masses. But I really tried hard to study. When I tried so hard to absorb the lessons, I felt like I'm going out of my mind. I had to understand immediately. Because in the movement, you really have to be quick in understanding, cannot afford to be slow. In the movement, the schedule is very fast and these lessons will not be repeated anymore. We only had one education session a year. You have to understand at once because the lesson will not be reviewed the following day. Education sessions must be finished fast because we must be quick and vigilant against a lurking enemy. You must absorb the instructions given by the teacher so you can immediately apply these later in your subsequent tasks. For we have a rule in the movement: when the commander says that you have to be deployed in a new area, you have to go. In the movement, you must obey the command of whoever is above you.

We attacked enemy detachments. We first underwent training. Only for a day. We were two thousand; we were many. You have to be swift, very swift. We were trained and taught how to move quickly. There are instructions to follow. You are really being taught. We were taught how to run with a full pack and M16 rifle. We wore colored clothes so as not to be seen. There were supplies, sometimes none, yet we cannot ask for food; the masses must give food voluntarily. We cannot force them to give us food. The masses were not even informed that it's prohibited. We had our hammock, complete with covering, the works. Heavy. We wore shoes or boots that we get from the cleaning, confiscated things from the enemy. When they get killed, we get their things.

I experienced so many problems regarding food, because there were times when we had no food to eat. During military operations, sometimes for a week, there were times when we could not eat at all. Cooking rice was not allowed to avoid producing smoke. Usually, we would be able to eat only during nighttime. But the next day, you cannot be choosy with food. You have to fill your lunch box with whatever leftover food is available.

As for long walks, it's really very tiring to walk under the heat, in the dark night, or through the rain. You'll really feel some crisis inside. Once, I wept when I fell off a cliff because I was so sleepy but still had to go on walking. It's not a life with few problems. But the worst is when you are sick and there are enemy troops around. It's likely that your condition will worsen into a very severe disease. That's the life in the group. Perhaps the hardest for me was about getting sick. Sometimes I get sick for a week. That's my most difficult crisis. I can go on without food, but I really cannot bear getting sick. What I really want to avoid is the situation where I'm so sick; of course I'm not a civilian but in the group [and] had to walk far and fast. But what if I cannot do it, what are they going to do with me? When we start walking, we really walk fast!

I experienced gunfire only once. There was one incident where we were supposed to be the one to conduct a raid, but instead we were the ones who were almost caught by enemy troops. They came right after we left the area. We had just left when the enemies arrived. I fired my rifle, but I had not killed anyone yet. I'm even afraid of looking at the dead, how much more in killing someone? I saw a comrade dying, but I never had the chance of killing anyone. Sometimes I wondered whether my bullet really shot somebody or not. When the shots are fired, you get the hang of it and killing people seems exciting. You become hotheaded. It's not just in a situation of battle. Even during military trainings, they also fire guns at us to train us with the idea that there's an enemy. Comrades are worse because they spray bullets on you, sometimes even using an M16. It's a good thing no one was injured by gunfire because we really crawled so hard. You just have to make your body move in whatever way and get used to it. Sometimes you have to race to a hilltop to train yourself to be faster than enemy troops.

Now I'm not with my mother anymore, I feel guilty and think that what I did was wrong. For example, while I was inside the movement, my mother was having a hard time. My cousin sent me a letter requesting me to come home because my younger sibling is sick. Or if I asked them if they can give some help, they would say, "What about?" "My father needs money." They would always say, "Don't worry because we will write down your request. But we need to find some money first." I told them, "That might be too late. My father's life is more important to me than money." I said maybe it would be better for me to go home first so that I'd be there whatever happens to my father. They tried to stop me by saying it's not my father who will die but rather it's me who might be killed by the military. The highest problem, they said, is capitalism. They said that if I get caught I will surely be killed. I really felt so bad that I cried. I was in such a miserable situation, I just thought of walking out of there because I wanted so much to see my mother, my siblings, and my father. The comrades refused my request to go home. They really prevented me from going and suggested that my mother come to me instead. I felt so bad and sorry for my life. I could not stop wondering about my father. I thought that if something happened to my father, I would really blame the comrades.

What I know in the movement is that they are not [now] accepting minors. But at that time, there were many minors who joined the armed struggle…they said even if I had killed someone, I would not be penalized because I'm still a minor. I tend to believe that's true. They also said that the leadership of the armed group receives money. There is a leader who receives all the money while we in the Philippines do not receive a single centavo. According to the soldiers, we are only being used. That is true anyway. And then we who stayed here in the Philippines, they said we are pitiful, because he continuously receives money while we do not receive even a peso.

In the armed group, I know that we have some right to say what we want to say. But I think there were also those who were deceived. Because in the movement, you just can't question things. That's a no-no. That's why whatever the soldiers said, I just kept quiet. I really don't know. We are afraid that we would be victimized, that's what we are afraid of. They said that those who discuss things like that were considered as enemies. For example, if I was given a task to get rice and I questioned it, they would question my being critical. Because you cannot really be disobedient, you have to follow their word.

I want to go home, not to join the movement again, but to just engage in some livelihood to help my mother. I would say to the staff in the center that I just want to go home because I can't take it any longer; I don't know what's going to happen here. I really can't bear going back to the movement. I think it's best for me to go home to give me the chance to think of what I should do, rather than stay here and remain uncertain about my life. The best is to go home. I have this feeling that I'd be able to forget about the movement. I cannot deny that I'm still interested in the movement, but some of the things I believed in have been disproved by my own experience.

I already decided that I would help my family. My mother used to wonder what would happen if I leave them. She would say, "Where are you my child? What will happen to us if you leave us?" I told her that I would not leave them, that I would just be around to help them. For me, if I can return home, I can go to school. My big problem is my mother, because she is quite old already and has no clear livelihood. I really want help, if there's anybody to help me continue schooling. How can I continue school when I'm torn between going to school and helping my mother? My mother is more important to me. In my mind, I imagine many untoward things that might happen. I really want to rest and to be with my mother.

I suppose what happened to me, regarding my experiences, there are some things I regret and lament. I feel so sorry. I have gone through such grave experiences. Imagine the stories I'll tell my children. I just want to forget everything because I really feel like dying inside when I remember my experiences in the movement. So when I just don't want to remember the experiences, I take a breather and go outside. I just want to forget…or else I'd go crazy. A soldier told me that in the movement I would just die without a future. They made me understand that I am still so young. That's really true. We're still so young to be in this struggle, and we end up not being able to follow the laws outside the movement. I just want to laugh. I am always crying because of my problem.

Dia (COLOMBIA, 2001)

I used to work. I chopped firewood and sold it; and I used to work in the fields—weeding, sowing, with my other brothers and sisters. We had to work hard. I had to go down to the village up to three times a day to sell firewood to get enough money together for food. I started when I was seven years old. My older brother used to beat us and swear at us. All of us have a different dad. As far as I know, when my mother was pregnant, my dad left. When I was a bit older my mother took me to his house, and my dad said that I was his daughter and that he would pay for my studies and he asked me to live there with him. He tried to abuse me when I was younger, and because I didn't let him he got angry. In the end I was with my mother at home. She said that I had to behave myself, that I had to study, to get on with things, not to go and fall in love or anything like that, and I didn't really pay attention to her because she was kind of crazy.…She talked nonsense. "Well, you must be stupid to go and fall in love because the same thing will happen to you as happened to me"— that's what she told us, that we shouldn't fall in love—look at how much she had suffered, now not even her children loved her. She said she hasn't even got children, she hasn't got anyone to love her.

At school there were some good teachers and some bad ones. Some taught you things. The teachers used to fight with the pupils, they used to expel people from the school, and they taught some people more than others. I had to be careful and do my homework so that we wouldn't be punished, because if you failed the grade you were given a thrashing and you couldn't study anymore. I didn't want to study anymore. A family member was already ill by this stage and there was no one there to stay with her at home, and so I said that I wasn't going to study anymore, so that I could be with her and do the housework.

Once I had a problem at home. I was scared, and so I went to the guerrillas secretly, so that no one would know, one day when I went down to the village to sell a bundle of firewood. I left at six in the evening. When I went down to the village the guerrillas called me over and told me that I had to go with them for about three days. And so, after being with them for three days, I asked to leave, but they said I couldn't…only those people that had been with them for three years could leave. Sometimes they say that it's just for three days, and then when you've been there for three days they don't let you leave; they say, "No, now you have to face up to the situation and carry on in the organization." I said I didn't want to,

I wanted to be with my family, that I wasn't going to join, and they said no, I had to join them. And so I had to join.

I was there for six months. I didn't get any training. When you arrive there with the other companions, you're given a different name. They told me they were the ones who were going to help the country to recover. To help make changes, to help the people. I was given a pistol. In case of a battle, I had to look for my comrades so that they would protect me and to go on ahead with the commander. I was also taught how to keep watch and how to talk to the people. The commander gave the orders and you had to obey them, and if you didn't obey them then you were punished. I was told, "You have to be at that house over there at ten o'clock, and you have to give them a talk about the organization." And sometimes I said, "Oh, I don't want to go and give talks," because I used to be embarrassed by it. Then I was told I had to go and give that talk. If not, I'd be punished with thirty hours of guard duty. In the case of a firefight, we had to leave all our things and just get the radio out of there. We were always a bit scared because if we lost that radio then maybe they'd kill us, because the commander used to say if that radio gets lost then you'll pay for it. Pay with your life or with a punishment, for example, doing thirty trips to fetch firewood, thirty hours of guard duty, and thirty days of cooking duty.

You had to watch over the camps, because if you weren't careful and the army attacked the camp and you managed to survive, you were blamed for everything that had happened. If something like that happened, if you cause a comrade to be killed, you were killed. The most difficult part was when there were battles with the army or when they said that they were going to attack a village. They came and called everyone together. "When you get there," they said, "we're going to attack this village, and you all have to be on the lookout." You feel nervous, and you think that maybe you'd be killed there and with family so far away.

At that moment I missed my boyfriend and my whole family. I used to think that maybe I'd be left there, and my family wouldn't realize. They leave you where you fall, and then the army collects you and brings you in. When someone else was killed, that made me sad, that a comrade should fall, and maybe you'd die as well, or get injured. If the wounds were serious that you'd got, then you could die from that, and you're in pain until you die out there. All of us went out; the ones that were killed were left there, and then you went back to the camp again.

Sometimes you could call your family or write to them, but you couldn't escape. You asked the commander for permission to call or write to your family. You wrote a letter and you showed it to him so that he could read it and see what you had written, and if he said, "You can't write this word," then you had to cross it out.

Everyone in the group was equal. For example, the equipment that we had to carry was about ten or eleven pounds, and everyone had to carry the same eleven pounds. For example, when a girl was ill, or at that time of the month, you said, she shouldn't have to carry so much, but then they said, "No, everyone is equal." You had to do what they said. I didn't like walking because that made me tired and they all walk fast, and if you didn't move fast then the commander said, "The person who doesn't step on it tonight will do six hours of guard duty as punishment." So you learn to walk quickly.

If you had a good behavioral record and they could see that you were an enterprising person, then they trained you to be a commander. The commander decided everything. If you didn't like the person that was going to be made commander, you just had to put up with it because it was an order and you had to. I didn't want to have any kind of rank. Once I was left in charge of three girls and I was nervous, in case one of the girls should escape, and I'd have to pay for that. I would have to run after them—I couldn't lose one of the girls. And there were a few who wanted to give themselves up to the army—they weren't happy in the group.

If you wanted to have a relationship with someone then you went to the commander and you asked him. If the commander said no, then you had to abide by that; if the commander caught you, if you carried on in secret, talking to the boy, he got angry and he punished you. The commander, [even] if he had…three girlfriends, then you couldn't say anything to him because he was the commander. A lad once told him, "You've got your girlfriend and then others," and he said, "But that's me, and no one can say anything to me. If I have ten girlfriends, then I have to be with all ten of them." The women with the commander were next to him all day so that he wouldn't give them guard duty. You had to respect them more than the other girls. He chose which one he wanted to be with.

All the women there, even if you didn't have a boyfriend, had to use contraception, because the commander used to say that no one could get pregnant there. If you got pregnant there, then that was your salvation be-cause you were sent back home; but then when the child was born and grew up a bit, you had to go back again. Those were the rules of the organiza-tion. If you were already pregnant and didn't want to tell the commander, then some had abortions. But if you told him, then he sent you home when you were about five months pregnant; he sent you home, and people used to come and visit you and were keeping an eye on you. You always get punished for getting pregnant, but the baby's looked after. Though, if you were pregnant without a partner, you had to manage by yourself, and at home you weren't really welcomed. If you were in an established relationship, the guerillas acknowledged the child, but if not, then they didn't. An established relationship is having talked to the commander and if he had given you permission to be in that relationship. That's why there were a lot of abortions, because no one acknowledged the child; and at home [your dad or mother] would get angry.

Here, where I am, they tell me that I have to respect myself so that others respect me, and to learn to respect and be with other people, and to learn to get ahead with what I want, that despite all those upsets that I had, I have to get up again and carry on. I wanted to be a computer scientist. When I joined the guerrillas all my dreams went up in smoke. But now I want to get back to that, I want to get further ahead in what I can...not to regress. I have a special dream that I was going to be a computer scientist and have a good husband, and I was going to be rich and have lots of money and many things; I wasn't going to be lacking anything. I thought that maybe the boyfriend I had was going to be my future husband.

The person that I loved the most and who helped me with everything isn't here anymore, but I have to carry on, and one day someone else will arrive who I'll love as much. At the moment I think I'm OK. I think I have to go further to be able to get along, to begin to express myself more, to talk to other people, and to be successful in everything that I can.

Manju (SRI LANKA, 2001)

I was told that my father left home as soon as I was born. He does not come home even now, but I meet him once in a while—outside home. Father and mother separated over a verbal quarrel. He never hit my mother in front of me. They only argued. One day they had a big argument and he left home. After he left my mother and us, his children, I heard that he had married again. He has children by that woman, they say. He does not come home. They are also living close by. He talks to me sometimes, but he does not come home.

When I was young my mother went away to find a job. My mother's relatives looked after us. My mother was very good at artificial flower making, and I, too, liked that. I used to sit by her side and watch her making flowers. I too can make flowers. I like cooking, too; even here I help and enjoy cooking. We, too, have our own house. We built this home; it is enough for us. I liked to go to school. I studied up to the ordinary level. There were many teachers. I liked all my teachers. Nobody hit me. They scold us to make us study well. I don't mind that. Sometimes they used to hit, even that I think it's for our own good. I played netball. I go for practices and enjoy playing.

Today I am here. Why? Not because I wanted to join; it is no fault of my own at all. I was forcefully taken away into the movement. One day three of us wanted to go to my grandmother's village. My cousins—the three of us got ready to go. While walking along the road there was a three-wheeler. We wanted the driver to take us to that village; the driver agreed. After a while he drove us into an unknown place and kept us locked in a house; later, he forcefully took us to a camp. We told our story, but nobody listened. They thought we came to join the movement willingly, and now we are making up stories. We were then taken to a training base.

There were some others like us who were taken in forcefully. Very often I got hit. They tried in every way to make me stay and I was forced into training. The training was for four months. I was not assigned for fighting. I have to take all the details of any group moving out for fighting, details of all the arms taken, what kind and who is taking it, and so on. For the four months I underwent training, I did only the basic physical training. It was difficult for me. Maybe because I didn't like anything there—I hated everyone and everything. There was another one who also wanted to run away. One of the three of us who were taken fell sick and she was sent home. I was sad and I used to cry and wished that I too became sick. I fell sick, but I was looked after by doctors; the treatment was good. I was kept there and looked after. They gave medicines. I was very unhappy and cried.

When we do physical training, if you don't do it properly they hit you. I have got hit by some leaders, but some were good. As we go along and if we do well they give more training. I was given a dummy rifle. I had to carry it all the time and look after it like a real one. I was not chosen to be given a real rifle—maybe they knew I was not happy there. Twice they gave me a rifle for my own protection they said. That was when I had to follow a group on a fighting mission. I have never been in the front line or even in the middle—I go only to record the situation. I was given a bag with a pen and a book. There were teams in that group with a leader in charge. The arms given are according to their experience, like T56 and other very sophisticated guns. The magazine rounds, even the cleaning material given out, I had to record.

When someone goes out for a hero's death, they are honored. I feel sorry for them. Many die and never come back. Some have come back after performing dangerous missions. They are then promoted and become respected. I have never shot anybody. I don't know why that I can't kill. I made up my mind not to kill anyone. I have had to carry dead bodies. I carry these bodies usually in the dark. Yes, I was filled with fear, fear that I can't talk about. Fear…fear…fear….What could I do? I carry the body on my shoulder, it is difficult, and I walk crying all the way.

I was given a uniform, jeans, shirt, and shoes. That was all right. You need comfortable clothes while you are doing all those difficult and terrible jobs. Two women gave me training. I learned to shoot but did not shoot anyone, not even an animal. All the time we are trained. We are trained up to the day of the hero's death. That is also training, that is, you go out on a dangerous mission. We get different types of food. Bread, lentils, rice, and curry. Different curries are given on different days. We have got even nice apples in the middle of the jungles. When we are on the job, water is brought to us for drinking purposes. Water was difficult to get. Somehow or the other we managed. We used water very carefully. I was not given a cyanide capsule. Only the fighters get cyanide, and they have to go through one-year training at least. I did not want to be a fighter and I never got the cyanide.

There is a day when you can see the relatives, [on] the hero's day. On that day my mother's sister came to see me. I was happy to see her and I was sad also. I cried and cried. My mother came to see me in the camp three times. They do not allow us to see them without any reason. She was sent away and I cried.

I found another friend like me who wanted to escape. So two of us used to get together and plan how we could get out of the place. This, of course, was in my mind from the day I was taken in forcefully. She has been closer to the camp than to where I lived. One day finally we ran away. We walked and walked and finally reached a village. When people asked us we said we were going home on leave. So we escaped. My friend knew how to get to her place, as she was close by. We did not want to go together beyond that. I spent the night with her people and started on my escape. I really didn't know how to manage….Now I made up my mind to tell the truth to someone and get help. I met an elderly woman, she looked somewhat friendly. I went into her hut. I told her the truth. She took pity on me and agreed to hide me till I could escape. I stayed with her. I never went out during the daytime. This kind lady was good to me. She cared for me. She understood my suffering and really cared for me. I will never forget her—she could have sent me out because her life was in danger—yet she cared for me. I wrote a letter to my mother, and one day my mother came and took me.

I am very worried about my mother. We have finished all the money. Everything from the bank is over. My mother is sick now; she's at home. She cannot look after me. I have no one except my mother. She had a big tumor and she was operated. Now she is a sick person and stays at home. She has to go for another operation. The stitches after the operation have come out and she is always in pain. She can't work; it's difficult for her now. When the time comes for me to leave this center I have no problem to get back home. Relations are all OK, but not all; some are good, but some don't like us. My sister and her husband are living a happy life.

For my future maybe I can start sewing to earn my living. The few good things I learned there is how to write and maintain records. This helped me to keep my mind occupied. This helped me to keep away from direct fighting, which I hated. Physical training also helped me somewhat. I got fever, and that type of shivering fever still continues, and even now I'm suffering from fever. I was in hospital; they said I was better and sent me back, but today I feel feverish and shivering comes off and on.

I had no romantic involvement; I didn't have a single boyfriend, and I am not going to have a boyfriend. I will marry someone who is arranged for me. I want to study; I don't know how to fit in. But I'll try. Everyone knows that I did not go on my own and I also came back by surrendering. I cannot really understand why this misfortune fell on me. This has changed my life entirely.

RESTAVECS IN HAITI

Jean-Robert Cadet, a former child slave in Haiti, confronts the problem of freedom. The slave experience is not over for him: "nightmares…haunt me well into my adulthood…the trauma lasts a lifetime." His childhood can "never be recovered," and he will "feel its absence for the rest of my life." The narrative quotes his wife's observation that sometimes the "reality from decades ago is upon us again."

As a restavec, Jean-Robert was one of thousands of Haitian children who are sent by their poor rural families to stay with wealthier families. Supposedly, they will be treated like one of the family and enrolled in school in exchange for domestic labor. But this rarely happens. Instead, they work fourteen hours a day for no compensation and are frequently abused. Slavery was initially abolished in Haiti after the revolt of 1794–1804, when African slaves fought and overthrew their French masters and declared the colony of Saint-Domingue on the island of Hispaniola an independent republic. But as Haiti's economy collapsed, and the country became the poorest nation in the Western Hemisphere, the restavec system exploded. The Haitian government estimates that 90,000–120,000 children are enslaved as restavecs, but the UN puts this number at 300,000—or one in ten children in Haiti. Some are as young as four years old, and 75 percent are girls, many of whom are sexually exploited.

Jean-Robert (HAITI, 2002)

Anyone of you sitting here at this very moment can go to Haiti and ask for a child to live with you. All you need to do is to find a family with too many mouths to feed and promise that you will send the child to school and she is yours. You can treat her the same way slaves were treated under the French colonists. You do not have to make her a part of the family, learn her name, send her to school, provide her with health care, buy her clothes, give her affection, or treat her like a human being. You can make her sleep outside, torture her to death and dump her body in the trash, and no one will question you, and there will be no government investigation to find out the cause of death. In fact, the same specialized whips that were manufactured to torture the slaves during the 1700s can be purchased today on

Jean-Robert Cadet (photograph by Adam Cadet, 2004)

the streets of Port-au-Prince to torture children in domestic servitude. This practice is a violation of Haiti's Constitution, the Convention on the Rights of the Child (CRC), which passed the UN General Assembly in 1989, as well as the ILO's Convention concerning the Prohibition and Immediate Action for the Elimination of the Worst Forms of Child Labour (Worst Forms of Child Labour Convention) of 1999.

One of the worst forms of abuse facing Haiti's slave children is exclusion. Slave children in Haiti set tables for meals in which they cannot partake, fetch water that they cannot use for their own needs, are denied medical care when they are struck by illness, are forbidden to speak until spoken to, and stay outside when adults are inside. While these slave children are forced to be invisible, they must remain within the reach of their master's voice. Otherwise, severe doses of physical punishment will ensue without mercy. This is a reality that provoked nightmares that consumed my own childhood and still haunt me well into my adulthood.

At night, when I was a restavec child in Haiti, the adults installed themselves in the living room and I would go behind the house to watch television through the window screen, standing on a concrete block in the dark while mosquitoes feasted on my exposed legs and arms. I had to be constantly within the reach of the grown-ups' voices in case they wanted to be served a cold beverage from the refrigerator within their reach. I then remained out of sight until everyone was in bed, arranged my bedding under the kitchen table, and woke before everyone would get out of bed.

Today, in the year 2002, on any early morning in Port-au-Prince, children in tattered clothes are seen hand in hand with children in bright uniforms crossing the street. The ones in tattered clothes are restavecs who must return to their duties as domestic slaves after escorting their counterparts to school.

This daily exclusion from any community or family often leaves no visible scars, but the trauma lasts a lifetime. These children all too frequently become victims of the abusive and institutionalized practice of domestic servitude. Since their most basic rights—to a family's love and protection, health care, and education—are denied, restavecs are invisible children, observers instead of participants in their own society.

As a slave child in Port-au-Prince, my day began at 5:30 in the morning and ended when the last adult went to sleep. I had to sweep the yard, water the plants, fill the tub for everyone's bath, empty and wash the chamber pots, hand wash diapers, boil baby bottles, wash the car twice a day, dust the furniture every day, serve people drinks in the front yard every evening, wash people's feet every evening, run errands, hand wash women's monthly napkins, fetch water from afar, be borrowed by the family's friends, and cook my own food. I worked seven days a week with no pay and no time to play. I was also excluded from all family activities, such as meals, birthdays, attending school and church, Mother's Day, Christmas, New Year's celebrations, weddings, first communions, and even funerals. I could not speak unless spoken to. For any minor infraction, such as not answering quickly enough when my name was called, I was beaten without mercy. Like all restavec children, I was only an observer rather than a participant in my Haitian society and culture.

It was by a twist of fate that I came to the United States. In 1970 the family that owned me moved to the United States and later sent for me to resume the same duties that I used to perform in Haiti. My birth certificate was purchased on the black market, and I was listed as my virtual owner's son only to fool the United States immigration officials.

In New York, my situation improved a great deal. My owners made sure that I wore shoes and clean clothes to hide the fact that they had a slave child living with them. However, by having to address everyone as monsieur, madame, mademoiselle, they made sure that I did not forget my status as a restavec. I no longer had to wash their feet, fetch water, or hand wash feminine napkins every month. But I continued my duties of washing dishes, cleaning the house, setting the table, babysitting three children, and washing the car.

One day, a family friend who knew me in Haiti came to visit and told the family that it was against the law in the United States not to send a minor to school. I was taken to Spring Valley High School in New York and placed in the ninth grade. I was about sixteen years old and I had the equivalent of a third grade education, with no English proficiency.

When the family realized that their children and I would be attending the same school, I was shown the door to fend for myself. However, the fact that I was attending school, participating in extracurricular activities, and eating in the cafeteria with my fellow students made me an integral part of American society. For the first time in my life, I could express my needs, feelings, and opinions.

After four years in high school, I graduated and joined the United States Army for three years. I then completed my university studies and eventually wrote my autobiography, *Restavec* (University of Texas Press, 1998), simply to raise international consciousness to the plight of Haiti's more than three hundred thousand slave children.

By looking at me, you cannot tell that I never had a childhood. It was stolen, and the accomplice is Haiti's institutionalized practice of domestic servitude. Since it can never be recovered, I will feel its absence for the rest of my life. To give you an idea what it is like to have never had a childhood, let me read parts of the foreword to my book that my wife Cindy wrote:

> My days and nights reverberate with the truth of this story that my husband has written. I was not there to witness the circumstances of his birth, the horrors of his childhood or his surreal assimilation into American society that form the basis of his memoirs, but I lie beside him now each night as he sleeps. And when that sleep is fitful—when I hear his labouring breath, his muffled cry, or feel his arms tremble and his legs thrash about—I know that reality from decades ago is up on us again.

Four months ago, while I was in Haiti to distribute clothes to street children who once were slaves, a Haitian acquaintance invited me to spend a weekend as a guest in his family's house. It was a two-story yellow and white brick house in an upper-class suburb in Port-au-Prince, protected by an eight-foot wall and a large red iron gate. I was awakened from a light sleep at around four in the morning by the crowing of roosters. I went to sleep again, and I opened my eyes to daylight when I heard a noise coming from the yard. It was quarter to six. I got out of bed and I looked down from the balcony. It was the sound of Celita's large broom sweeping the cement yard. Everyone else in the house was still in bed.

Celita was an eleven-year-old slave girl who had been living with the family for the past two years. Her mother, who lived in the countryside, had handed Celita to the host family because she was no longer able to provide her daughter with what every child needs—three meals a day and a decent school. Celita was dressed in an oversized, sleeveless T-shirt and a skirt.

She cleaned up after the dog, washed the yard with buckets of water and dried it with a rubber squeegee. Then she repeatedly carried water from a bucket upstairs to flush toilets and to fill up bathtubs. After each of the four adults and one child bathed, she set the table and made a trip to the bakery, while the cook prepared breakfast. As everyone ate, Celita stood near the doorway with her hands behind her back, waiting for requests to pass the butter, the sugar, the salt, or whatever someone did not care to reach for. After breakfast, Celita cleared the table and ate the leftover food sitting on a cement block near the gate. Then she washed dishes and went upstairs to make the beds, dust the furniture, and mop the rooms.

While doing these tasks, she was interrupted with several requests: "Celita fetch my slippers," "Celita bring me a comb," "Celita bring my purse." Besides being the doer and the fetcher of everything for everyone, Celita also cared for the family's bright-eyed nine-year-old daughter, Maida, whose face looked healthy and was always ready to smile. She was often praised and affectionately touched by her mother, father, and grandfather, who spoke to her only in French. A large picture of her first communion in a gold frame graced the small coffee table in the living room. Maida was Catholic, she had toys, and attended an expensive private school.

Celita was a dark-skinned child with a thin, scarred, and hardened face that did not seem able to smile. Her eyes were deep and dull. She was often criticized and threatened with the back of a hand. She had no picture of herself in the house. She did not go to school, and her owners never took her to any church. She had no religion. She entertained Maida instead of playing with her. She obeyed Maida's every command.

As her owner began to back his brown car out of the driveway, he honked his horn and Celita ran at full speed to open the heavy iron gate that kept the house and everyone inside safe from intruders. As soon as Celita finished her other house-cleaning duties, she sat on a cement block and began to wash by hand a huge pile of clothes. And again, she was constantly interrupted: "Where is Celita—come wash this pot," "Celita come dry the floor," "Celita come flush the toilet," "Celita come set the table." By late afternoon, the brown car returned again and the horn was honked again. Celita rushed to the front yard and pulled opened the heavy iron gate. The car entered, and she pushed the gate shut.

By late evening, the family sat on the front porch relaxing in the warm tropical breeze. Celita carried a bucket of water to the side of the house where the dog was tied. She bathed there, changed to an oversize dress, and remained out of sight but within the reach of everyone's voice. Soon the requests began again until everyone went to bed: "Celita bring me a glass of water," "Celita fetch my slippers." Celita's sole purpose was to slave. Her right to be a child ended the very moment she walked through the red iron gate. Her masters' comfort was her hell.

Haiti's institutionalized practice of using children as domestic slaves violates every article of the Convention on the Rights of the Child, which passed the UN General Assembly unanimously, along with Haiti's ratification in 1989. Haiti is now making preparations to celebrate its 200th year of independence in 2004. Leaders of many nations will be invited to attend the ceremony, and every Haitian will take to the streets to celebrate, except the children forced into domestic slavery.

CHILD SEX SLAVERY IN CAMBODIA

Chantha and Chariya became child sex slaves in Cambodia at the respective ages of thirteen and seven. Chariya was trafficked with her sister, who was only four. Both narrators emphasize the abrupt shattering of their childhoods. Chantha notes that the dreams of a "little girl" were over when she entered slavery, and Chariya reveals that she saw "things that children should never see."

Both narrators also communicate that slavery continues to cast a long shadow. For Chariya, who spent four years in slavery before being rescued, freedom includes "nightmares." And for Chantha, freedom brought no restored sense of self; she observes that her life has "had no significance, no value" (though she hopes that it might finally achieve "meaning" through the telling of her story). Instead, freedom brought rejection by her family, prostitution, AIDS, and—six months after she told her story—death from an AIDS-related illness.

Chantha (CAMBODIA, 2003)

When I was a little girl I dreamed of going to school, and then finding someone to love, to have a family. That was my dream, when I was a little girl. Then I was forced to become a prostitute at age thirteen. My mother died when I was very young. My stepmother was mean; she would beat me and refuse to give me food. So I left my father's house to find work. When I arrived in the big city, a woman said she can give me a job at her house. I was very happy to have some work and a place to stay.

But at this woman's house, men would come. If I tried to refuse, the woman would beat me or shock me with electricity. And there was always someone watching, so I could not escape. In this house I was one of fifteen girls. After two years I convinced the woman to let me go, so I can find my father and stepmother.

When I found them, they despised me and told me to leave. For three days and nights I slept in the fields along the road without any food. Hungry and alone I sat near a garden and waited for men to come to me. After several customers I had enough money to get some food and a bus ticket. In the city a man found me and said he had a safe place for me to stay. Then he sold me to another brothel. When I was a prostitute I was required to have fifteen men each day. If I did not, I would be beaten and refused food.

This is the story of my life. I am now twenty-four and I am dying from AIDS. One of my greatest fears is that when I die no one will come to my burial. When I talk to God, I ask him to give me peace. My life has had no significance, no value....I hope that by sharing my story, my life will finally have meaning and can help prevent others from the deep sadness of my life.

Chariya (CAMBODIA, 2003)

My name is Chariya. I am twelve years old and I have seen things that children should never see. When I was seven, my mother died. When she was living she made thatched roofs for people's houses. She was a wonderful mother. I miss her very much. My father was unable to care for me and my little sister, so my auntie took us. She was not a nice woman. One day she sold me and my little sister to a brothel. I was aged seven. My little sister was aged only four.

We were locked in a room where we could not escape. We were forced to watch pornographic movies to learn what to do. We were forced to watch couples through a hole in the wall. If we refused, they would shock us with an electrical rod. I still have nightmares.

SEX SLAVERY IN GERMANY

In the aftermath of her enslavement, Mariana still felt trapped. She couldn't return to her Ukrainian village because her neighbors believed she had been a "prostitute in Germany" and because pimps were looking for her. She moved to her uncle's house, then to a friend's house, seemingly on a perpetual journey from slavery to freedom.

Masha Gnezdilova and Irina Veselykh encountered the same problem of freedom after slavery. "Even two years later, I was depressed," explains Masha. Though ten years might have passed since her trafficking, "the situation has still not changed," she says, confronting the ongoing fact of slavery for others. Equally, Irina continues to grapple with the fact that her traffickers "continue to traffic women." Irina also outlines a more practical problem. After her escape she "began a long, terrible process of multiple questionings and misunderstandings," was placed in prison for three months, and only received assistance from an NGO.

Both Masha and Irina were trafficked to Germany from Russia, where traffickers abduct an estimated fifty-five thousand women each year. Corrupt police officers and border guards reportedly accept bribes to facilitate trafficking. Irina was taken along the so-called Eastern Route through Poland. This is a key overland corridor for trafficking women to the European Union from Russia, Ukraine, Romania, and the Baltics.

Mariana was trafficked to Germany from Ukraine in 1997 at the age of sixteen. She had accepted the offer of a job. The push for women to leave Ukraine and other former Soviet areas is powerful, for women account for up to 90 percent of the unemployed and are usually the first fired. Traffickers abduct an estimated thirty-five thousand women from Ukraine each year; and by some estimates four hundred thousand Ukrainian women under the age of thirty have been sold abroad. Ukrainian consulates have brought 11,000 trafficking victims back to Ukraine. The International Organization for Migration says it has helped more than 2,100 Ukrainian victims since 2000, but it estimates that this is a small portion of the total number.

Almost fifty countries serve as destination points throughout Europe and eastward. Germany, where all three women were taken, is one of the most popular destinations in Europe for women trafficked from Ukraine and Russia, though victims who arrive in Germany also come from Africa (mainly Nigeria) and Asia (mainly Thailand). Prostitution was legalized in Germany in 2002, in part to stop human trafficking—as a legitimate trade, prostitution would presumably be safer and healthier. But the UN still rates Germany "very high" as a destination for sex slaves, and in 2006 the Parliamentary Assembly of the Council of Europe expressed concern that between thirty thousand and sixty thousand women might be trafficked for sexual exploitation during the 2006 World Cup championship in Germany (most likely there was no significant increase in sex trafficking).

Mariana (GERMANY, 2003)

I was born in 1981 in Poltava region, Ukraine. I had never known who my father was. My grandmother told that he had worked at the collective farm and had died there during the fire. My mother died when I was three years old and my grandmother brought me up. I studied at school and worked hard at the collective farm and at home. In 1997 I finished the ninth form. I couldn't continue studying, because I had to go to the region center.

Once in summer my friends and I went dancing. There were a lot of young people and some boys from Kiev among them. The boy from my school came up to me and said that one of the Kievites wanted to speak to me. His name was Rostik. He proposed for me to work in Germany as a nurse. When my friend Nadja learned about this work she also was very interested in it. We decided to go together, but Rostik didn't come to our village for a long time. My grandmother got very little pension and I worked at the collective farm. I was waiting for Rostik.

He came to the village only before Christmas and proposed for me to go to Germany at once. He persuaded my friend and me that everything will be good. But Nadja's parents didn't allow her to go. I also started to hesitate, but he persuaded me. Rostik promised that one woman who also wanted to work in Germany would go with me. I considered him to be a reliable and thoughtful person. So I agreed to go and promised to my grandmother to be back in a month. Rostik asked me whether I had a foreign passport. But I hadn't even a Ukrainian passport. Then he said that he would take care of the affair by himself.

We went by car. There was a woman in the car, but she disappeared somewhere during the trip. I didn't notice that we crossed Poland border. In Poland we stopped for a night in the house of one of Rostik's friends. His name was Stefan. He helped us to cross a river at night and we got to Germany. We continued our trip by car. Guys brought me to some house and told me that the owner was waiting for me inside and that I had to take care of the affair by myself. I left all my things in the car and came in.

The owner was a middle-aged man. He told me some words in bad Russian and pushed me in a room and locked me there. I couldn't understand what had happened with me. I'd sat there for a long time and didn't know what to do. Then a nice woman came to me and brought me some food. She asked about my parents and my birthplace. The woman was Polish and I understood her quite well. She asked me whether I knew I had to work as prostitute. I began to cry.

Two weeks passed. I was crying all the time. I wasn't allowed to go out and I was scared. The same women brought me food. Once the women asked me how old I was. She didn't believe that I was sixteen. Next morning she came to me again and said she was very sorry for me. She gave me some money and explained how to escape. She asked me not to tell anybody that she had helped me. The woman said that the owner paid big money for me.

So I've escaped to Holland. The police helped me to make contact with an NGO that helps those women who were sold. They helped me to come back to Ukraine. Now my grandmother has died. I can't live in my village because the pimps are looking for me. They are very angry that I escaped. They said to my neighbors that I was a prostitute in Germany.

I don't have any place to live. Two months I have lived with my uncle, another two months with my friend. I would like to enter a hairdresser school, but it costs money. I don't have any.

Masha (GERMANY, 2006)

My name is Masha. I am thirty-three years old. By education I'm a lawyer in the field of social services. I previously worked as an inspector in the social security services department and as a human resource manager in a medical college.

In 1996 I visited my relatives in St. Petersburg. While standing in a line at the railway station to buy a ticket home, I met a middle-aged woman who seemed very nice. During our conversation she mentioned that she has good friends in Germany who are looking for a young Russian girl to assist them with housekeeping. She offered me a chance to go to Germany to see the country and learn the language as well as to earn some money. At the time, I had not been to a foreign country and was unemployed. The opportunity seemed interesting and I agreed. This woman helped me fill out the necessary paper work, and in the beginning of 1997 I left for Germany on a bus.

In Hamburg I was met by a young Russian woman named Janna. She brought me to her home and immediately took my passport away, acting as though she wanted to show it to the people I was supposed to work for. The next day, she met three more Russian girls at the bus station and brought them to her home as well. Their passports were also taken away. Later that day, Janna informed me that the job I had been promised did not exist. However, she said that there was no need for me to go home as she would provide me with another job. Janna took all of us by car to a bar called Sixty Four where prostitutes worked. Janna told us that we would work as prostitutes and that there was no sense in resisting or complaining—in fact, it would be dangerous to do so. She threatened that if anyone tried to escape to the police she would be severely beaten, since they have their own people in the police and runaways would be returned regardless and punished.

I decided not to behave aggressively and pretended to be completely compliant; I even tried to demonstrate frustration when clients did not select me. Janna believed my act and began looking for an appropriate bar for me. This is how I came to work in several German bars.

One day, Janna brought me and three other girls to a bar in a small city on the highway Hamburg-Hanover. I don't remember the name of the city, but it was close to Bielefeld. The bar's name was Savoy and it was closed. Two day later, we found out that the reason the bar was closed was that several Russian girls had recently been murdered there. Now that the situation with the police had been cleared up and the club reopened, we were brought in to replace the murdered girls.

There we found the clothes, underwear, and purses of the murdered girls. At the bar's grand opening, we worked as hostesses and prostitutes. We were not allowed to leave this place and had no documents. Fortunately, approximately a week later the bar was raided and we were taken to the police department in Bielefeld. At the police department, a Russian female lawyer questioned us. She pitied us and we were released into the streets. We did not have anywhere to go. No one told us about any shelters or services. We were lost and afraid in a strange country. We didn't know the language and had no money, so we went back to the bar.

We had hoped that we could get our things, call for help, and arrange our escape, but there was someone at the bar waiting for us who called Janna. That evening, Janna came to take me back to Hamburg. There she sold me to another pimp for $1,000, and again I was put to work in one of the German bars as a prostitute. In a week this bar was also raided by the police and I was again detained at the police department. Later, I was released and was supposed to pick up my documents at another place. I did not know German or the city but kind local people helped me get there. When I finally got there, they did not have a translator, but my documents were ready for my deportation from Germany. I wanted to explain what had happened and that I shouldn't be deported, but nobody wanted to listen or talk to me and I ran away.

Usually, when a girl's visa expires or when she is detained by the police, the traffickers provide her with a false passport (at that time for me it was a Polish one) and they immediately traffic her to the Netherlands. Most of the criminal groups have clubs in both Germany and the Netherlands, where they also sell drugs.

The other girls from the German night club were given false passports and trafficked to Holland, but I could not tolerate it anymore. I stopped eating and told my pimp that I would jump from the fourth floor. He believed me and was afraid that I would draw more attention from the police; I don't know exactly why, but this man helped me buy a ticket home and come back to Russia. Thus, in two months I was back home. But even two years later, I was depressed and had many troubles. Then I found an ad in a newspaper for the St. Petersburg Crisis Center for Women, which provides psychological assistance to the victims of human trafficking. I contacted them and they invited me to come in. This is how I came across the Angel Coalition. From them, I received psychological, moral, and material assistance. I went back to my town and started an NGO that is a member of the Angel Coalition. It seems like we Russian women are placed in impossible economic conditions and are not needed by our own country. In other countries, we are spit on as prostitutes when we are really victims. Ten years have passed since I was trafficked, but the situation has still not changed. Is the German government really not aware of what is happening in their country? Or are they happy to profit from our suffering?

Irina (GERMANY, 2006)

My name is Irina Veselykh. In 1983 I graduated from the construction college in Amur, and from 1984 until 1991 I worked as an engineer in the department of production at a construction company. I was married in 1996 and I have two daughters. During perestroika (1992–1997), I requalified to be an accountant and later worked as a senior accountant at a hospital.

Afterwards, I divorced my alcoholic husband, took a one-year course in massage and cosmetology, and moved to Volgodonsk where I worked in a clinic as a physiotherapist. I was only making $100 per month and supporting two children on my own.

Because I needed more income and was in debt, I began looking for advertisements for short-term work abroad. I had hoped to work for a maximum of six months to one year and send the money home to my children.

I came across an advertisement offering work abroad in the newspaper *Chance*. The company that I turned to for help finding work appeared to be entirely legitimate and I didn't feel any apprehension. The Agency for Employment Abroad offered me work as a waitress. I was given 500 euros [$650] for a visa, tickets, and travel with the understanding that I would return 1,000 euros [$1,300] when I was working. I was to earn 800–900 euros [$1,000–1,150] a month. Everything was arranged from the company's offices in Volgograd and Moscow. I was told that I would have a six-month contract once I arrived in Germany. I signed their contract since everything seemed trustworthy and they assured me that the work in Germany was legal.

I traveled by bus through Poland without any money for food. When I arrived in Germany in the city of Bremen, I was met by two extremely rude young Russians named Evgeny and Tatiana. They took my passport and informed me that there was no waitress job and that I was expected to work as a prostitute. When I objected, they told me that if I wanted to go home I had to pay back the 1,000 euros. I tried to refuse and they beat me. When I threatened to go to the police, I was warned that the police had been bought off and that without my documents I would be considered the criminal. They said that all the pimps are working under the protection of the police. They control girls with the help of the police. They showed me photographs of dead girls who had tried to go to the police.

I was terribly shocked and afraid. I decided that the only way to survive was to cooperate. Almost immediately, Tatiana and Evgeny left for a vacation in the Canary Islands and I was sold to another man, Viktor, who was running a business in Bremen selling young Russian girls to Belgian pimps for $15,000 apiece. I started working in a brothel managed by a German woman named Tony. This was a kind of point of dispensation—some women were sold to Belgium, some to the Netherlands and other places. I was popular with German and Dutch men so they kept me there. The majority of men were Germans.

Tony's place was a legal brothel, but she knew that most of the women there were illegal and had no documents because all of their documents had been taken by the pimps. Viktor and a Lithuanian woman named Monika gave me a fake Lithuanian passport. All the new Russian girls who came were forced to buy the fake Lithuanian passports for 2,000 euros [$2,600]. However, Viktor kept the actual passports and the false ones. In addition, Viktor and the other pimps reminded all of us constantly that they knew where our families were and they would kill our children if we tried to escape.

I complained that I could not pay my debts, so they sent me to a different club where I could service more clients and pay lower rent. I was then taken to a club called Diplomat, which is in the Netherlands on the border with Germany. But I saw right away that no matter how many men there were, I could never repay the debts. I immediately made the decision to run away. There were three other women, also terrified, who had already been living there for a few months (also on false documents). A beautiful Russian girl by the name of Tatiana helped me try to run away by stealing my fake passport and all of my real documents from the pimps. She said she could not go with me because the pimps had threatened to kill her two-year-old son back in Russia. She wanted me to get away and get help for her and her family. But I later learned from Russian men who were trying to help me that she was killed for helping me.

Other girls in the club helped me escape and I took a taxi to the town of Van Shoten, looking for a man named Ben who owned a nightclub called Antenna and was known to help girls escape from trafficking and the Russian mafia. He helped hide me, but the Russian mafia found me working as a hostess and told me that I was going to be killed. That night Ben took me by car to his Dutch friends, who hid me for two weeks in their garage and brought me food while I was being hunted. I was moved from one place to another, working in nightclubs as a waitress but not as a prostitute.

Many good Dutch people tried to help me, but I was always followed by the Russian gangsters. I needed to get to the police, but it was dangerous. The Dutch people I was staying with brought my twenty-one-year-old daughter to the Netherlands to help me. With my daughter, who speaks English, I went directly to the police. But at the police station, I was immediately separated from my daughter and detained for five days by the Dutch national police.

So began a long, terrible process of multiple questionings and misunderstandings by the authorities.

The authorities wanted to charge me for using the false passport that I was provided by the criminals. I gave the Dutch police all of the information about what had happened, including information about the traffickers, the Russian mafia. I told them everything I knew, and I thought they would help me. I was not provided with a lawyer and I was suddenly told that I had to work out the fine levied by the judicial system of the Netherlands for the use of a false passport. I hadn't even used that passport and did not agree with the decision of the court. But who listened to me? After all the assistance that I provided the investigators, I was placed in humiliating conditions and remained in serious danger without protection from the Russian gangsters.

After determining that the crime had taken place in Germany, the Dutch national police turned me over to the immigration police and they placed me in a shelter. I provided the authorities with all of the information again while the police investigated and verified every part of my story. After two weeks, I was released from the shelter and I returned to my daughter.

But, eventually, my daughter had to go home to work. I stayed in the Netherlands for two years, living only on the small benefits I received with the help of kind Dutch people. Finally, I grew tired of this situation. I could not wait any longer for my appointment in court living in such circumstances. I told the Dutch authorities that I wanted to go home. I said that I would return if they needed me to testify, but I was very, very tired. My health was poor. I missed my daughters. I was constantly depressed and often thinking about suicide.

But instead of helping me go home, the Dutch government decided I had not suffered enough and placed me in prison for three months because I didn't pay the fine for using a false passport—a fine that I didn't know about. There was a contradiction between the Dutch national police who wanted the fine paid and the immigration police who acknowledged that I was a victim of trafficking.

For one month, I was not allowed to get in contact with lawyers or with my relatives. I started a hunger strike to defend my innocence, but as a result I was put into solitary confinement with only a mattress on the floor.

I was only able to get help when my daughter contacted the Russian consul in the Netherlands with the help of the Angel Coalition in Moscow. My daughter had called the Angel Coalition Trafficking Victim Assistance Center on their toll-free helpline, and the Angel Coalition contacted the Dutch law enforcement liaison officer at the Dutch embassy in Moscow. He began investigating with the Dutch police while the Angel Coalition worked with my family. I was released on the street with 30 euros [$40]. The police were supposed to take me to the consulate, but they gave me no help. Local people helped me get to the consulate. From there I was sent for a short time to a shelter and then returned home to Russia. The Angel Coalition met me at the airport, gave me a ticket home, and provided me with medicine. This is the only human assistance that I received during the entire time that I was in this terrible situation. The Angel Coalition is still helping me cope with all the terrible things I went through in Germany and the Netherlands.

I did not commit any crime in those countries and I was put in prison for absolutely nothing. The people who involved me in that situation are still free and continue to traffic women under government cover. My rights were violated—who will pay me back for all of my suffering? In those countries, the rights of immigrants in difficult situations are violated and their governments do not want to take responsibility for what is happening on their territory.

SEX SLAVERY IN SOUTH AFRICA

Faith was taken from her home country of Zimbabwe to South Africa in 2004. Like many young Zimbabwean women, she was trafficked through the false promise of employment. Other Zimbabwean women are tricked into slavery through promises of marriage and education, and some are simply abducted. Zimbabwean women are also forced into prostitution in the United Kingdom, the United States, and Southeast Asia; and some are trafficked internally from rural to urban areas for forced domestic labor. High levels of poverty and unemployment are factors in Zimbabwe's trafficking problem, and the low status of women in Zimbabwean society perpetuates gender violence. The situation has worsened since 2005, when the Zimbabwean government began Operation Murambatsvina (Operation Clean-Up), a campaign to forcibly clear slum areas. This has displaced hundreds of thousands of people and left an estimated 223,000 children vulnerable to trafficking.

In South Africa, where Faith was still in slavery when she narrated her story, the number of trafficking victims remains unknown, but the International Organization for Migration reports that trafficked women and children arrive from the Democratic Republic of the Congo, Malawi, Mozambique, and Zambia (trafficked through Zimbabwe), and that several major criminal groups in South Africa now traffic women: Bulgarian and Thai syndicates; the Russian and the Chinese Mafia; and African criminal organizations, mainly from West Africa.

For Faith the problem of freedom is not an ongoing fear of re-enslavement, rejection by her family, traumatic memories, AIDS, or an awareness that slavery continues for others. Freedom for Faith simply doesn't exist—she has tried to escape but "had no place to go," so "had to go back" to her enslavers. Forced to continue prostitution, she concludes: "This is my life."

Faith (SOUTH AFRICA, 2005)

I am twenty-six years old. I was going to school, but I fell pregnant and had to quit. After having my baby, I had no job. Then, my uncle was living in South Africa. On one of his visits home, he informed me that he had friends in Johannesburg who owned companies and he could get a job for me there if I came with him. I followed him. We traveled with a Kombi driver and four other men. I was the only girl. We left Bulawayo at about 2 P.M. and arrived at Beitbridge at 10 P.M. Since the other men and I had no travel documents, we were dropped at Beitbridge while my uncle and the driver crossed the border. At about 12 midnight, we started to cross the border by foot and swam across the river. At 3 A.M., we reached the other side, and the men placed a white plastic bag on the road so that the Kombi driver would recognize that we had reached there. The driver saw it, drove up, and picked us up. We continued the journey and got to Pietersburg early in the morning. We then drove straight to Hillbrow. My uncle left me at the minibus driver's house because he had not paid the fare.

After two days, my uncle came back, paid the driver and took me to a club in Hillbrow and said that is where I would live. He said I had to pay my own rent. Then he had a discussion with the owners of the club and abandoned me there.

That night, the runners asked me to go up to my room. Then they sent a white man to sleep with me. That is when I realized that I had been tricked by my uncle. I was very confused. The white man asked me to give him a blow job. I resisted, so he went down and complained to the owners. They started forcing me to drink alcohol so that I could please the customers. Finally, I had to accept that I had become a prostitute.

My uncle came to see me for the first week or two to collect his money, but after that, he disappeared. When I called home, they told me that he had said that I had run away from him and he did not know where I was. I could not tell my family that I had become a prostitute. I just told them that I was working somewhere. I am very unhappy, but now this is my life. I tried to escape once, but I had no place to go to, so I had to go back there.

THE SEVERED CHAIN

Freedom after Bondage

The contest was now ended; the chain was severed.
> Frederick Douglass, *My Bondage and My Freedom,* 1855

We named it Azad Nagar—"the land that is free."
> Ramphal, a former quarry slave, India, 2004

AGRICULTURAL SLAVERY IN THE UNITED STATES

Joyce Grant is an African American woman who was born in Ocala, Florida. She subsisted on migrant work from the age of nine and from 1985 was enslaved by the Bonds family, who operated a ring of labor camps from Florida to the Carolinas. After seven years in bondage she escaped with her husband Huey.

Sometimes the experiences of twenty-first-century slaves encompass not only the narrator's turn from slavery to freedom but also a reversal for their enslavers. In 1993 members of the Bonds family were charged with conspiracy to hold workers in a state of peonage, distribution of crack cocaine, and two violations of the federal Migrant and Seasonal Agricultural Worker Protection Act. The Bonds were released from prison in 2000, and Joyce recently received word of their fate. While she had experienced stasis and entrapment ("there's nowhere to run"), the Bonds now spend *their* days trapped by the side of a highway, picking up cans for a living. In her narrative, Joyce further inverts slavery's power dynamic by using the vague and threatening third-person pronoun "they" to counter her own dehumanization ("treated like a dog").

Joyce (UNITED STATES, 2002)

Was doing migrant work since I was nine or ten. Went to school with Mormons. Only black in the school. Picking tomatoes, cucumbers, string beans. Wages still the same, and now I'm forty-three years old. It ain't went up no more than about ten, fifteen cents.

Lake Wells, near Orlando, is where I was mainly working. With my husband. Worked many years on the camp. And they be beating on you and pistol-whuppin' you. Leaky showers, the water be cold. Half-fed people, unlivable camps. Ain't no sheets on the bed. The mattress don't be fit to sleep on. The food is slop. Some of the time it be cold. For lunch, they bring you a little sandwich, sauce, and baloney. It already melted in the sun. It make your blood pressure high. Treated like a dog. They used to spit in the food. Once, the Bonds girl wrung out a tampon into the food.

Got you way down a clay dirt road; mosquitoes eat you up. You so far back out there in the woods you can't walk to town. Never got paid a cent. You go to bed at nine or ten o'clock. Sun up to sun down. They have you working in the rain at 5 A.M. Sometimes till 9 P.M. with the truck lights on picking sweet potatoes in North Carolina. Locked up each night in a compound with barbed wire, guarded by dogs. They'd make a count of everyone before bedtime, and they'd be walking with a rifle outside the hall when people slept. All the men stayed in the bullpit. Wind blows and turns over the trailer.

They take you to town in a van; they count you. They stay right there with you when you go to the store. The town's so small there's nowhere to run. They'd just come get you, and they'd tell the other crew leader man that they done stole their people.

Once they took me to Atlanta, to get homeless men by offering crack. I was tired, didn't wanna go work in the fields that day. I was telling those men how we had swimming pools and how nice the camp was. Pool tables, this that and the other.

Sometime around '91 or '92 we decided we needed to get away. We made a plan. At night, when we could, we went into the peach fields, started stowing our belongings. Got another camp leader to help us with that. The guards went and drank at night. When Huey said start running, you start running. The dogs started chasing; I fell in a ditch; Huey fell with me. The cars were chasing and the dogs were chasing, and we went to some other camp, and the guys at that second camp protected us. The way the brothers got caught was a guy came on the camp pretending to be a worker, but he was a cop or something.

The big farmer, they're the ones making the money. Maybe a contractor, like, say, Goldteeth, off one truck of sweet potatoes, he made ten thousand dollars. He probably makes sixty or seventy thousand a season. He's got his own camp now, eight miles outside Benson.

HEREDITARY SLAVERY IN MAURITANIA

Like her mother and grandmother before her, Salma Mint Saloum was born into slavery in Mauritania, one of the last places on earth where chattel slavery is practiced. Slavery was first abolished in Mauritania in 1905 by the colonial French rulers, and again when Mauritania joined the UN in October 1961. It was abolished for the third time in 1981 by the Military Committee for National Salvation. But the situation didn't fundamentally change. Masters don't have to pay their slaves or provide any sort of social security; the ban did not address how masters were to be compensated or how slaves were to gain property; and there was no provision for enforcement. This arrangement allows the legal fiction of slavery's abolition to continue. In 2003 Mauritania passed a law that made slaveholding punishable by fines and imprisonment, but no slaveholder has been prosecuted. As Salma explains in her narrative, "It doesn't matter what the laws say there, because there they don't apply the laws."

In 1997 Salma decided not to wait any longer and liberated herself. She crossed the river border to Senegal, but she still didn't feel free. As she notes, "I was free. I still wasn't free." She felt that to be "truly free," beyond the danger of re-enslavement, meant going to the United States, and so began a journey that retraced the route of the transatlantic middle passage, though with a very different outcome. She smuggled herself across the Atlantic on a cargo ship to freedom, arriving in the United States in 1999. The following year, she sought legal asylum through the New York Association for New Americans (NYANA). An immigration judge ruled that Salma was a slave entitled to U.S. protection.

In the United States, Salma observes, she experienced "total liberty." Her narrative includes a long section that compares her life as a slave with her life as a free person, and Salma defines this new freedom. She focuses on freedom of expression and being able "to talk with people I choose to talk to...to be free to go where I want, to eat what I want, to sleep where I want." Freedom also means being able to "make decisions concerning my own children," for in Mauritania she "never had the right" and had to "watch the children of the master's wife" instead of her own. Most important, however, freedom means being paid for her work. This, she emphasizes, is "really liberty."

Salma (MAURITANIA, 2003)

My name is Salma. I want you to read this attentively. If you want to meet me—I am here. I am a witness, before the whole world, to the fact of slavery in Mauritania.

I was born a slave. I was born in Mauritania in 1956. My mother and father were slaves for one family, and their parents were slaves of the same family. Ever since I was old enough to walk, I was forced to work for this family all day, every day. We never had days off. We hardly knew that it was Saturday or Sunday, because we had to work every day. Even if we were sick, we had to work.

When I was still a child, I started taking over my mother's job, taking care of the first wife of the head of the family and her fifteen children. Every day at 5 A.M. I had to make their breakfast. First, I had to get water and wood to make a fire. We were in the desert, and the well was far away, so often I had to walk a long way. I had to cook all their meals and clean their clothes and watch all the children. Even if one of my children was hurt or in danger, I didn't dare help my child, because I had to watch the children of the master's wife first. If I didn't, they would beat me. I was beaten very often, with a wooden stick or leather belt. One day they were beating my mother and I couldn't stand it, I tried to stop them. The head of the family got very angry with me, and he tied my hands and branded me with a burning iron, and he hit me across the face. The ring on his finger left a scar on my face.

When I was a slave, I was never allowed to go to school or learn anything more than some Koran verses and prayers. But I was lucky, because the eldest son of the master had gone to school away from our village and had different ideas than his father. This eldest son decided to help me. He saw that I was smart, and he secretly taught me to speak French and to read and write a little. I think that everyone thought he was raping me, but he was teaching me.

The first time I tried to escape was about ten years ago. When I left the family's village, I didn't know where to go, and I went in the wrong direction. I didn't know how close I was to Senegal, just on the other side of the river. So instead of going to Senegal, I walked for two days in the wrong direction. I found another family with slaves, and I hid with the slaves, but that family found me and sent me back. The head of the family punished me terribly. They bound my wrists and ankles and tied me to a date tree in the middle of the family compound and left me there for a week. He cut my wrists with a razor, so that I bled terribly. I still have scars on my arms.

Finally, I managed to escape. I met a man in the market who told me that Senegal was not far away, that it was just across the river, and that I could escape. So I decided that I had to try. I ran away from the family compound and went to the river. At the river, a man with a small wooden boat agreed to take me into Senegal. There I made my way to a safe house run by a former slave from Mauritania.

I stayed in Senegal for a few years. But I never felt safe there. I knew that Mauritania wasn't far away. Always I had in my head that the master of the family could come and pay people to look for me and bring me back to his house. I was afraid all the time in Dakar. I was free. I still wasn't free. The man whom I met in Rosso [on the Senegal River in Mauritania] told me that I had to go to the United States to be truly free. I saw this man again in Senegal, and he told me that I had to go to the United States. I spent several years in Dakar. I worked to live. I cleaned the house, and I washed clothes.

When I got to New York, to the United States, I found liberty. I worked when I got here, braiding hair. That was the first time I had been paid for work I had done. To be paid for my work, that was really liberty. To work for someone and be paid, I can't even explain it. I had never believed in that. Even here, in New York, I believed that I would be treated like I was in Mauritania. The first time I was paid here, I cried that day. That really helped me. I didn't know that. I had never seen a person paid for her work before in my life. It was a very, very good surprise. Now I am used to that. It has really made me happy. To work, and to learn things, to go to school, to learn, to talk with people I choose to talk to—these things are liberty to me. To have the liberty to discuss with people, to be free to go where I want, to eat what I want, to sleep where I want. Before, I didn't have that. Really, seriously, before, I didn't have that. Also, to have my children with me. One of the hardest things for me was leaving my children behind in Mauritania, but I knew that I had to escape first and then figure out how to get them out of there.

In the three years I have been here, I have been working to secure the liberty of my children, so that they would be as free as me. I had to pay people in Senegal so that they would find them and bring them to Senegal. Now most of my children are in Senegal. Every morning I get up early and buy a phone card, and I speak with my children. All my children tell me that they would rather die in the street than to return to Mauritania. Also I have been paying for them to go to school in Senegal. They never went to school in Mauritania—there they got nothing. For them, they love to go to school, to learn. One of my children is now in the United States with me. My children were like dreams for me. Since I have had my first daughter here in the United States it has become reality. I want very, very much that the others will join us. That is also liberty for me. In Mauritania, I never had the right to make decisions concerning my own children. Here, it is incomparably different.

I myself went to school in the United States. I have been learning English. I want to continue learning English. I want to learn many things. I want to learn to speak English well, like everyone. I want my children to learn English better than me. I want to become an interpreter somewhere. I also want to learn how to use computers. These are things that would never ever have been possible for me in Mauritania. In Mauritania, I didn't dare go to the government, because they wouldn't listen. Because, for them, slavery is normal. It doesn't matter what the laws say there, because there they don't apply the laws. Maybe it's written that there is no slavery, but it's not true. Even in front of the president of Mauritania I can say in full voice that there is slavery in Mauritania, because now I'm as free as he is.

When I arrived in the United States, I was in Harlem, with Africans who took me for a while. Then I went to the Bronx. The Africans with whom I was living explained to me that I should apply for asylum, that I should go to immigration. I made an application with the help of some Africans. Then I went to immigration for my interview. Immigration sent me to Federal Plaza, to court. I went to immigration court, and the judge asked me if I had a lawyer. I told him that I had a lawyer, but he didn't come. The judge told me I should get my money back and that I should go to a different lawyer who was honest. I saw the name New York Association for New Americans, and I liked that name, and I went there.

In the beginning, in the United States, I was afraid of going to immigration. I was so afraid that I would be sent back to Mauritania. After I met my lawyer, I learned that that wasn't true. Here, if you are honest and correct and you tell the truth, you will really have your liberty. Here, it's freedom. The judge was honest, and he did his job. The judge demanded proof, but then he paid attention and listened. I met a doctor who helped me, and professor Kevin Bales, and the Bellevue/NYU Program for Survivors of Torture. It was a big difference from Mauritania, and a big surprise to me. A big difference.

The hard things in life now are not understanding English and finding work. To live here, you really have to work. Those are my difficulties. In Dakar, I was in a house, and I didn't pay, I just did a little work. Here, people don't help you that way. You have to pay for everything. At NYANA people helped me. At a certain time, they gave me money to pay my rent.

I would like to be a citizen of the United States one day. I want my children to be citizens. I came here and got total liberty. I see that here there is democracy, which to me means freedom of expression. In Mauritania, there was no liberty of expression. In Dakar, I was afraid to speak out, because we were so close to Mauritania. I had to be cautious. I had to be far, far, far from Mauritania. Here in America, I can speak out.

For me, liberty was a thing that was necessary, that all the slaves must dream of. I always thought about liberty. The other slaves were afraid of being free. They were afraid that they wouldn't know where to go or what to do or who to talk to. Me, I knew that it wasn't good to be afraid, and I was never afraid of liberty. I always believed that I had to be free, and I think that helped me to escape.

I know many people who are still slaves there, from my family and other families. I never knew people in my family who escaped before me. In my family, I was the first one. My mother and father died slaves. I told my mother that one day I would be free.

DOMESTIC SLAVERY IN SUDAN AND THE UNITED KINGDOM

In 1994, when Mende Nazer was about twelve, Arab militia stormed her village in the Nuba Mountains of central Sudan. They raped and massacred the villagers and sold Mende and other children into slavery, as part of the Muslim-dominated government's war strategy against rebels in southern Sudan. For about six years Mende was beaten, sexually abused, fed food scraps, and kept prisoner as a domestic slave for a family in the Sudanese capital of Khartoum. At the age of nineteen she was taken to London and passed on to the family of a Sudanese diplomat, becoming one of an estimated six thousand women who have been trafficked to Britain in the past few years (mainly from countries in eastern Europe, Africa, and South Asia).

Mende's achievement of a free life after slavery was a highly publicized process. She escaped after several months, in September 2000, and claimed asylum, then suddenly found herself at the center of an international uproar: she published a controversial full-length autobiography in 2002, and the British government rejected her claim in October of the same year. She faced deportation and feared reprisal from the Sudanese government. Human rights and abolitionist groups appealed on her behalf, and the Sudanese embassy in Washington, D.C., denounced her as a fraud. In November 2002 the British government announced that it would reconsider her case, eventually granting her asylum and permanent residency. Mende began to spread awareness about slavery in Sudan. Her narrative explains that "the reason for talking out is to help make another slave free," and in an interview she observed of her decision to tell her story: "They treated me as less than a human being. I'll only forgive them if all my friends enslaved in Sudan are freed....I want people to know about my past."

Mende (SUDAN/UNITED KINGDOM, 2003)

I was living in a village, Karko, in the Nuba Mountains with my parents, two sisters, and two brothers. We had a very simple life. One night, when I was twelve or thirteen, we heard a noise outside. The village was under fire. People were screaming and there was confusion. We didn't know what we had to do. My dad said, "Mende, trust me, grab me hard." I clung on to him and he told my mum to stay close to me. We had to run, we had to survive.

When we finally reached the mountains, raiders were everywhere. We couldn't escape. Many people were dead. We ran and ran; we had nowhere to hide. It was very crowded and I lost my dad. Somebody caught at me and said, "I will protect you, and I will take you back to your parents later." I said OK. I believed him really because it was very dangerous. I saw people being killed in front of me; they killed the people at night and raped the girls.

He took me from this place to somewhere in the forest. When I got there I found some girls and boys there and stayed with them; he said to stay there. They were around ten and twelve years old.

We were happy because we all thought we were going back to our parents later. But after a while, all the raiders came and took everybody to a place called Geling, about a day's walk away. I was there for a few days; every day people came and took children away. A man came to the camp and chose us; I was taken in a car with five other girls to a house in a place called Khartoum. He would not let us out. We had to work all day. One by one the girls were taken away. One day, a woman came and took me away. This is my new life…this is a hard time; I stayed with this woman for six or seven years.

I had to do very hard work; I had to do everything: clean the house and big yard, wash clothes by hand, and look after her children—over time there were five. After she saw I was clean she had me cook.

Everything that was mine was kept separate. After a while, I started to play with the children, and the children liked to play with me; I liked to play, I was still a child. Before being captured I was in school; now I am not. I was beaten for every single thing, even for something that was not my fault.

At first I wanted to leave, but I couldn't because there was nowhere to go and I had no money and I could not go to the police.

From the beginning in my master's house I didn't realize I was a slave, I was confused; I wondered why I was here. Later on, my master was talking to her friend and she said two things that made me realize it. One was she mentioned she owned me. The other, she called me "abda" to her friend. She called me her slave. From that time on I understood who I am. From the beginning she treated me badly and beat me; even then I couldn't understand why. It was only when she said she was my owner and that she called me "abda" then I understood.

One day she told me I was going to London. I cried because it meant I would be farther from my family. My master told me what to say for the visa. She told me a name to give of the person I would work for and told me to say that I was only cleaning and washing dishes. I was asked how long I was going to stay and what I would earn. I said I didn't know—he was surprised so the interview ended. I was given a letter to give to my master with these questions. She said I would be there six months and the amount I would earn.

She took me to the airport and said I would be collected. I worked in London as a domestic. My master in Khartoum instructed me to behave myself and obey the new master and do the same sort of work I did for her.

Now I feel I'm free because I am doing things I never used to do before. For me the reason for talking out is to help make another slave free—not just a slave from Sudan, but from anywhere in the world. By talking out, people will be more aware and more able to help people become free.

I am studying to improve my English. My hope first is to see my family and to be a nurse.

DEBT BONDAGE SLAVERY IN INDIA

In 2000, some of the 220 residents of Sonebarsa, a quarrying village in Uttar Pradesh, India, revolted against their slaveholders. About forty families lived in Sonebarsa, all of them Kols, an ethnic group near the bottom of India's steep ladder of caste and discrimination, and all locked into hereditary debt bondage. Children worked from the age of three or four, and infant mortality was high.

Ramphal, Choti, Shyamkali, and Sumara were four of the slaves who rebelled. The villagers had begun meeting with organizers from Sankalp, a grassroots NGO that has so far helped four thousand slaves free themselves from slavery in the stone quarries of Uttar Pradesh. Seeyawati, who works for Sankalp, recently explained that organizers offered the villagers two things initially: "an example of another village where we'd been able to get some progress done," and the question how long could they live this life as a slave. Bala, who also works for Sankalp, added: "Earlier on, there was no hope at all amongst the people. They didn't believe they could be free. We gave them a new hope and said to them, 'What has happened has happened. The past is past. But it's up to you to make a change, because it's your life and the lives of your children.'" The slaves began to organize.

Women were particularly central to this process of self-liberation. As Bala explained: "When one of the slave owners came to a house and raped a man's wife, fifteen females came out of their houses and said, 'No more!' formed their own self-help group, and joined us in the movement." The narratives focus on the role of women in the process of self-liberation. Choti observes that the women "played a very big role in getting revolution," and Shyamkali says that "because we are also bread earners...we also have [an] equal role to play in fighting for our freedom."

The slaves called a mass meeting and were joined by 3,500 people from sixty villages. Slaveholders interrupted the meeting, attacked the villagers, and shot guns into the air. The villagers retaliated by throwing stones, and one of the contractors was killed. His friends set fire to Sonebarsa. "Not a thing was left, everything was gone," recounts Choti. Eight men from the village were scapegoated and jailed. Ramphal was one of these eight, along with Choti's husband. After the burning of Sonebarsa, Sankalp assisted the forty refugee families and helped them form microcredit unions. The villagers pooled their money and petitioned for a mining lease. But the Allahabad Mining Corporation wouldn't allow leases, and so the villagers moved on to unoccupied land in Uttar Pradesh and began mining it. Authorities protested this in court. A judge ruled that no unauthorized work was being done and signed leases. Today the villagers—including Ramphal, Choti, Shyamkali, and Sumara—continue to build their community, which they have named Azad Nagar, "the land that is free."

Ramphal (INDIA, 2004)

My name is Ramphal. I am twenty-seven or twenty-eight years old. I was born a bonded laborer, and I remember my earliest childhood days. Way back, we were farmers. We all worked in the field, and we were bonded laborers under the contractor. Then we came to the stone quarry and we became slaves. But there is actually no difference between being a bonded laborer and being a slave. It is the same thing. When my grand-parents were born, they were slaves. When my parents were born, they were slaves. When I was born, I was born a slave, and the situation really didn't change until recently—about five or six years ago. When my son was born, he was born a slave. And when I went to prison, my daughter was born a slave.

Ramphal (photograph by Peggy Callahan, Free the Slaves, 2004)

When I say I was a slave, or that my parents were slaves, I want you to understand what I'm talking about. If I wanted to cycle on the road, the moment I stepped onto my cycle I would be stopped and thrashed. The reason? I didn't get the slave owner's permission to use the road. If I walked out of my house, if I wanted to sit somewhere, if I wanted to eat, if I wanted to drink, any single action at any point in time, anything that I wanted to do, I required permission. That's what I mean when I say I was a slave. Freedom of movement was something I didn't know existed. And it was not just me. My mother, my father, my grandparents had to live through this, generation after generation. It was deep in the psyche.

But it was only when we thought about it and became aware, that we realized that we were slaves. The realization came when we looked at the contractor and saw we did all the hard work. We were responsible for loading the trucks. For all the stones we would load onto the truck we would get the measly sum of 250–300 rupees [$5–6] and he would pocket the rest of the 1,500 rupees [$30]. At no time were we free to do what we wanted to do or to make our own choices. That's when we realized we were slaves.

Each time I think back and look at the life that I led in that village, my heart is filled with grief and with sadness. There was just no relationship between the slave owner and us. It was a matter of their mood or their fancy. They would just pick up anyone on the road, anyone cycling, someone's brother, someone's son, myself, anyone. Any single individual at any point in time could be just picked up and beaten, no rhyme or reason. My mother, my sister, somebody else's mother, sister, wife, daughter. It made no difference to them. There was no feeling within them that "this is my employee, this person works for me." Almost that you weren't human. That's the level of torture for us, the indignity that we suffered from. Understand the fact that everyone was under their control. The slave owners had complete authority. There was not a moment when they would think, Oh my God, look who's sitting there, a person. We weren't individuals. You have to understand that. Whatever they wanted to do, they could do. We were in total fear of them.

The level of violence against the females was always very high. There were always the situations when we, the men, would go to work. We would go to load the lorries, and very often the slave owners would just come inside and do as they pleased with the females. There was nothing you could do. An incident happened in a district not very far from here. An eight-year-old girl was sitting in a house and these landlords came and they just set fire to the house. The girl died. They could do what they wanted to do. As simple as that. The level of fear, the level of constant control that we were under, was so high that we were just shaking each time anyone would approach us. There was just no dream. Anything else was an impossibility.

Now the situation has changed. All my children are being born free. They are free men. What happened was that the level of torture and harassment was escalating. There was no end; it kept going on and on. And into this environment people from the municipality came in and talked to us about forming a committee. We got together as an awareness group. Then people from Sankalp came from outside to talk to us. Committees forming made the contractors jittery, and because of their jitteriness, they began labeling us as rebel leaders and politicians. The contractors even harassed the Sankalp people and beat them up a couple of times. But somehow something had sunk in at some level. When Sankalp left, about ten mothers thought together and started talking.

There was a thought process about how we should get together and form an organization, this informal committee. The thought processes got conceptualized and formalized, and the entire village joined in unanimously. There was a rally in Falatna and a lot of us went there—almost the entire village got together and went there. There, a lot of issues were raised. It wasn't an easy rally, but as a result there was this feeling spreading among the people, that "yes, something was happening, something was possible." These ripples were moving over everyone.

After that, the people of Sankalp would come in repeatedly. They would talk to us; awareness spread, and on the basis of what they told us and what we thought among ourselves, we started walking along a path. A direction was shown and we were moving toward it. Then there was a huge meeting in Ramgarh. A large number of people came. The villages adjoining our village flocked together. The meeting came at a time when the ripples were escalating so there was an expectation in the air that something was going to give, something would happen. That was the feeling that was prevalent among everyone. There was electricity in the air. The slave owners in turn also knew that the meeting was going to happen so they were prepared. Violence was what they had on their agenda. We had an inkling that they knew.

We had all assembled together, about five thousand villagers. We had a meeting peacefully. But as the meeting was about to terminate, we noticed that about ten of the slave owners were circling around the entire congregation. The meeting began to disperse. Some people went to nearby shops to buy stuff, and the slave owners came to these shops and used their bare hands, their shoes, their slippers, and randomly began to beat these shop owners and the people buying provisions. There was uproar; people were screaming and shouting. We all turned around and came back to check what was happening. But even then, violence did not erupt. People were asking, "What's up? What's happening? What's wrong? Why are you beating us up?" Then the entire flock turned around and came back toward this commotion. Now there were five thousand people. A discussion began between the elders of the mob and the slave owners, but the slave owners took pistols and shot them in the air. When the mob heard these shots in the air, that's when all controls broke loose. Now they were scared, scared for their life and also angry. The mob lost its cool and completely surrounded these ten people. There were sticks being used, blows being thrown around, and basically violence erupted. In the chaos and confusion, the chief of the slave owners died and about four others were wounded. The moment the mob realized that death of someone had taken place, calmness resumed.

We all congregated again and moved slowly toward the police station in Bara, but there were over five thousand of us and we were on foot. We were walking around the mountain, which is a longer winding path, so by the time we reached the police station, the slave owners had already reached there. Since their version of the story had reached the police first, they refused to lodge any of our complaints or accept our story. We made a silent protest. We just sat...we just sat on the doorstep of the police station and refused to move, hoping that this demonstration would compel them to register our complaint. In the meantime, the slave owners who had been injured had been rushed to the Allahabad hospital. Over there, in front of a doctor, they named about eight or ten villagers they could think of or who were popular as the people responsible for the mob attack.

On the basis of the testimony that the police got from the slave owners, they took about eight of us and they put us in prison for six months. The families of my fellow inmates were left high and dry. There was no one to look after them. I was at least safe. I was in prison, there was no fear of any landowner, any slave owner. But at the same time all of the fellow mob members were severely harassed by slave owners. They were under constant pressure. I had no hope that I would see the earth again, that I would be free; but after six months, I was released. My release was a combined effort of a lot of people—the members of Sankalp, my self-help group, fellow villagers, people from other villages. They all tried very hard, spoke to a lot of officials, gathered money for my bail application. Sankalp moved every single rock to get me freedom. But afterwards the slave owners had banned my reentry into my own village.

Right about that time of the Ramgarh meeting, a girl was burnt alive by the landlord for no rhyme or reason. It's all connected, these incidents that took place one after the other. And, as a result of that, the houses were burned by the landlord. When the looting happened, eight of us men were in prison. Houses were looted; the women weren't protected; the men weren't there. Every household item that you can think of—clothes, suitcases, food, baskets, water—was completely destroyed, burned, looted. In all forty houses, not one needle and thread could be found. Gone, all gone. That was a bumper year; there was a great amount of crop. Every house, no matter how poor, had about ten or twenty quintals [2,200–4,400 pounds] of rice and wheat all stocked up. Even if the crops had failed for the next two years we would have survived. But all of that, every single speck of grain, was gone. You think we would have complained to the police, taken some legal action, but they were hopeless. They had taken so much money as bribes that they were standing while the houses were looted, just standing and watching.

We all moved to land close to my former village. The belief was so strong among all of us, this feeling of brotherhood that we now share, that we all actually formed this entire village just by ourselves, and we named it Azad Nagar—"the land that is free." This means so much to us, the fact that it self-proclaimed, that we all led a march one day. If you just stretch your eyes one day, you might catch a glimpse of it.

I'm so happy with this new life that I've got. It gives me so much joy—the fact that I can control my own mind, my own thoughts, my own movements. I can't even look back at my earlier existence. Now we are in control, to do what we want, when we want, how we want. I had taken a loan of about 5,000 rupees [$100], but today I'm a debt-free man. The work is the same, but there's a fundamental difference. Earlier I could not control the hours I wanted to work, when I went to work, how I wanted to work. Now I can. Before, if the vehicle came, I would load it right there and then, no matter what I was doing. Now I can go and work in the mountain and work for as long as I want. If I don't want to work I can come back and rest. I can go outside the village, go meet someone, talk to someone. I'm master of my own mind, my own destiny. That's a big difference. I can do what I want to do. I am free. The very fact that I'm sitting here and I'm able to take time from my hectic day's work speaks about today.

Today I'm free to not only live as I want to live but hope for a better future. My dream is now to start some kind of business, to have earnings and savings for myself and for a better future for my children. The dream is very big. I'm a little scared that it might not come true. I want my child to study, to become big, to do something, to be successful in all that he does. It's so grand, so big a dream.

I have a dream that tomorrow we'll be able to continue the unity we have awoken, and take this unity toward a more progressive future for us and everyone in my village. Ever since we have obtained our freedom, we've talked to the other people who are still slaves. We keep telling them that all we want is for them to live an independent life like we do, and that's what we want for anyone and everyone who's under slavery. We are trying. I am trying, and all the fellow volunteers of Sankalp are also trying very hard to get them out of bondage.

When I was a slave, I never dreamt I could go to Delhi, and now I have. In fact, I've been put in charge of all the running around that has to be done between the big cities. Whenever I go to these places, I learn, I become aware, and I come back and I impart this awareness to my fellow villagers and also to the other people who are working in bondage. We meet them and talk with them and they listen. It's not like they don't. They do. But then they forget, or they're too scared of the landowners. That doesn't matter. We keep telling them, showing them our life, the life we lead now, and they're keen to get out of bondage, so it'll happen. It's just a question of time. My life today is so much better that all I can think about is coming generations—they will be even better than mine. I don't know exactly what will change, but there will be a change. That's my wish. That's my desire. We are doing this in spite of being free. You know our motto for the villages? Just like we are able to break this hard hard rock with the hammer, any enemy is going to be shattered because of the unity that we now have.

Choti (INDIA, 2004)

My name is Choti. I think I'm about twenty years old. When I was getting married, I took a loan from the slave owners. At that point I ended up becoming a bonded laborer. Before my marriage I was not a slave. I was free. I would work in the fields, but I was a field-worker. I think I got a loan of about 5,000 rupees [$100] for ceremonies, the guests, the miscellaneous expenses of my marriage. But I took 5,000 and I repaid 10,000 [$200] for a long, long time. From the time when my kids were tiny to the time when they could work, that's the amount of time I was a bonded laborer. I would go back and ask them, "Is the debt over? Have I repaid it all?" They would say, "No, no, now it increased. It was 10,000. Now it is 20,000." Then,

"No, no it is not 20,000 anymore, now it is 30,000." I was not earning anything. I was barely earning some grain, some rice. How was I to repay the loan? I had no idea. This carried on and carried on and carried on.

Life was very tough. I was made to work in the fields the whole day, whether the children were crying or not, or when anyone was sick. I was not allowed to go home. Every single day, for long hours, I was expected to be working very hard. Not only were we made to work in the fields, we were also made to work in the stone quarry, to break up the stones and make them into tiny pieces. For all our effort we were hardly paid. Once the breaking of stones was over, we were also forced to lift them up and load them onto the truck. I was very scared of the slave owners because they would issue directions: "Go and work here. Go break the stones." You could not refuse because the next step was: "I'll burn your house." That's it, every day. The threat was so strong, and I knew they could carry it out. Therefore I had no choice. We had to go and work. Life under the slave owners was complete hell.

The females were especially harassed. The men would go off to work, either to the fields or the stone quarries, and the slave owners would come to our house, show us a huge knife and compel us to work. If you would refuse, saying the males had already gone, they would just drag us by the hair and compel us to work. Things got so bad that when the slave owners came to one woman's house and she refused, he had a huge knife and he just killed her. We never knew when a tractor would come and just drive over us and kill us. And once in the night, the contractor came to a woman's house and raped her. There were no rights, nothing.

One day a girl had gone to work in the fields and when she came back, the contractor wanted to misbehave with her. She tried running away and as she was running he burned down her house. He burned down a lot of houses and a girl was burnt right inside. They burned our houses, our food, our clothes. Everything was burned down. It seemed certain that they would lock us inside the house and burn us. They almost did. Sacks of grain were burned, everything was completely destroyed. We had to run away. Not a thing was left; everything was gone, completely evaporated. We had to all come out and move to a village. We were left to live below plastic sheets. No walls, no roof, nothing. It was very tough. That's what we had come down to. The basic utensils weren't there; the utensils on which we cook chapati weren't there—nothing.

The night that the houses burned down, not only were my eyes weeping, my very soul was torn, shattered. We saw crying and wailing. It was sheer agony. My husband was in prison and my son died during that time. But I did think things would get better because the interaction with Sankalp had begun. So I knew there was a ray of hope. There was an expectation that something would give and change would come about. My children were homeless. But something was going to happen. I knew it.

The females played a very big role in getting revolution. When we had initial meetings with the local authorities and with Sankalp, they told us to coordinate with each other. That didn't mean very much to us at that point. But slowly, when we had a couple of meetings here and a couple of meetings there, things began to sink in, and we came to realize we were doing all the work. We are the ones who are cutting the stones, we are the ones loading the lorries every single day and not getting any assistance or any monetary benefit. That's when we all met the Sankalp members and took action into our hands. Initially when Sankalp would come down to the village and interact with us, the contractors did not like the idea. "You motherfuckers," is what they would scream at us. "What are you doing?" So on and so forth. Seeing this just got our enthusiasm more aroused, and that's when we started taking Sankalp more seriously.

The Sankalp people said, "Look, you have food that you grow yourself; you have labor that you do by yourself." They made us aware of the fact that it was possible for us to be self-sufficient, for us to be able to sell and buy our own food grains, for us to be able to educate our children. They made us realize that we were exploited and that we were under the control of the slave owners. We knew that, of course. We were aware that there was an evil person who would come and beat us up, but they made us aware there was something we could do about it, that it was possible for us to get together, move toward the cities and the towns, and then bring about a revolution. The Sankalp people helped us a lot after the burning. They came together and gave us a vessel on which to cook our food; they gave us medical help and assistance for our children.

I love my life now. I just simply love it. My children are going to school. I have food in my stomach. Ever since I held the hand of Sankalp, I love my life. There is so much happening in it now, so many good things. I've got a lease on a house; I'm free; there's education; my children are happy; I'm happy.

My dream for my children is that they grow up, they become people who can read, who can write, who can live in the cities and have a job. They shouldn't be like us, any of us. They should not be working to break stones; they should not be dying like we do, day in and day out, under the hot sun. They should be people who live a life in the cities, big people. That's my dream.

I have five kids and I don't work now. Before, when my children woke up, they would be rubbing their eyes and I would be far, far away in some field, working under the slave owners. Now I don't work. I get up; I feed my kids and send them to school. They come back. I relax in the afternoon. In the evening I make sure they're OK—you know, a regular wife. That's what I do now. That's my life. All I want is that nobody remains bonded anymore. That every child is free, free to study, free to learn, free to live their own life.

Shyamkali (INDIA, 2004)

My name is Shyamkali. There's a whole story from the beginning to the end about what happened to me. I took one loan. My son needed medicine; the roof was falling down; I needed some money. I was illiterate, so the documentation was something I could not read. He probably made it for his own purposes, and because of that loan I became a bonded laborer. Every time I went back to the money lender, the amount of the loan had always increased. The last I heard, my family owed him 10,000 rupees [$200].

My husband would work very hard and so would I. I had to run my household and try to save some money for a bleak day. That's how I would lead my life. It was extremely hard and there was no freedom at any point. We were made to do two forms of labor. We had to work in the fields and we had to break stones. For all this hard work, we were barely paid, sometimes 300 rupees [$6], sometimes 400 rupees [$9].

The people of Sankalp came and told us that unity is our strength: "If you only unite together, there is nobody who can do anything against you." They told us that the individual by himself is going to be weak, he's not going to be able to defend himself against the slave owner, but if we all form an organization, get together and form a group, a self-help group, then we'll be able to defeat the slave owners.

Today is very different. There's a huge, huge difference. Earlier on we were slaves, either agricultural slaves working in the fields or slaves working in the stone quarries. But now we are free. We work if we want to, and not if we don't want to. And this freedom makes a big difference. I now want my children to study. I want my girl child to study. I want her to be able to read, to write, to do a job somewhere as well as to manage a house. I want her to be able to do both of these things together.

When I ask the children what happened in school they tell me about the day. Recently, she could count from one to ten, and all by herself she came up to me and wrote out the numbers on her slate. I don't know how to write. I never went to school, so never in my life did I have a chance. My children teach me, but they lose patience very fast. They come and write some kind of message and I can only write half, and then it's enough and we walk away.

Before, when I was a slave, I had no dreams and no ambitions. Later on, when we started forming a committee, there was hope. The hope was shattered when they burned the houses and everyone was refugees. There was again this sadness creeping in. But the unity that we had kept going. I believe in unity. It has become a lifestyle. The next step for all of us is to ensure that the cooperation and coordination, the unity, remain strong. We want to get a government hospital built somewhere close by. We also want to improve the conditions of our school and make it more safe.

Women have a huge role to play. We feel very important because we are also breadwinners. Since we earn, we also have equal role to play in fighting for our freedom. Freedom means economic independence as much as it means freedom of movement.

Sumara (INDIA, 2004)

I want to talk about my life as a bonded laborer, as a slave. It was very tough living under the control and exploitation of the slave owners. During those days, my husband was in prison. I tried to go to Bara to file a report. The police refused to file one. I didn't know what to do. My eyes were red from weeping uncontrollably day in and day out. I went every single day for four days and asked them to file a report, to hear my account of the story. Nobody was there, nobody paid any heed. I then went to Allahabad, sat on a car all the way. It was only then that somebody heard my side of the story. I was asked to come and produce myself as a witness. I did. I cried repeatedly, "What to do? Where to go? Whom to meet?" Everything was such a mess.

Things began to become a little better, however, when Sankalp came into my life. Because of them, there were regular meetings conducted. But even that was something that slave owners could not tolerate. They refused to let us hold meetings in the village itself. We all started meeting at a place called Ramgarh, a huge open ground.

Sankalp told us, "You're under the obligation and the exploitation of the slave owners." They said that life could be better; that if we heard them out and listened to what they had to say, we would be able to live free from

Shyamkali and Sumara (photograph by Peggy Callahan, Free the Slaves, 2004)

any form of exploitation—have basic freedom to do what we wanted to do. They told us we could all collect together, fight against the exploitation of the slave owners, and then live our own life. Later they promised our children education, so that they would not be laborers; but, initially, the first step was to get us together so we could think of how to get out of the clutches of the slave owners.

We were barred entry into our own village. After four whole days we were finally allowed inside and we saw there was nothing left of the houses, there was not one single piece of clothing to wear, no food to eat, no utensils, nothing. We were left to fend for ourselves, without any means of livelihood. Sankalp came in to help us. They would organize food from other villages and give us food to eat. It was during this time that we acquired a lease.

We're happy now here. We have a lease; we work; we get our money; we earn our own livelihood; we have food to eat. Now I can dream about a future and live a happy life. I feel a little lazy—it's so easy. Our kids go to school. For my son, my dream is that he does well, he learns, he studies, he reaches high up, and he's not like me—he doesn't break stones.

That's my dream. I'm very happy. You all sing; you dance. There's joy in our life now.

SEX SLAVERY IN THE UNITED STATES

Trafficked into sex slavery in 1988 at the age of fourteen from her home-town of Chicago, Tina Frundt is one of many survivors who become activists after liberation. Calling herself "a voice among the many who have been unheard," she explained in an interview that "once people are aware of this issue, they can write letters to Congress, find out what areas have a trafficking problem, and take notice when they're coming home from a club or are out late." As a street outreach coordinator for the Trafficking Intervention Program at Polaris Project, an NGO that provides services to trafficking victims, she told Congress in 2005 that "sex trafficking of U.S. citizens is a reality in every city in the United States, including right here in our nation's capital." Tina added, "If we are judging the efforts of other countries to combat trafficking, we certainly must aggressively fight the trafficking of our own citizens."

Tina decided to tell her story because, as she noted in a 2005 press interview: "Testimony sheds light on a problem that has been going on for so long in the United States. Yes, it's going on in other countries as well, but we also need to focus on what's been going on here in the United States for years." She knows, as she explained to Congress, that "when we see a woman on the street here in the United States, we think, 'Why is she doing it? This must be her choice. She can walk away any time she wants. She can leave.' There is less sympathy for the domestic victims." But like victims who are foreign nationals, Tina said, domestic victims are also moved away from their homes: "They can't go back because they don't know where they are, or they are ashamed to tell their families of what has happened to them....How can you ask help from the police when they have done nothing but arrest you, not recognizing you are a victim of sex trafficking?"

Tina (UNITED STATES, 2005)

When we hear the words "sex trafficking," as Americans we immediately think of women and children overseas who are being forced into the sex trade or who are brought into the United States for the purpose of sexual exploitation. We don't usually think closer to home—Americans trafficked by Americans. But I want you to think about young women and even girls that you have seen late at night when you come home from work or a social event. Maybe you have seen them in the streets in short dresses and spike heels. You turn your heads to look away. We do not look at the faces of these young women and girls who are forced to be out in the street. Maybe we think this is what they want to do or they wouldn't be out there. Maybe it is easier to believe that it is an empowering choice they have than face the harsh reality of child sexual abuse, physical and mental abuse, and the pimps that prey on the young women and girls.

To understand all aspects of sex trafficking in the United States, you have to open your mind and let go of what you have seen or heard on television. You need to let go of the media's portrayal of the "joys" of street prostitution and open your eyes to the violence and control the pimps and sex traffickers exercise over their victims, who are mostly girls and young women.

I was fourteen years old when I was forced into prostitution. Like many teens at that age, finding my own identity and defying my parents were top on my list. So when a man came into my life and showered me with attention and listened to me when I complained about my parents, I did not think twice that he was ten years my senior. After all, he said I was mature for my age and told me I understood him better than anyone his own age. Little did I know, he was laying down the seeds of manipulation. It did not matter what my parents said, to me they did not understand me and he was the only one that "got me." After six months, I thought I loved him, at least that is what he told me, so I did what I thought my heart was telling me and ran away to be with him. We ended up in Cleveland, Ohio. He told me we were going to meet the rest of the family.

I had no idea the "family" meant myself and three other girls. After I was introduced to the "family," I was told what my role would be. I would go out to "work" that night and bring him back the money. How else would we build our dream home? He assured me he would always love me no matter what, but he needed to know how much I loved him by making sure I would do anything for him.

Later that evening, his friends came by the motel. At first, he told me to have sex with someone. I did not want to, so his friends raped me. Afterwards, he said that wouldn't have happened if I would have just listened to him at first. I blamed myself instead of being angry at him for being raped. I was angry at myself for not listening to him in the first place. After that, he picked my clothes out, told me what to wear, what to say, how to walk, what to say to johns, and how much money I was to bring back to him. He then forced me to go out into the streets.

When I first went out into the streets, when I met my first john, I felt like this was something I did not want to do. I walked around the streets back and forth for hours. Finally, I got into a car because we were always being watched and I knew I had to get into a car sooner or later. Our quota was $500 and I had only made $50 that night to give back to the pimp. As a result, he beat me in front of the other girls to make an example out of me and then he made me go back out until I had made the money. This is the same man that took me out to eat, listened to me when I wanted to complain about my parents, gave me words of advice. I was now seeing a side of him that I never saw before—a brutal side where he repeatedly hit me in front of the other girls to teach us all a lesson.

Not only was I shocked, I was scared. What would happen to me if I did try to leave, and who would believe me if I told them what was going on? I worked from 6 P.M. until 10 P.M. the next night without eating or sleeping. I came back with the $500, but in his mind I still had not learned my lesson. He sent me back outside until 5 A.M. the next morning. After the second day, he finally bought me something to eat, but as a punishment to learn never to defy him again, he locked me in the closet. Since that night, I was locked in the closet on numerous occasions and had my finger broken, which never set right. None of us were ever allowed to see a doctor, so we endured our pain by pushing it deep down inside and trying to forget it ever happened.

I can't count the number of times people have asked me, "Why didn't you just leave? Couldn't you escape?" To that, I simply say, "Do you ask a child that is kidnapped why they didn't try to leave?" No, we automatically say they are a victim; it wasn't their fault. Now I know it was not my fault that a pimp manipulated a child. Under federal law, a child under eighteen years who is commercially sexually abused is a victim of trafficking. However, under local law a child is charged with child prostitution.

The pimps who are trafficking young women and girls on the street have a great marketing tool—the media. You can turn on the TV now and see pimps glamorized in TV shows, music videos, and movies. Young people use "pimp" in everyday conversation: "My ride is pimped out," "Your clothes are pimping." They do not understand the reality behind the term.

Pimps prey on young women and girls by finding their weakness and then exploiting it. It is easier to manipulate children, and by the time children become adults, they are broken down and dependent on a pimp. After the pimp gets into your mind, it's easy for him to maintain control, much like a domestic abuser. From then now on you have to call him

"Daddy," and he will punish you if he feels like you have stepped out of line. You are required to bring him $500–2,000 every night. You are not a woman, you are always a "bitch" or a "ho" and are reminded of that daily. You are part of his "stable." If you do not want to follow the rules, then he may sell you at any time to another pimp.

Polaris Project, a nonprofit antitrafficking organization in Washington, D.C., reported that a pimp who had three young women and girls in his "stable" who each were bringing back $500 every day. Do the math—the pimp was making about $24,000 a month or $642,000 a year tax free by selling sex with girls and young women he controlled and then keeping all the money.

In the dictionary, the definition of slavery is the "state of one bound in servitude." If someone sells you to someone else, is that not slavery? If someone forces you to do things against your will and you are not allowed to leave, is that not slavery? Then I ask you why, when pimps traffic young women and girls on the streets of America, isn't this a form of modern-day slavery?

What happened to me fifteen years ago is still going on today. I now work as a street outreach coordinator for Polaris Project, and I can see that it is not getting any better—it is only getting worse. We see girls and young women every night being forced onto the streets, beaten, and raped to make money for the pimps.

There are organizations all over the world that work with young women and girls helping them escape from trafficking situations. I urge you to learn how you can stop sex trafficking in the United States and overseas. To stop the problem we have to understand and help make stronger laws to get these traffickers.

I hope that next time you see the young women and girls on the street you will have more understanding of the reality of their situation. Now that you have the knowledge, what will you do with it?

SEX SLAVERY IN LIBERIA

Settled with freed slaves from the United States after 1822, and founded as a republic in 1847, Liberia was named to mean "the country of the free." But today, men, women, and children are trafficked into slavery within Liberia, and children are brought into the country for domestic and sex slavery from Sierra Leone, Guinea, and Ivory Coast. Children are also trafficked out of Liberia to Guinea, Gambia, and Nigeria for domestic and sex slavery, as well as to Ivory Coast for use in combat.

And during Liberia's civil war, which ended after fourteen years in 2003, both government forces and rebel factions forcibly recruited many thousands of children for use in combat and as messengers and porters.

Ruth Kamara was trafficked into sex slavery in Liberia's capital, Monrovia, in the early 1990s. She was brought from Sierra Leone, where women and children are also trafficked out to Guinea, Ivory Coast, Nigeria, Guinea-Bissau, Gambia, the Middle East, and Europe. As in Liberia, a civil war in Sierra Leone between government and rebel forces has prompted forcible recruitment for combat. In addition, that war of 1991–2002 displaced more than two million people, many of whom became at risk of exploitation by traffickers. There are no reliable statistics for either Liberia or Sierra Leone, but more broadly, across all the countries of West and Central Africa, around three hundred thousand children are trafficked into slavery each year.

Now imagining the abolitionist movement as a mini–civil war that she is "ready to fight," Ruth explains that her weapon in that war is her testimony as a survivor. She speaks to people in her country, defines human trafficking for them, and then will "always back it up with my story."

Ruth (LIBERIA, 2006)

At the time I was nineteen, and a friend of mine asked me to go and spend time with her in Liberia. We went to a man, and she introduced me to the man like, "This is the one that we are going to Liberia with." Then all of a sudden she told me, "Oh, I forgot one document. Let me go home so that I will go and collect it." I said, "OK. I hope you will come later." She left. That was the end. I never saw her again.

We left in the car, me and the man. So, after a day or two, we reached Monrovia. He took me to a big compound, telling me that's the room that they found for me. That night he asked me to have sex with him. I said, "No, this is not the arrangement, because my friend said we are just coming to spend time here." Then, in that room, he told me, "Don't you know I am your boss? I bought you from that lady." After having the sex with him, he kept me in the room, employing other men to come. I was there for two years.

I'm a survivor. So I'm not ashamed to tell them: "I was there, but God brought me out for a special purpose." And this is the purpose, to tell my testimony, and tell people that this thing is happening. Now I talk in villages and schools, telling them about my past experience. After giving them the definition of human trafficking, I always back it up with my story. So people will know that this thing is a real thing. It is happening. I am hoping that this thing will come to a stop. We are ready to fight what is going on now.

CHILD SLAVERY IN GHANA

Along Ghana's Lake Volta, slave children work long hours mending, setting, and pulling nets, cleaning and smoking fish, and rowing the fishing boats. Boys as young as six are forced to dive to disentangle nets caught on tree stumps below this large man-made lake. The fishermen tie weights to the children to help them descend more quickly. When the water is too cold or the children get caught in the nets below it is not uncommon for them to drown, and later their bodies are found washed up on the shores. If sick or injured, the children receive no care or treatment. While most of the enslaved children are boys, some girls are used for domestic work and to sell the fish in the market. Like other trafficked girls in Ghana, they are likely to be sexually abused as well.

Lake Volta is one of the world's largest lakes and used to be a source of fish for both the national and export markets. But in the 1960s a dam slowed the vigorous flow of water and destroyed the fishing potential of nearby communities. Facing a newly impoverished environment, some fishermen began to enslave children rather than pay adult workers. With schooling hard to obtain and family incomes around the starvation level, parents will sometimes agree to let their children go in order to gain a 200,000 cedi ($28) "advance" on their child's labor. Normally, the fishermen promise that another 400,000 cedi will be paid to the parents over the next year. The money never comes.

Kwame was trafficked in 1998 and spent eight years with the same master as a slave at Lake Volta. Kwasi spent three years in slavery. Both boys were rescued in 2006 by the Association of People for Practical Life Education (APPLE), a small nonprofit organization that works directly with the fishermen and children. Since 2001, APPLE workers have been approaching the fishermen, explaining why their child slaves should be freed. Although thousands of children remain enslaved along Ghana's Lake Volta, some five hundred children have been freed by APPLE so far.

Kwame and Kwasi look beyond slavery to freedom. Just as APPLE's strategy is one of education (of communities, local leaders, and, most strategically, fishermen), so both boys now plan to become teachers.

Kwame (GHANA, 2006)

I come from Mafi Dugame where I live with my parents. A man came to our village and requested from my parents to take me to help in selling. I didn't know him. The first time I saw him was when he came to my parents to ask for me. The man mentioned that I was going to be involved in his selling business and I was a bit interested. When we got to Atitekpo, in Yeji, he said he didn't have any thing to sell but rather we shall be fishing.

We woke up around 4 A.M. to go to the river to pull the net into the boat and bring the fish to the riverside by 8 A.M. After delivering the fish we returned back onto the river to work, and it's after all this before we were given food. Then we attended to the fish, mended the nets, and returned to fishing after 8 A.M., came back in the afternoon. Then went back to the river about 3 P.M. and returned around 6 P.M. We didn't eat on the river, only when we returned were we allowed to eat. We ate *banku* [cooked fermented cornmeal, a staple] twice a day, in the afternoon and before we went to bed.

They beat us. At times, as a form of punishment, they paddled the boat away from us while on the river and we had to swim a long distance to catch up with them. Sometimes if you were not lucky you drowned in the river.

I will inform my parents that where I was sent to work was very bad and full of suffering. I was made to go fishing very early till late in the evening. I was not fed well and was often beaten over little things, at times even made to swim long distances which could lead to my death.

I believed I would one day escape. My parents allowed us to come here to suffer, and even when the contract days were up they wouldn't allow us to leave. My plan was to get the chance to work for another master who would pay me and I could use that money to run away, back to my family.

We were informed that the government wanted to collect us and send us back to our families to go to school. Having been released I am very happy. I like the food here much better and I am well treated. I do not have anything to complain about.

I hope to go to school and train to become a teacher. I am very much interested in school, and, given the opportunity, I will pay attention in class so that I can grow to become somebody.

Kwasi (GHANA, 2006)

I am called Kwasi. I was with my father when one of my uncles came to ask for me to stay with him and attend school. When I came he put me in school all right, but we normally woke up and went fishing at about

3 A.M., and by the time we returned and I went to school it was already too late. It wasn't my own decision to go to school late, but we often returned very late and this was the routine. The teachers used to get angry, and my master finally told me to stop school and concentrate on the fishing. Then we were made to go fishing at about 3 A.M. and only returned at about 1 P.M. in the afternoon.

My uncle took me with my parents' consent. But he made my parents believe that I will work and go to school. I was made to fish and farm, including throwing nets, diving, paddling the boat. Apart from the work itself my major difficulty was lack of proper food. We ate very little in the morning or sometimes none at all before going to fish, and we were made to work long hours till we get back home before we are allowed to eat again. I will tell my parents that I was suffering a lot where I was sent. I was made to work for long hours and I never had a chance to go to school.

I had hope that one day my father will come and bring me back home. I was there one day when my master received a letter from my parents saying that the government is asking for me to come back and attend school. Now I am happy, especially because I no longer have to do the work I used to do. I hope to become a teacher. I believe that if I pay attention in class and I am serious, with God's help I can become a teacher in the future.

AGRICULTURAL SLAVERY IN SUDAN

In 1985 William Akoi Mawwin was captured and forced into slavery at the age of six. During raids by Muslim militia from northern Sudan on the villages of the Christian Dinka tribes during the 1980s, tens of thousands of other boys between the ages of four and ten had the same fate. As well, babies and toddlers were killed, and girls were raped, killed, or forced into slavery. Some boys who escaped capture headed to refugee camps in Kenya, but it is estimated that only one in three survived the journey.

After seven years in slavery, William escaped and lived on the streets of the capital. He worked to earn money for a passport and left for Cairo, where he found work in a rubber factory before a machinery accident took his hands. In 2001 the U.S. government granted 3,600 Sudanese orphans refugee status. Some 500 boys, including twenty-one-year-old William, were placed in Arizona.

William describes his capture as a sudden disappearance: "You're gone for good." But his narrative confronts this problem of erasure and offers a solution. "I'm here," he insists. This assertion of ongoing presence is part of William's call to action. While his family gave him up as dead after he disappeared—"nobody believed," he observes—William refuses to give up on other slave children. "I'm not going to give up. I believe," he concludes. For while he still doesn't feel entirely liberated, explaining that his "heart's not free," William seeks a final sense of freedom through activism that might lead to a large-scale liberation of Sudan's slaves. Reminding his reader about "the kids who are slaves today," he asks, "What are we going to do…?"

William (SUDAN, 2006)

My family means a lot to me, means everything. You need to have a hug from your mom, a kiss, hang out with your father, laugh. I was six years old when I was captured. People came, and boom boom, running by with horses and shooting people, killing people, capturing kids, taking kids away, and tying them to horses. When I saw a person shot, bleeding, it scared me more than anything. You're a little kid, you're thinking, Grandmother will come along and yell at them and get you out. But, no, you're gone for good. Because I was a little boy I had to accept it, because I don't have my family around me, to survive I had to accept it. You have to lie: "I look at your wife like my mom, I look at you like my father."

In the capital I was so excited, not thinking about the past—you're a poor man, trying to survive. Then I thought, you go to Egypt, you make good money and buy what you want.

I still need to get a hug from my mom, but it's not going to be the same. Right now I am not free. My heart's not free.

When we talk about slavery and don't take action, it feels like, why should I say my words? I should just stay at home and forget about it. But I can't forget about it. I can't. When I was captured I was six years old. I saw four three-year-olds getting killed because they didn't have mothers. Who was going to be the mother of those kids? So they just took them and killed them. And when they kill them, they don't kill them in a way you can't see—they put them in front of you, and say, "You see that?" They want to get you to be scared. So when you're six years old and you don't have a family around you, when you have no one to protect you, what do you think? In my situation, I built a lot of trust with my master—got him to trust me to be a leader in front of other kids. But I didn't tell the other kids my plan. You just have to do it.

I planned it for five years. I saw people getting cut in the feet when they tried to escape. They cut their toes, and when they cut your toes you cannot run. You can't even walk far.

They want you to watch their cattle in a field every day. You sleep out-side like animals—rain, cold, no shoes. You're not a human being. You have to forget about your life. You're not thinking about your family anymore. You have to think about yourself. So the kids in Sudan have a mentality that they don't even want to leave anymore, because they don't believe in their family—they don't know where their family is. They don't care anymore. Some people blame their families.

And what about the mothers, whose children are captured? Even if their child makes an escape and comes back, what is she going to do? He's going to have no culture, he's going to be a weird person in the family. He's going to see himself alone, always. He's not going to be happy.

Sudan is not a country that has education. Do I know my story? Some people don't even know their birthday. Some people don't know what money is. When I was in my village, I thought I was in the only village in the world. But if kids have education, they will not be enslaved today. They will now what a "human right" is.

Today, "human rights" is about talking. It's not about action anymore. When you think that the United Nations is speaking up today—a UN res-olution, section this, number that—what does that mean? Will it help me in the village? I don't have TV in the village. I have my resources, people are killing me for my resources, but I don't know what the resource is be-cause I'm not educated. I don't know where the oil is—I'm not educated. I'm getting wiped out in my land.

But when we have education, paper keeps the story. When you write something down, you pass it down to generations. We don't have that. Do we know if our great-grandfather was a leader? Do we know if he was a thief? We don't know, because we're not educated.

Politicians in Southern Sudan, their kids are in London, America, first-world countries. What about the poor kid? The person who doesn't know how to use soap, to wash his clothes, to wash his hands? What are we going to do for him? Are we going to help them, or just let them die like a dog?

I don't count myself as disabled. I have a brain—I don't have hands. It doesn't bother me. What bothers me is when I see people hungry and I'm here eating, I have a TV, I'm sleeping.

For twenty-two years I haven't seen my mom or my dad. My grand-mother, who I was visiting when I got captured, died in 2004. Do you think she died happy? I didn't find my family until 2004. I didn't meet my brother until 2005. My brother told me people believed I died and was buried a long time ago. Nobody believed.

People have to take action, but we just do research. I don't have anything to do with my people anymore, but I won't give up. I'm here in America. I was in Egypt and my hands got lost, and I didn't know where to go, but I made it to America. I'm here today, talking to people. Because when you don't talk about your problem, I tell you that's your problem. You have to speak to people, to let them know. We don't need Sudan to be a perfect country. But the kids who are slaves today, are we going to get them out? I'm not going to give up. I believe. I escaped and I'm here today.

APPENDIX

Antislavery Organizations and Agencies

Angel Coalition; Moscow, Russia; [7] (495) 783-5865, www.angelcoalition.org

Anti-Slavery International; London, England; [44] (0207) 501-8920, www.antislavery.org

Anti-Slavery Society of Australia; Melbourne, Australia; [61] (3) 964-2101, www.anti-slaverysociety.org

Association of Albanian Girls and Women; Tirena, Albania; info@aagw.org, www.aagw.org

Association of People for Practical Life Education (APPLE); Accra, Ghana; [233] (020) 819-5709

Astra Anti Trafficking Action; Belgrade, Serbia; [381] (11) 3347-817, www.astra.org.yu

Bal Vikas Ashram; Uttar Pradesh, India; (202) 588-1865, www.freetheslaves.net

Bonded Labor Liberation Front; New Delhi, India; [91] (11) 336-6765/7943, www.swamiagnivesh.com

Break the Chain Campaign; Washington, D.C.; (202) 234-9382 ext. 244, www.ips-dc.org/campaign/index.htm

Christian Solidarity International; Zurich, Switzerland; [41] (44) 982-3333, www.csi-int.org

Coalition against Slavery in Sudan and Mauritania; New York, N.Y.; (212) 774-4287, http://members.aol.com/casmasalc

Coalition against Trafficking in Women; Amherst, Mass.; info@catwinternational.org, www.catwinternational.org

Coalition of Immokalee Workers; Immokalee, Fla.; (941) 657-8311, www.ciw-online.org

Coalition to Abolish Slavery and Trafficking; Los Angeles, Calif.; (213) 365-1906, www.castla.org

Comité contre L'Esclavage Moderne (Committee against Modern Slavery); Paris, France; [33] (1) 4452-8890, www.ccem-antislavery.org

End Child Prostitution, Child Pornography and Trafficking of Children for Sexual Purposes; Bangkok, Thailand; [66] (2) 215-3388, www.ecpat.net

Faith Alliance against Slavery and Trafficking; Alexandria, Virginia; (888) 466-4673, www.faastinternational.org

Free the Slaves; Washington, D.C.; (866) 324-FREE, (202) 588-1865, www.freetheslaves.net

Foundation against Trafficking in Women; Utrecht, the Netherlands; [31] (302) 716-044, www.bayswan.org/FoundTraf.html

The Future Group; Calgary, Canada; smajumdar@thefuturegroup.org, www.thefuturegroup.org

Global Alliance against Traffic in Women; Bangkok, Thailand; [66] (2) 864-1427, www.gaatw.org

Global March against Child Labour; New Delhi, India; [91] (11) 4132-9025, www.globalmarch.org

Human Rights Commission; Lahore, Pakistan; [92] (42) 586-4994/583-8341, www.hrcp.cjb.net

Human Rights Watch; New York, N.Y.; (212) 290-4700, www.hrw.org

Informal Sector Service Center; Kathmandu, Nepal; [977] (1) 427-8770, www.insec.org.np

International Justice Mission; Washington, D.C.; (703) 465-5495, www.ijm.org

International Needs—Ghana; Accra, Ghana; [233] (21) 226-620, www.africaexpress.com/internationalneedsghana

La Strada—Ukraine; Kiev, Ukraine; [38] (044) 205-3695, www.lastrada.org.ua/?lng=en

Laogai Research Foundation; Washington, D.C.; (202) 833-8770, www.laogai.org

Lost Boys Center; Phoenix, Arizona; (602) 262-2300; www.azlostboyscenter.org

Maiti Nepal; Kathmandu, Nepal; [977] (1) 449-2904, www.maitinepal.org

Payoke Shelter; Antwerpen, Belgium; [0032] (0) 3201-1690, www.payoke.be

Perm Center for Assistance to Persons Suffered from Violence and Human Trafficking; Perm, Russia; no-violence@narod.ru, www.cavt.ru

RugMark; Washington, D.C.; (202) 347-4100, www.rugmark.org

Shakti Samuha; Kathmandu, Nepal; [977] (1) 449-4815, www.shaktisamuha.org

SOS Slaves/SOS Esclaves; Nouakchott, Mauritania; [22] (252) 54-602, www.sosesclaves.org

South Asian Coalition on Child Servitude; New Delhi, India; [91] (11) 621-0807, www.cridoc.net/saccs.php

World Hope International; Alexandria, Va.; (888) 466-4673, www.worldhope.org

PERMISSIONS AND CREDITS

Section 1

Shengqi: Narrative as told to the U.S. House of Representatives Subcommittee on International Operations and Human Rights of the Committee on International Relations, May 22, 1997, in Washington D.C.

Sam: Narrative as written by the narrator, October 16, 2003, in Atlanta, Georgia.

Ying: Narrative as told to participants at the 60th session of the UN Commission on Human Rights joint forum with the Falun Gong Human Rights Working Group and the NGO International Education Development, March 31, 2004, in Geneva, Switzerland.

Jennifer: Narrative as told to the U.S. Congressional-Executive Commission on China, June 22, 2005, in Washington, D.C.

Bin: Narrative as told to the City Council of Chicago's Human Relations Committee, October 20, 2005, in Chicago; revised for publication in November 2005.

Abuk A., Abuk G., Abuk K., Achai, Ajok, Anyang, Marco, Mary, Yei: Narratives as told to Christian Solidarity International, January 1999, in North Bahr al Ghazal, Sudan.

Isra: Narrative as told to the Toronto Network against Trafficking in Women, 1999, in Toronto, Canada.

Vi: Narrative as told to the U.S. House of Representatives Committee on International Relations, session on Implementation of the Trafficking Victims Protection Act, November 28, 2001, in Washington, D.C.

Shanti: Narrative as told to Peggy Callahan for Free the Slaves, November 10, 2001, in Son Barsa, Uttar Pradesh, India.

Munni: Narrative as told to Peggy Callahan for Free the Slaves, November 3, 2004, in Son Barsa, Uttar Pradesh, India.

Maria: Narrative as written by the narrator, 2002, in Bulgaria.

Ada, Adelina, Elira, Flutura, Kimete, Miranda, Odeta, Sanije, Valdete, Zamira: Narratives as told to the International Organization for Migration, with the Association of Albanian Girls and Women, 2005, in Tirana, Albania.

Patience: Narrative as told to International Needs—Ghana, February 2004, in the Volta region of Ghana.

Arvind, Rambho: Narratives as told to Peggy Callahan for Free the Slaves, August 19, 2004, at Bal Vikas Ashram in Allahabad, Uttar Pradesh, India.

Rama, Ravi: Narratives as told to Peggy Callahan for Free the Slaves, October 31, 2004, at Bal Vikas Ashram in Allahabad, Uttar Pradesh, India.

Shahnawaz: Narrative as told to Peggy Callahan and Supriya Awasthi for Free the Slaves, April 6, 2005, at Bal Vikas Ashram in Allahabad, Uttar Pradesh, India.

Ashok, Battis, Sandeep: Narratives as told to Peggy Callahan and Supriya Awasthi for Free the Slaves, July 19, 2005, at Bal Vikas Ashram in Allahabad, Uttar Pradesh, India.

Section 2

Nuch: Narrative as told to Human Rights Watch, March 3, 1995, in a shelter in Bangkok, Thailand.

Pot: Narrative as told to Human Rights Watch, June 1, 1995, in Ibaraki Prefecture, Japan.

Kaew: Narrative as told to Human Rights Watch, September 13, 1997, in Chiang Rai, Thailand.

Nu: Narrative as told to Jean D'Cunha for the United Nations Development Fund for Women (UNIFEM) and the Coalition against Trafficking in Women (CATW), 2000, in a shelter in Bangkok, Thailand.

Seba: Narrative as told to Kevin Bales, December, 1996, in Paris, France.

Christine: Narrative as written by the narrator, 1997, and presented as a lecture to antitrafficking activists, with the title "Surviving Sexual Slavery: Women in Search of Freedom" in St. Petersburg, Russia.

Dina: Narrative as told to participants at the First National Conference on Gender and Development, September 7, 1999, in Phnom Penh, Cambodia.

Anita: Narrative as told to the U.S. House of Representatives Subcommittee on International Operations and Human Rights, session on Trafficking of Women and Children in the International Sex Trade, September 14, 1999, in Washington, D.C.

Rita: Narrative as told to Sangeeta Lama for the Panos Oral Testimony Programme, 2002, in Kathmandu, Nepal.

Olga: Narrative as told to the U.S. Senate Foreign Relations Committee's Subcommittee on Near Eastern and South Asian Affairs, session on Trafficking of Women and Children, April 4, 2000, in Washington, D.C.

Alina, Amasya, Farida, Iliona, Shahnara, Tamara: Narratives as told to the International Organization for Migration, 2000, in Yerevan, Albania.

Bahar: Narrative as told to Siddharth Kara, October 31, 2005, in Comrat, Moldova.

Alana, Maria, Milena: Narratives as told to Siddharth Kara, November 1, 2005, in Costesti, Moldova.

Section 3

Kavita: Narrative as told to Peggy Callahan for Free the Slaves, November 3, 2004, at a women's shelter run by Sankalp, in Uttar Pradesh, India.

Miguel: Narrative as told to Peggy Callahan for Free the Slaves, February 13, 2005, at the headquarters of the Coalition of Immokalee Workers, in Immokalee, Florida.

Roseline, Christina: Narratives as told to Peggy Callahan for Free the Slaves, February 24, 2005, in Washington, D.C.

Tamada: Narrative as told to Romana Cacchioli for Anti-Slavery International, with the Timidria Association, February 2005, in Ayorou, Niger.

Beatrice: Narrative as told to the U.S. House of Representatives International Relations Committee's Subcommittee on Africa, Global Human Rights, International Operations, March 9, 2005, in Washington, D.C.

Maria: Narrative as told to Peggy Callahan for Free the Slaves, May 13, 2005, at the headquarters of the Coalition to Abolish Slavery and Trafficking in Los Angeles, California.

Joy: Narrative as told to E. Benjamin Skinner, February 16, 2006, in Amsterdam, the Netherlands.

Selek'ha, Oumoulkhér: Narratives as told to Romana Cacchioli for Anti-Slavery International, with SOS Esclaves, August 1, 2006, in Nouakchott, Mauritania.

Section 4

Jill: Narrative as written by the narrator, 1997, with Katherine DePasquale.

Ragaa: Narrative as told to the Egyptian Center of Human Rights for National Unity in Cairo, 1997, in Cairo, Egypt.

Inez: Narrative as told to the U.S. Senate Foreign Relations Committee's Subcommittee on Near Eastern and South Asian Affairs, session on Trafficking of Women and Children, February 29, 2000, in Washington, D.C.

Maria, Rosa: Narratives as told to the U.S. Senate Foreign Relations Committee's Subcommittee on Near Eastern and South Asian Affairs, session on Trafficking of Women and Children, April 4, 2000, in Washington, D.C.

Aida, Dia, Manju: Narratives as told to the Quaker United Nations Office, 2001, in the Philippines, Columbia, and Sri Lanka.

Jean-Robert: Narrative as told to the International Institute for Labour Studies, November 2002, in Geneva, Switzerland.

Chantha, Chariya: Narratives as told to World Hope International, 2003, in Phnom Penh, Cambodia.

Mariana: Narrative as told to La Strada—Ukraine, April 2003, in Kiev, Ukraine.

Masha, Irina: Narratives as told to the U.S. House of Representatives International Relations Committee's Subcommittee on Africa, Global Human Rights, International Operations, at the Briefing and Hearing on "Modern Day Slavery: Spotlight on the 2006 'Trafficking in Persons Report,' Forced Labor, and Sex Trafficking at the World Cup," June 14, 2006, in Washington, D.C.

Faith: Narrative as told to the International Organization for Migration, 2005, in Hillbrow, Johannesburg, South Africa.

Section 5

Joyce: Narrative as told to John Bowe, 2002, in Orlando, Florida.

Salma: Narrative as written by the narrator, 2003, in Cincinnati, Ohio.

Mende: Narrative as told to Beth Herzfeld for Anti-Slavery International, October 2003, in London, England.

Ramphal, Choti, Shyamkali, Sumara: Narratives as told to Peggy Callahan for Free the Slaves, November 2, 2004, in Azad Nagar, Uttar Pradesh, India.

Tina: Narrative as told to the U.S. House of Representatives Subcommittee on Domestic and International Monetary Policy, Trade, and Technology, and Committee on Financial Services, session on the End Demand for Sex Trafficking Act, April 29, 2005, in Washington, D.C.

Ruth: Narrative as told to the Faith Alliance against Slavery and Trafficking (FAAST), with implementing partners World Hope International and World Relief, January 2006, in Makeni, Sierra Leone.

Kwame, Kwasi: Narratives as told to Jack Dawson, director of the Association of People for Practical Life Education (APPLE), October 2006, in Lake Volta, Ghana.

William: Narrative as told to delegates at "Slavery and Antislavery: A New Research and Teaching Workshop," October 13, 2006, Arizona State University, Tempe, Arizona.

INDEX